California Employment Law 2026

SHRM®

James J. McDonald, Jr.

California Employment Law 2026

*The **SHRM** Guide for Employers*

KoganPage

First published in the United States and Great Britain in 2026 by Kogan Page Limited

Society for Human Resources Management (SHRM)
SHRM, Alexandria, Virginia, shrm.org
SHRM, India Office, Mumbai, India, shrm.org/in
SHRM, Middle East and North Africa Office, Dubai, UAE, shrm.org/mena

Kogan Page
Kogan Page Ltd, 2nd Floor, 45 Gee Street, London EC1V 3RS, United Kingdom
Kogan Page Inc, 8 W 38th Street, Suite 902, New York, NY 10018, USA
www.koganpage.com

EU Representative (GPSR)
eucomply OÜ, Pärnu mnt 139b–14 11317, Tallinn, Estonia
www.eucompliancepartner.com

ISBNs
Hardback 978 1 3986 2893 9
Paperback 978 1 3986 2891 5
Ebook 978 1 3986 2892 2

Library of Congress Cataloguing-in-Publication Data
A CIP record for this book is available from the Library of Congress.

British Library Cataloguing-in-Publication Data
A CIP record for this book is available from the British Library.

Typeset by Hong Kong FIVE Workshop

Contents

About the Author

James J. McDonald, Jr., J.D., SHRM-SCP, is a partner in the Irvine, California and Tampa, Florida offices of the labor and employment law firm Fisher & Phillips LLP. His practice involves trials, arbitrations, and appeals of employment law claims. He also has more than 40 years of experience advising employers about all aspects of labor and employment law, strategic human resource issues, and how to avoid employment claims and lawsuits. He has spoken before many human resource, business, and industry organizations, and he taught labor and employment law in the Human Resources Management Program at the University of California, Irvine for 16 years. He received his undergraduate degree from New College of Florida and his law degree cum laude from Georgetown University. He is a member of the California and Florida Bars.

About SHRM

SHRM is a member-driven catalyst for creating better workplaces where people and businesses thrive together. As the trusted authority on all things work, SHRM is the foremost expert, researcher, advocate, and thought leader on issues and innovations impacting today's evolving workplaces. With nearly 340,000 members in 180 countries, SHRM touches the lives of more than 362 million workers and their families globally. Discover more at SHRM.org.

Acknowledgments

The author gratefully acknowledges Alaina Leadbeter of SHRM, Lucy Carter and Martin Hill of Kogan Page, and the entire SHRM and Kogan Page book publishing teams for their support of this project. The author also gratefully acknowledges Benjamin M. Ebbink, Todd A. Lyon, Warren L. Nelson, John K. Skousen, and Robert Yonowitz of Fisher & Phillips LLP for their review and suggestions regarding chapters in this book. Ultimate responsibility for the contents of this book rests with the author, however.

CHAPTER 1

California Employment Law: How Did This Become So Difficult?

It is often said that it is impossible for an employer to fully comply with all of California's employment laws. They are just too numerous and too complicated. They are frequently changing, and rarely for the better. There are so many traps for the unwary. Unfortunately, this is mostly true.

1.1 Why California Employment Laws Are So Difficult

Part of the problem is that California deems itself to be special. All the employment laws that serve the rest of the country just fine, such as Title VII of the Civil Rights Act, the Fair Labor Standards Act, and the Americans with Disabilities Act, are not considered adequate for California. Instead, California has its own versions of these laws—its own Labor Code, its own Fair Employment and Housing Act, and its own bureaucracies to enforce these laws. Sometimes these agencies interpret California law consistently with similar federal laws, sometimes not, and sometimes it is not really clear. California's wage and hour laws are among the most difficult to follow. Many of them were written by a body called the Industrial Welfare Commission, which no longer exists. In some instances, they are enforced by the Division of Labor Standards Enforcement (aka the Labor Commissioner, or what many call the "Labor Board"). That agency has written a lengthy *Enforcement Policies and Interpretations Manual* that contains some useful hints on what the laws mean, but courts routinely refuse to follow it because it was never subjected to public notice and comment. The same goes for the opinion letters the Labor Commissioner issues occasionally. The courts' refusal is sometimes a good thing because the agency's positions are often not employer-friendly, but it leaves many employers scratching their heads as they try to figure out which interpretation of often-ambiguous laws they should follow.

Another part of the problem is the Private Attorneys General Act (PAGA). Enacted in 2004 because the legislature felt the Labor Commissioner lacked the resources to fully enforce California's wage and hour laws, the law deputized disgruntled employees and their lawyers as bounty hunters to extract penalties from unwary employers for violating obscure laws, some dating back to the 1800s. The penalties are supposed to be shared with the state, but no similar split is required for the attorneys' fees recovered, so PAGA lawsuits have become lucrative ventures for the plaintiffs' bar and an expensive headache for employers.

Unpredictable court decisions are part of the problem too. Clever lawyering by plaintiffs' attorneys and sympathetic judges occasionally produce abrupt changes in the way California's employment laws are interpreted. Court decisions finding that piece-rate workers must be paid at least minimum wage for the time they are not doing piece-rate work, and rejecting the long-applied (and commonsense) rule that employees need not be paid for the time they spend sleeping, are two examples. These decisions imposed substantial retroactive liability on employers because they were premised on the notion that employers should have been complying with the new interpretation of the law all along.

Another part of the problem is that California has a full-time legislature. In states with part-time legislatures, legislators typically run businesses or work in jobs when the legislature is not in session, so they have some passing familiarity with the real world of work. California's legislators are not burdened with such distractions, so they stay busy churning out new laws. Many of these laws affect the workplace and make managing employees within the law that much more difficult. Examples include a law protecting undocumented immigrants who present fake documents to become employed and then present real ones later, and a law awarding an extra hour of pay to workers who work outside and can claim they did not get to spend enough time resting in the shade. It is almost as if every time somebody in the legislature says, "Hey, I have an idea!" it becomes law because employers have so little leverage in Sacramento. The premise behind most of these laws is that employees are commonly abused by bad employers and need ever more protections. So the legislature passes yet another law, which may or may not overlap previously enacted laws addressing the same evil. It is true there are some unscrupulous employers, but few in state government seem to heed the effect that this ever-thickening web of laws has on the vast majority of employers that are doing their best to comply.

1.2 Which Law?

Both federal and California law applies to California employers, but which law applies is not a difficult question. Whichever law is most favorable to employees is the law that applies. Ordinarily, that will be California law, but not always. This book will address the law that is applicable, usually without specifically identifying it as state or federal unless the distinction is important. Also, in recent years some local governments in California have enacted ordinances regarding such matters as minimum wage and paid sick leave, and many of these laws apply not only to employers located in the jurisdiction but also to employees who work there even though their employer is located elsewhere. It is important, therefore, to determine whether any of these local laws will apply to your employees.

It is true there are some unscrupulous employers, but few in state government seem to heed the effect that this ever-thickening web of laws has on the vast majority of employers that are doing their best to comply.

1.3 The Cost of Getting It Wrong

The stakes are high for California employers. A simple mistake can lead to a seven-figure jury verdict or a class action lawsuit.

One reason for this is that under California law, unlike under federal law, there are no limits on the amount of emotional distress damages and punitive damages that may be recovered in most employment lawsuits. There is no rational explanation for this beyond the influence of the plaintiffs' bar on the legislature. Is it really more traumatic to lose a job in California than in Indiana? The lack of damage limits often leads to outsized jury verdicts that courts are not likely to reduce except in extreme cases. When juries side with plaintiffs in employment cases, they often decide to make them millionaires—with the employer's money, of course.

California's overlapping laws are another reason employment lawsuits are more expensive in California. For example, let's say you terminate an employee who has been out on a medical leave for a long time and does not appear likely to return. You will probably be sued, not once but five times over, for: (a) disability discrimination, (b) failure to provide a reasonable accommodation, (c) failure to undertake the interactive process of accommodation, (d) failure to prevent discrimination, and (e) wrongful termination in violation of public policy. Each of these causes of action addresses the same termination decision, but they give a jury five separate grounds for awarding damages.

Numerous overlapping laws often apply in the wage and hour context as well. Suppose you pay your employees on a piece-rate basis, which is perfectly legal under federal law, and they earn well in excess of the minimum wage for all the hours they work. In California such a method of paying employees is illegal, however, if employees spend any part of their workdays not actually producing piecework. Virtually all piece-rate employees have downtime, such as training time, time spent waiting for a new assignment, and paid rest breaks. California courts have decided that these employees must be paid separately for these intervals in which they are not producing piece work. Dividing their total earnings by hours worked, as is done under federal law, will not suffice. Thus, almost every employer that has paid employees on a piece-rate basis has been (or is being) sued, but not just for unpaid minimum wage. Employees can also recover "liquidated damages" equaling the amount of unpaid minimum wage, plus interest and attorneys' fees. Former employees may also recover 30 days of pay as a "waiting time penalty" for not being paid all wages due when their employment terminated. In most wage and hour lawsuits, moreover, additional penalties are recoverable under PAGA.

Because wage and hour violations typically affect many employees, lawsuits for these violations are usually brought as class actions with the exposure for a particular error multiplied by the number of employees in the class. Class actions are a thriving industry in California. They started in the employment context with alleging that retail and restaurant managers were misclassified as exempt from overtime. Eventually most employers, some having been sued multiple times, properly classified their employees, so the class action lawyers moved on to attack missed meal and rest breaks. Then inaccurate paystubs became the focus, then piece-rate employees, and so on. As soon as employers get their houses in order with respect to one law, the class action lawyers switch their focus to another.

Even absent a class action lawsuit, simple mistakes can be costly. Say you have an employee who earns $52,000 annually. They quit their job, and when you calculate their accrued vacation due at termination, you erroneously undercalculate the amount due by a half day. That half day of vacation is worth $100. Suppose the former employee files a claim with the Labor Commissioner for unpaid vacation. They will likely be awarded the $100 *plus* $6,000 in waiting time penalties—$200 per day for each of the days (to a maximum of 30) that they had to wait to receive their $100.

1.4 This Book's Purpose and Approach

This book is written for those who must contend with employment law in California as part of their work. It is written primarily for business people and HR professionals, not lawyers, although in-house counsel and lawyers who practice outside of employment law will find it useful. This book's approach is practical. There is no lengthy analysis of court decisions, and there are no footnotes. This book is grounded in the law as it is found in statutes, regulations, and case law, but its focus is on how the law works in the real world. This book is written from the perspective of a lawyer who has spent a career advising employers, so it has a point of view. The purpose of this book is to help those who must deal with California employment law understand it better, but this book does not provide legal advice. Most of the time the right legal answer depends on the facts of a specific situation. Although this book will provide you with an overview of the law, it is not the substitute for competent advice from a lawyer who is knowledgeable about your business and is fully apprised of the facts of a particular situation.

CHAPTER 2

Employment at Will: What It Really Means

California's Labor Code contains a presumption that employees are employed at will. This means that either the employer or the employee may terminate employment at any time, with or without cause or prior notice. This is important for employers because "cause" is defined under California law as "a fair and honest cause or reason, regulated by good faith on the part of the employer." Employers would be significantly burdened if they had to prove to a court or jury that they acted "fairly" and "in good faith" in every employee termination.

2.1 Exceptions to Employment at Will

Exceptions to employment at will include:

- Public-sector employees, most of whom are protected by civil service laws and by a "memorandum of understanding" between their union and the agency that addresses discipline and termination.
- Employees represented by unions and covered by a collective bargaining agreement that contains a "just cause" standard for termination.
- Employees (usually executives) who have written employment contracts requiring "good cause" for termination.
- Employees whose employers have said or done things that overcome the presumption of employment at will.

Courts in some cases have found that employer policies or manager statements have overcome the presumption of employment at will, such that an implied contract to be terminated only for good cause arose. One such policy is a rigid "progressive discipline" policy under which employees cannot be fired until a series of prior warnings and lesser sanctions have been imposed. Managers' assurances of secure or long-term employment might also be found to overcome the presumption of employment at will in some circumstances.

2.2 Reinforcing Employment at Will

California courts will not find employer policies and manager statements to overcome the presumption of employment at will when an employee has signed an express employment-at-will acknowledgment. To retain the freedom to terminate employment without cause that employment at will affords you, therefore, you should do everything you can do to preserve employment at will. This means:

- Include an employment-at-will statement on the employment application and in offer letters so that a prospective employee understands, before leaving another job or moving from out of state, that the new job will be employment at will.
- Have new hires sign an employment-at-will acknowledgment on their first day.
- Include an employment-at-will statement in the employee handbook.
- Avoid rigid progressive discipline policies, and instead say that conduct violations "may lead to disciplinary action up to and including termination of employment."
- Train managers and supervisors not to make careless assurances of job security during job interviews or in response to questions from employees or applicants.
- When presented with an employment verification form in connection with a mortgage application, do not respond to questions asking about the employee's prospects for future employment.

fyi **Model Employment-at-Will Statement**

"I acknowledge that my employment is at will and for no specific duration. Either I or the company may terminate my employment at any time, with or without cause or prior notice. My employment-at-will status cannot be changed except in a writing signed by the president of the company."

2.3 The National Labor Relations Board and Employment at Will

The National Labor Relations Board (NLRB) is vigilant regarding employer policies that may tend to interfere with employees' exercise of their right to engage in concerted activity for mutual aid and protection under Section 7 of the National Labor Relations Act (see Section 19.2 in this book). In one case, an NLRB judge found unlawful an employment-at-will statement that said that it could never be changed. The judge found fault with this statement because employees have the right to decide to be represented by a union, and most union labor agreements contain a clause requiring just cause for termination. In another case, however, the NLRB approved of an employment-at-will provision stating that it could be changed only in writing by the president of the company, noting that this language did not foreclose employees choosing to be represented by a union and having a collective bargaining agreement with a just cause termination standard that would be signed by the president of the company.

It is not clear how far the NLRB will go in scrutinizing employment-at-will provisions. For now, employers should heed the agency's concerns by including language stating that employment at will cannot be changed except in a writing signed by the company president (or similar official).

2.4 Employment at Will vs. "Right to Work"

Sometimes employment at will is confused with the "right to work." They are different concepts, however. In states with right-to-work laws, union-represented employees cannot be forced to pay union dues or fees as a condition of employment. California is not a right-to-work state, so the term has no significance in California employment law.

2.5 The Limits of Employment at Will

Employment at will simply means that an employer cannot be sued for breach of an implied contract requiring a showing of good cause for termination. It does not mean that an employer may not be sued for other employment wrongs, such as discrimination, retaliation, violations of specific statutes (including those protecting whistleblowers or employees who take family or medical leave), or for terminations that violate public policies set forth in statutes or regulations.

Employers should do everything they can to preserve employment at will. It is not a good idea, though, to tell an employee only that "we are exercising our employment-at-will rights and terminating you." Because there are so many other grounds for employee lawsuits, you should still be sure to document the reasons for terminating an employee. This includes providing prior warnings, when appropriate, for poor job performance and less serious types of misconduct such as attendance policy violations. These warnings should not be given pursuant to a formal progressive discipline policy but rather simply to establish that misconduct or performance issues occurred and that the employee was put on notice of them, to rebut a later claim that the termination was motivated by an unlawful reason such as discrimination or retaliation.

CHAPTER 3

Arbitration of Employment Disputes

The U.S. Supreme Court and California state courts favor arbitration of employment disputes. Numerous court decisions over the last few years have strongly endorsed arbitration of employment cases, including class actions. All California private-sector, nonunion employers, therefore, should consider implementing arbitration of employment disputes.

3.1 Why Arbitration Is a Good Idea

There are several reasons to consider implementing arbitration agreements, including the following.

The Employer Is Likely to Get a Better Result in Arbitration

Multimillion-dollar jury verdicts in employment lawsuits in California are hardly news. An employer goes into a jury trial with the deck stacked against it. This is because jury trials of employment cases usually take several weeks, and the jurors who can afford to sit on jury duty for such a long time tend not to be owners or managers of businesses. More frequently they are public-sector employees who get paid for jury service, students, and retired persons. Most public-sector employees come from an environment where strict due process applies, and no one gets fired without multiple warnings and thorough documentation. Recently naturalized citizens are appearing with greater frequency on juries too, and some of them face language difficulties or come from countries with different legal systems than ours. Whatever their background, jurors tend to identify with the employee, and they may not view misconduct at work harshly. Some jurors may themselves have been mistreated by a boss. Many of them may view the company as a "big corporation" regardless of its actual size. Jurors tend to focus less on the evidence and more on what is "fair." By contrast, an arbitrator (who typically will be a retired judge) will be less likely to be swayed by bias or emotion and more likely to rule on the evidence.

It's not a jury of your peers. It's a jury of theirs.

The Exposure for a Case in Arbitration Is Generally Less than in a Jury Trial

Unlike in federal employment discrimination cases, there are no caps on non-economic (that is, emotional distress and punitive) damages in discrimination cases brought under California state law. Moreover, California jury instructions are often vague and generally favorable to plaintiffs, and the standards for mitigation of damages and for recovery of future lost wages are extremely indulgent to plaintiffs. Also, California laws give plaintiffs multiple shots at winning—and at winning multiple times. Separate causes of action for discrimination or harassment, as well as for failure *to prevent* discrimination or harassment, are permissible, as are separate causes of action for disability discrimination, failure to accommodate a disability, and failure to engage in the interactive process of accommodation. As a result, California juries typically award large sums when they rule for plaintiffs, and except in extreme cases, courts are not usually inclined to reduce damage awards. In arbitration, damage awards tend to be substantially more modest and reflect a plaintiff's actual losses. Whereas juries often want to punish an employer found liable for some workplace wrong, arbitrators are more likely to focus on making the plaintiff whole.

Arbitrated Cases Are Generally Less Expensive to Try

In the typical California jury trial, the case may trail for several days until a free courtroom is located; then two or three days are spent on arguing pre-trial motions and picking a jury. Because judges must deal with other matters, rarely will you have more than four or five hours of trial time per day, and many judges hold trial only three or four days per week. The typical employment case, therefore, takes at least three or four weeks to try. In arbitration, the case starts on the scheduled date, and you have eight hours of the arbitrator's time every day. No time is spent on jury selection or jury deliberations, and opening statements and closing arguments are streamlined. Most employment cases can be tried in between two and five days, substantially reducing the amount of attorney time needed. Even though under current law employers are required to pay the arbitrator's fees in full, given that arbitration hearings are usually shorter than jury trials and that no time is spent waiting for a courtroom to become available, arbitration is usually less expensive overall.

Arbitration Occurs in Private, So There Is Little or No Media Coverage

Although nothing prevents a plaintiff's attorney from attempting to gain publicity for an arbitration win, in practice, the media pays little attention to arbitration cases not involving celebrities or other famous people. Lack of media coverage reduces the likelihood of negative exposure and copycat lawsuits.

The Settlement Value of Arbitrated Cases Is Less than That of Cases Tried Before Juries

For all the above reasons, arbitrated cases are usually valued less for settlement purposes than jury cases. Plaintiffs' lawyers know that a jury trial will be expensive and that a sympathetic jury may award a substantial verdict, and they use these points as leverage to negotiate high settlements. They also know that an arbitrated case will cost the employer less to try, that the case will be decided on the evidence, and that they will not be able to appeal to a jury's emotions. This creates a discount of the settlement value of most arbitrated cases.

3.2 Potential Negatives Regarding Arbitration

Arbitration has some potential negatives. One is that the employer must pay the entire arbitrator's fee, win or lose. Most arbitrations are conducted by retired judges, whose fees can be substantial. Also, a bad arbitration result is not generally appealable in the courts, although a provision may be included in the arbitration agreement for appellate review by a second arbitrator. Finally, some arbitrators—but not all—are less inclined to award a summary judgment (that is, dismiss the case without a full hearing), but a summary judgment is often difficult to obtain in California state courts in employment cases in any event. On balance, the advantages of arbitration generally substantially outweigh the disadvantages.

3.3 Enforceability of Arbitration Agreements

California courts will enforce arbitration agreements so long as they are not unconscionable and they satisfy the requirements set forth by the California Supreme Court in *Armendariz v. Foundation Health Psychcare Services, Inc.* (2000).

With respect to unconscionability, the courts look for both *procedural* and *substantive* unconscionability. *Procedural unconscionability* involves oppression or unfair surprise in one party's entering into an arbitration agreement. A court will not find an arbitration agreement unconscionable simply because the employee was required to sign it as a condition of employment, however. Though courts often cite the "take it or leave it" nature of mandatory employment arbitration agreements as evidence of procedural unconscionability, they ordinarily do not refuse to enforce the agreement unless it is also substantively unconscionable. Nor will a court find unconscionability in an employee's assertion that they did not read or understand the agreement before signing it. It is important that you give the employee sufficient time to read the agreement and to ask questions of an employer representative knowledgeable about arbitration before signing it. In situations in which the arbitration agreement appears to be deliberately misleading, is prolix, contains too much unexplained legal jargon, is written in very small font, or is not provided in a language that the employee can understand, the likelihood of a court refusing to enforce it is greater.

Substantive unconscionability involves contract terms that are one-sided. The most common situation in which a court will refuse to enforce an arbitration agreement as unconscionable is when the employee is bound to arbitrate disputes with the employer over discrimination, harassment, or wrongful termination, yet the employer is free to litigate in court claims it has against the employee, such as theft or misappropriation of trade secrets. In addition, the *Armendariz* requirements also address issues of substantive unconscionability. Those requirements are:

- *The agreement to arbitrate must be mutual.* The agreement cannot require that only the employee arbitrate claims. The employer must similarly be bound to arbitrate all claims it may have against the employee. However, California law provides that either party may seek a temporary restraining order or a preliminary injunction in court without waiving arbitration.
- *The employee's rights and remedies may not be limited.* Statutes of limitations cannot be shortened, recoverable damages cannot be limited, and there cannot be a provision that the loser pays the winner's attorneys' fees. The employee must have all rights and remedies that would be available in court.
- *The arbitrator must be neutral.* The arbitrator may not be aligned with either party.
- *Adequate discovery must be available.* The agreement may not severely limit discovery. The parties must be able to take at least a few depositions, obtain documents from one another, and subpoena documents from third parties.
- *There must be a written arbitration award.* It must provide the arbitrator's reasoning in sufficient detail to allow for judicial review.
- *The employee must not be required to pay for the cost of the arbitration.* The employer must pay the arbitrator's fee in its entirety, but the employee typically must bear the same costs for court reporters, expert witnesses, and other expenses that would have been incurred had the case been heard in court.

Additionally, an arbitration agreement must be limited in scope to cover only claims arising out of or related to the employee's application for employment or employment. An agreement that is too broadly written to cover "all claims" between the employee and the employer entity (such as personal injury claims unrelated to the employee's employment) might be found to be unenforceable.

Electronic Signature

Arbitration agreements may be signed electronically. Under California law, an electronic signature has the same effect as a handwritten signature. On occasion, however, a plaintiff may attempt to avoid arbitration by claiming never to have electronically signed an arbitration agreement. In such an event you will need to prove that the plaintiff did in fact electronically sign the document. This requires more than just stating that all new employees are required to sign onboarding documents electronically. Courts require proof that only the plaintiff could have signed the document. This typically requires that a unique username and initial password be given to each new hire who will sign onboarding documents electronically. Then the employee must change the password to a personally selected password and enter a personal password before being permitted to sign documents electronically.

3.4 Requiring Arbitration as a Condition of Employment

Employers in California may require an applicant or employee to sign an arbitration agreement as a condition of employment or continued employment. The California legislature in 2019 attempted to block employers from doing so in Assembly Bill 51 (AB 51), but that legislation was struck down in court. Employers therefore remain free to require arbitration agreements. Before you fire an employee or decline to hire an applicant for refusing to sign an arbitration agreement, however, you should review the situation with your legal counsel. Among other considerations, you will want to be sure that your arbitration agreement is enforceable under current law.

3.5 Use of Arbitration Agreements to Block Class Actions

In *AT&T Mobility LLC v. Concepcion* (2011), the U.S. Supreme Court held that class action waivers in arbitration agreements are valid and enforceable. The California Supreme Court reached the same conclusion in *Iskanian v. CLS Transportation Los Angeles, LLC* (2014), specifically with respect to a class action waiver in the employment context.

Class and collective action waivers are lawful, and they should be included in all arbitration agreements in California. If your employees have only signed older agreements lacking such waivers, you should implement a new agreement that includes the waivers. These waivers are a potent tool for fighting class action lawsuits alleging wage and hour or other employment law violations.

3.6 Arbitration of Private Attorneys General Act Claims

The United States and California Supreme Courts have issued a series of decisions addressing whether claims brought under California's Private Attorneys General Act (PAGA), in which employees pursue penalties for violation of the California Labor Code, may be waived under an arbitration agreement. Unlike a class action suit, which is brought in the interest of the individual class members, PAGA lawsuits are brought in the interest of the state government (65 percent of the penalties recovered in a PAGA lawsuit must be turned over to the state). The net result of these court decisions is that a class and collective action waiver will require a plaintiff in a PAGA lawsuit to arbitrate their *individual* claim under PAGA, but the plaintiff's *representative* PAGA claim on behalf of other affected employees may still be pursued in court.

3.7 Arbitration of Sexual Assault and Sexual Harassment Claims

On March 3, 2022, President Biden signed into law the Ending Forced Arbitration of Sexual Assault and Sexual Harassment Act. Under this law, a pre-dispute arbitration agreement is not enforceable against a plaintiff in a lawsuit claiming sexual assault or sexual harassment should the plaintiff elect to proceed in court instead of arbitration. Likewise, a class action waiver in an arbitration agreement is not effective against a class or collective action alleging sexual assault or sexual harassment. "Sexual assault" is defined as a nonconsensual sexual act or sexual contact as defined in 18 U.S.C. Section 2246 or similar state or tribal law, including when the victim lacks capacity to consent. "Sexual harassment" means conduct that is alleged to constitute sexual harassment under federal, state, or tribal law. Under recent court decisions, *none* of the claims in a lawsuit are subject to mandatory arbitration if one of the claims is for sexual assault or sexual harassment.

3.8 Transportation Workers

The Federal Arbitration Act (FAA) covers all employees working in interstate commerce with one important exception. Transportation workers, defined as workers "actually engaged in the movement of goods in interstate or foreign commerce," are not covered by the FAA. Courts have ruled that workers such as truck drivers who do not drive across state lines are still engaged in the movement of goods in interstate commerce if the goods carried are part of the stream of interstate commerce. A truck driver who picks up goods at the port and transports them to destinations within California thus would qualify as engaged in the movement of goods in interstate commerce. The consequence of an employee not being covered by the FAA is that the FAA's preemption of California laws hostile to arbitration would not apply. Class action waivers are not enforceable under California law, for example. Likewise, Labor Code Section 229, which allows employees to sue in court to recover unpaid wages regardless of an applicable arbitration agreement, would prevail in the case of a transportation worker. In other respects, however, an arbitration agreement not subject to the FAA would still be enforceable under California law.

3.9 Temporary Employees

A California court has held that an employer that utilizes temporary employees provided by a staffing company may not rely on the staffing company's arbitration agreement with its employees to compel arbitration of claims brought against the employer by the temporary employees, absent a provision in that agreement that it covers claims against client employers. Therefore, if you use temporary employees, you should either ensure that the staffing agency's arbitration agreement covers claims against client employers, or else have temporary employees sign your arbitration agreement.

3.10 Drafting and Implementing Arbitration Agreements

Arbitration agreements may be implemented in a number of ways. Applicants for employment may be required to sign an arbitration agreement as part of, or along with, the employment application. Such an agreement would cover any claims of wrongful failure to hire, as well as employment claims should the applicant be hired. If an applicant is going to refuse to sign an arbitration agreement, it's better to know at the application stage so that time is not spent interviewing and making an offer only for the person to refuse to sign an arbitration agreement during the onboarding process.

All new hires may be required to sign an arbitration agreement during onboarding. Arbitration agreements should not be offered on a rushed "take it or leave it" basis during onboarding. Rather, new hires should be given time to read and understand the arbitration agreement, and a representative of HR or a manager familiar with arbitration should be available to explain the agreement if necessary and answer any questions. Employees who ask to be able to take the arbitration agreement home, to show it to a lawyer, or to have some time to consider it should be allowed to do so, but you should set a deadline for them to sign the agreement if they want to continue their employment.

All new hires should sign an arbitration agreement, even if they signed such an agreement during a prior period of employment with the same employer. A California court has held that an arbitration agreement signed during one period of employment does not necessarily apply to a later period of employment where there has been a break in service.

Current employees may be required to sign an arbitration agreement (or an updated agreement) at any time, but the ideal time to have current employees sign an arbitration agreement is when a new employee handbook is distributed. Requiring current employees to sign an arbitration agreement in the absence of a new employee handbook might arouse suspicion, cause insecurity, or lead to unrest among employees. Yet, if you have to get a new agreement signed (that includes, for example, a class and collective action waiver) and you are not ready to introduce a new employee handbook, go ahead and get as many employees to sign it as you can and then address those who are resisting.

Guidelines for drafting arbitration agreements include the following:

- The arbitration agreement should be a separate document. It should not be combined with other acknowledgments or agreements or be a part of the employee handbook.
- Avoid legal jargon, tiny print, long-running sentences, and unexplained references to statutes or regulations. For example, instead of referencing the California Fair Employment and Housing Act, refer to "claims of unlawful harassment, discrimination, and retaliation." Break the agreement up into digestible paragraphs. To the greatest extent possible, the agreement should be written so that laypersons can understand it. If applicants or employees cannot read English, an agreement translated into the language they can read and understand should be offered.
- The "Company" should be defined in the agreement as including parent, subsidiary, affiliate, and client entities, as well as all of their owners, directors, officers, members, managers, employees, agents, contractors, attorneys, benefit plan administrators, and insurers of the Company and of its parent, subsidiary, affiliate, or client entities.
- The agreement shall also state that it covers claims against any person or entities alleged to be a joint employer with the Company as well as claims brought against staffing companies, employee leasing companies, professional employer organizations, or payroll processing vendors that the Company has utilized.
- The agreement should state that the Company and the employee are engaged in interstate commerce (assuming this is true) and that the agreement is governed by the Federal Arbitration Act.
- The agreement should waive the right of the employee and the Company to bring a class or collective action and it should state that all claims shall be brought in the individual capacity of the employee and the Company. The agreement should state that any individual PAGA claims must be pursued in arbitration. The agreement should state that it shall not be construed to allow or permit the consolidation or joinder of claims of other claimants in arbitration, and that no arbitrator shall have authority under the agreement to order any such class or collective action or joinder of claims. The agreement should state that any dispute regarding the validity, scope, or enforceability of the agreement or the arbitrability of any particular claim shall be resolved by a court, not by the arbitrator.
- The agreement should identify a person within the company whom the employee can contact to commence an arbitration. Ideally a position ("Director of Human Resources") rather than a specific individual should be identified.

- The agreement should state that the company and the employee have the right to be represented by an attorney at the arbitration hearing but that neither side is required to have an attorney.
- The agreement should describe the process for selecting the arbitrator. It should state that the arbitrator will be selected by mutual agreement and must be impartial. It should state that if agreement cannot be reached upon a particular arbitrator, the company and the employee will select an alternative dispute resolution provider and request from that provider a list of an odd number of potential arbitrators from which the company and the employee will strike names until one arbitrator is left.
- The agreement should state that the employer will pay for the arbitrator and the forum costs for the arbitration.
- Consider whether to include a provision that the arbitrator's award is subject to review by a second arbitrator acting effectively as a court of appeal. The advantage of such a provision is that it would provide protection against an adverse ruling by the arbitrator. The disadvantage is that it would prolong the nature of the proceedings and place a favorable award by the first arbitrator into jeopardy.
- The agreement should state that the employee had time to review the agreement and ask questions of the employer's representative before signing it.
- A company representative does not need to sign the arbitration agreement for it to be enforceable. It is best not to include a space for a company representative's signature due to the potential that a company representative might not actually sign every arbitration agreement, thereby raising the question whether the company really agreed to arbitrate. Alternatively, use an electronic reproduction of the signature of a company executive to ensure that it appears on each arbitration agreement.
- Finally, the agreement should state that, to the full extent permissible under the law, if any term, provision, or portion of the agreement is deemed invalid or unenforceable, it shall be severed and the remainder of the agreement shall remain enforceable.

Have experienced employment counsel draft, or at least review, the arbitration agreement before implementing it. The law in this area continues to develop, and an agreement borrowed from another employer or acquired from a commercial source of legal forms may be outdated and potentially unenforceable. Also, do not copy a commercial arbitration provision for use in the employment context. Commercial arbitration agreements often contain provisions, such as prevailing party attorneys' fees clauses, that are not enforceable in an employment dispute.

After an employee has signed an arbitration agreement, give them a copy of it and retain the original in the employee's personnel file. Retain the whole agreement, not merely the signature page, so there is no dispute later about what the employee read and signed.

CHAPTER 4

Employee Handbooks

Employee handbooks fill several important roles. First, they set forth what the employee may expect from the employer, such as employee benefits, leave policies, reviews of performance, and duration of employment (that is, employment at will). Second, they set forth what the employer expects from the employee, including attendance and conduct with regard to such things as substance abuse, harassment, and computer use. Particularly where conduct policies are concerned, standards should be established that can be enforced consistently, versus ad hoc enforcement by different supervisors that may lead to claims of discrimination.

An employee handbook generally is a positive tool for employers, and it is essential that the handbook be kept current with changes in the law and that it be reviewed by employment counsel before it is distributed. An employee handbook can become a liability for an employer if it:

- Contains gratuitous language that provides unnecessary rights and protections for employees, such as a pledge always to treat employees fairly, or a rigid system of progressive discipline requiring oral and written warnings before termination;
- Contains outdated language covering matters such as how a complaint of harassment should be reported, paid sick days, or medical and family care leave; or
- Contains language that courts or government agencies such as the National Labor Relations Board (NLRB) deem to be illegal, such as a policy that prohibits criticism of the company on social media.

These potential problems can be avoided by careful drafting. An employee handbook should be written in layperson's style, without legalese, and it should contain no more words than are absolutely necessary to achieve its purpose. Briefer is better. Handbooks that are too wordy are likely to be confusing and internally inconsistent, and they might inadvertently vest employees with rights beyond what the law requires.

The NLRB's current standards must be taken into account in drafting handbook policies. These standards tend to shift back and forth depending on the political party in power. The current NLRB subjectively examines whether a workplace rule or policy "has a reasonable tendency to interfere with, restrain, or coerce employees who contemplate engaging in" concerted activity for mutual aid and protection regarding wages, hours and working conditions. In other words, if an employee, who is economically dependent on the employer, could reasonably interpret the rule to be coercive (even if a noncoercive interpretation is also reasonable), then the burden shifts to the employer to justify it.

The employer may justify the rule by showing that it advances a legitimate and substantial business interest, and that such interest cannot be protected with a more tailored version of the rule. A handbook rule remains overbroad when it could be narrowed to lessen the infringement of employees' statutory rights while still advancing the employer's interest. The better approach in drafting or revising an employee handbook is to steer clear of the policy prohibitions of the current NLRB so that you do not become a test case in litigation.

The goal of this chapter is to identify those elements of an employee handbook that will make it a useful tool for managing employees and for defending against employee claims and lawsuits, while avoiding gratuitous language that might lead to unnecessary claims and remaining inside the policy guardrails of the current NLRB.

4.1 Introductory Language

Many handbooks begin with an introductory section that provides some history and general information about the company. Such language is not problematic if it provides only background, but it should avoid statements about how many employees have enjoyed long and successful careers at the company or that express a desire that all new employees have a long and successful tenure. It should also avoid language about "company philosophy" or "company values" that contains references to employees always being treated "fairly" or to the company, with respect to its employees, always doing the "right thing." These statements can be taken out of context and used against an employer in a lawsuit alleging discrimination or wrongful treatment of employees.

4.2 Employment at Will

The first substantive policy statement in an employment handbook should be one that reinforces that all employees are employed at will, for no specific term, and that the employment relationship may be terminated either by the employee or the employer without cause or prior notice. The NLRB has taken issue with statements that employees' at-will status may *never* be changed, so the best approach is to state that an employee's at-will status cannot be changed except in a written document signed by the president (or other senior executive) of the company. The employment-at-will provision should also state that it supersedes any and all prior statements and representations of the employer, as well as any and all policies in the handbook that might be interpreted as being contrary to the principle of employment at will.

4.3 Introductory Period

Many employers establish an introductory period, typically lasting ninety days, for new employees to demonstrate their fit for the job. During that time, special attention is paid to the new employee's job performance, attendance, and overall interest in the job, and employees who fail to demonstrate the expected performance may be terminated at the conclusion of, or at any time during, the introductory period. A statement should be included that completion of the introductory period does not change the at-will nature of the employment relationship. This provision should also include language stating that in the event of a leave of absence or unsatisfactory performance during the initial introductory period, the period may be extended as necessary at the employer's option to give the employee an opportunity to demonstrate the ability to perform the job.

Use of "introductory period" rather than "probationary period" is preferred because in the case of the latter, employees may believe that they are "off probation" after ninety days and that their performance no longer matters as much as before.

The introductory period should be used to address early in the employment process those employees who are not likely to succeed. HR should check in with the employee's supervisor as the ninetieth day approaches to determine whether the employee is a good fit and should continue to be employed.

Use of "introductory period" rather than "probationary period" is preferred because in the case of the latter, employees may believe that they are "off probation" after 90 days and that their performance no longer matters as much as before. Also, the introductory period policy should not state that at the end of the period a successful employee will become a "permanent employee," as such wording is inconsistent with at-will employment.

4.4 Equal Employment Opportunity

The employer's commitment to equal employment opportunity (EEO) should appear early in the employee handbook. The policy should state a commitment to providing EEO to all employees and applicants without regard to race (including traits associated with race, such as hair texture and protective hairstyles, including braids, locks, and twists), ethnicity, religion (including religious dress and grooming practices), color, sex (including childbirth, breast feeding, and related medical conditions), gender, gender identity or expression, sexual orientation, national origin, ancestry, citizenship status, uniform service member and veteran status, marital status, pregnancy, age (40 and over), protected medical condition (including cancer and genetic conditions), genetic information, disability (mental and physical), reproductive health decision-making, domestic violence victim status, political affiliation, off-duty cannabis use, or any other protected status in accordance with all applicable federal, state, and local laws. The policy should specify that nondiscrimination will apply to all aspects of the employment relationship, including hiring, discipline, termination, promotions, transfers, reductions in force, compensation, benefits, and training.

The EEO policy should additionally state the employer's commitment to providing reasonable accommodations for qualified individuals with disabilities, as well as for employees' religious beliefs and practices. The policy should further state that an interactive process to identify possible accommodations will be conducted upon the employer's learning of the need for an accommodation.

4.5 Policy Against Unlawful Harassment

The policy against unlawful harassment is another crucial part of the employee handbook that should appear toward the beginning. It should state the employer's commitment to providing a work environment that is free of *unlawful* harassment. Sometimes policies against harassment are drafted too broadly to prohibit all forms of harassment. Such a broad prohibition should be avoided so that the employer need not investigate complaints rooted in petty personality conflicts between employees or legitimate but unpleasant supervisory action. By prohibiting only unlawful harassment, a policy addresses only such harassment that is based on sex or other categories protected under law.

The policy should strictly prohibit all forms of unlawful harassment, including harassment on the basis of race (including traits associated with race, such as hair texture and protective hairstyles, including braids, locks, and twists), ethnicity, religion (including religious dress and grooming practices), color, sex (including childbirth, breast feeding, and related medical conditions), gender, gender identity or expression, sexual orientation, national origin, ancestry, citizenship status, uniform service member and veteran status, marital status, pregnancy, age (40 and over), protected medical condition (including cancer and genetic conditions), genetic information, disability (mental and physical), reproductive health decision-making, domestic violence victim status, political affiliation, off-duty cannabis use, or any other protected status in accordance with all applicable federal, state, and local laws.

The policy should state that its prohibition against unlawful harassment applies to all employees, including supervisors and managers. The prohibition against harassment should also apply to unpaid interns, volunteers, customers, vendors, suppliers, independent contractors, and others doing business with the employer. This is because California law allows unpaid interns, volunteers, customers, contractors, and others having a business relationship with an organization to sue for unlawful harassment. Likewise, the policy should prohibit harassment of employees by customers, vendors, suppliers, independent contractors, and others doing business with the employer.

The policy should provide examples of prohibited sexual harassment. It should state that sexual harassment includes a broad spectrum of conduct, including harassment based on sex, gender, gender identity or expression, and sexual orientation. The policy should provide examples of unlawful and unacceptable behavior such as:

- Unwanted sexual advances.
- Offering an employment benefit (such as a raise, promotion, or career advancement) in exchange for sexual favors, or threatening an employment detriment (such as termination or demotion) for an employee's failure to engage in sexual activity.
- Visual conduct, such as leering, making sexual gestures, and displaying or posting sexually suggestive objects or pictures, cartoons, or posters.
- Verbal sexual advances, propositions, requests, or comments.
- Sending or posting sexually related videos or messages via email, text, instant messaging, or social media.
- Verbal abuse of a sexual nature, graphic verbal comments about an individual's body, sexually degrading words used to describe an individual, and suggestive or obscene letters, notes, or invitations.
- Physical conduct, such as touching, groping, assault, or blocking movement.
- Physical or verbal abuse concerning an individual's gender, gender identity, or gender expression.
- Verbal abuse concerning a person's characteristics such as pitch of voice, facial hair, or the size or shape of a person's body, including remarks that a male is too feminine or a woman is too masculine.

The policy should additionally provide examples of other types of prohibited harassment, such as harassment based on race, ethnicity, or religion. Such examples might include:

- Racial or ethnic slurs, insults, and any other offensive remarks based on a protected characteristic.
- Jokes, whether written, verbal, or electronic, that are based on a protected characteristic.
- Mocking or ridiculing another's religious or cultural beliefs, practices, or manner of dress.
- Threats, intimidation, horseplay, or other menacing behavior that is based on a protected characteristic.
- Inappropriate verbal, graphic, or physical conduct, including practical jokes based on a protected characteristic.
- Electronically sending or posting text messages, videos, or images that are harassing based on a protected characteristic.

The policy should explain what an employee should do in the event unlawful harassment occurs. Employees should not be directed to report harassment to their supervisor because the supervisor might be the alleged harasser. Ideally, employees should be directed to report harassment to HR, but the objective is to make it as easy and comfortable as possible for employees to report harassment internally, versus complaining to a government agency or obtaining a lawyer. In larger or multisite organizations, a "hotline" telephone number answered by HR should be provided for employees to use in reporting harassment. A designated email address for employees to use to report harassment should be provided as well.

fyi **Reporting Harassment**

Your policy against harassment should provide multiple means for employees to use to submit a complaint:

- Report harassment to the HR department;
- Report harassment via a "hotline" telephone number monitored by HR; and
- Report harassment via a designated email address that is routed to HR.

In an organization that is not large enough to have its own HR department, the policy should direct employees to report harassment to a company official outside the chain of command, such as the controller or chief financial officer. Alternatively, a small employer without an onsite HR department should consider contracting with an outside HR consulting firm for an employee hotline service to which complaints of harassment and other misconduct may be directed. The hotline number for that service should appear in the policy.

The policy additionally should direct managers and supervisors to report all complaints of harassment they receive to HR or a company official immediately. The policy should state that all complaints of unlawful harassment will result in a fair, complete, and timely investigation. The policy should state that the employer will maintain confidentiality to the greatest extent possible, consistent with the need to conduct an adequate investigation. The policy should state that employees will not be retaliated against for bringing a complaint of harassment or for participating in an investigation.

Finally, the policy should state that remedial action will be taken if a violation of the policy is found to have occurred. It should specifically state that a violation will subject an employee to disciplinary action, up to and including immediate termination. It should additionally warn that, under California law, managers and employees may be held personally liable for harassing conduct that violates the California Fair Employment and Housing Act (FEHA).

If ten percent of employees or more in a given location speak a language other than English, you must translate the policy against unlawful harassment into that language. This is best done by providing a free-standing translated policy to employees in their language. There is no legal requirement that you translate the entire employee handbook, although that may be advisable where a substantial portion of the workforce does not read English.

4.6 Policy Against Retaliation

Due to the increase in the number of retaliation claims and lawsuits, an employee handbook should also contain a specific policy against retaliation. The policy should state that the employer is committed to prohibiting retaliation against employees who report, oppose, or participate in an investigation of alleged wrongdoing in the workplace. Some examples of activity protected from retaliation might be listed, including:

- Filing a complaint with a federal, state, or local law enforcement or administrative agency regarding an alleged violation of any federal, state, or local law, rule, or regulation.
- Filing a complaint with a federal, state, or local law enforcement or administrative agency regarding allegedly unsafe or unhealthy working conditions.
- Participating in or cooperating with a federal, state, or local law enforcement agency conducting an investigation of alleged unlawful activity or allegedly unsafe or unhealthy working conditions.
- Testifying as a party, witness, or accuser regarding alleged unlawful activity or as a witness regarding allegedly unsafe or unhealthy working conditions.
- Making or filing an internal complaint with the company regarding alleged unlawful activity or allegedly unsafe or unhealthy working conditions.
- Assisting another employee in making such a complaint.

As with complaints of harassment, employees who feel they have been retaliated against should be directed to complain to HR, some other official of the organization such as the controller or chief financial officer, or an employee hotline or designated email address maintained by HR or by an outside HR consulting firm.

4.7 Employee Definitions

Many employee handbooks include definitions of the various types of employees in the organization. The most common are the definitions of full-time and part-time employees. Under the Patient Protection and Affordable Care Act (ACA), employers that are subject to the law's "pay or play" employer mandate must provide health plan eligibility to all "full-time" employees. The ACA defines "full-time" as working at least 30 hours per week. Full-time employment is commonly the prerequisite for other employee benefits as well, such as paid vacation and holiday pay. Employers must decide, therefore, whether to use the 30 hour ACA threshold to define "full-time" for all employee benefits, or instead to use the ACA threshold for eligibility to participate in the health plan and use a higher threshold (35 or 40 hours per week, for example) for eligibility for other benefits. Note that under California's paid sick leave law, all employees, including part-time and temporary employees, who work 30 or more days within a year of hire are eligible to accrue paid sick leave.

4.8 Overtime

An employee handbook should set forth two basic rules concerning overtime. First, nonexempt employees should be informed that they are not permitted to work unscheduled overtime without the prior express approval of their supervisors and that working overtime without prior authorization may result in disciplinary action. Second, employees should be advised that scheduled overtime may be required of them as the employer's needs dictate, and that they must work overtime when assigned to do so.

4.9 Meal Periods

An employee handbook should set forth the employer's policy regarding meal periods for nonexempt employees. That policy should state that all nonexempt employees who work more than five hours must take an uninterrupted 30-minute meal period free from all duty to begin no later than the end of the fifth hour of work, and that they must take a second uninterrupted 30-minute meal period free from all duty to commence no later than the end of the tenth hour should an employee work more than ten hours in a day. Employees should be required to record the beginning and ending times of their meal periods in the timekeeping system. Employees should be prohibited from performing any work during meal breaks and should be allowed to leave the premises. Employees should be prohibited from altering, falsifying, or manipulating any aspect of their timekeeping records to inaccurately reflect or hide meal periods or time spent working during meal periods.

The employee handbook should describe the circumstances under which a meal period may be waived; that is, if an employee will complete their workday in six hours, the meal period may be waived. An employee who works more than ten but less than 12 hours in a workday may waive the second meal period only if the first meal break was taken. An employee who works more than 12 hours in a workday may not waive the second meal period. Employees should not be allowed to waive or skip their meal breaks to shorten their workdays.

In limited situations, certain employees may be authorized to work an on-duty meal period when the nature of the employee's duties prevent the employee from being relieved of all duty. The employee handbook should state that employees will be permitted to take an on-duty meal period only if the nature of their job duties requires it and if both the employee and the employer have agreed in writing to an on-duty meal period. Any on-duty meal period must be paid and treated as hours worked.

4.10 Rest Breaks

An employee handbook should also set forth the employer's policy regarding rest breaks. It should provide that all nonexempt employees must take a 10-minute paid rest break for every four hours worked (or major fraction thereof), which should be taken so far as practicable in the middle of each work period. Rest breaks should be provided according to the number of hours worked, as seen in Table 4.1. The policy on rest breaks should state that employees are relieved of all duty while on their rest breaks, and that they should not answer work-related text messages, emails, or phone calls while on their rest breaks. Additionally, it should advise employees that they are free to leave the premises during their rest breaks if they wish.

Unless all employees take their rest breaks at the same time, the employee handbook should direct employees to schedule their rest periods at their own discretion under these guidelines, except that (a) a supervisor may schedule rest breaks to best ensure coverage of workflow, and (b) rest breaks may not be combined with other rest or meal breaks, or used to shorten the workday.

Table 4.1 Number of Required Rest Breaks

Shift (Hours Worked in Day)	Number of Paid Rest Breaks
At least 3.5 but less than 6 hours	1
At least 6 but less than 10 hours	2
At least 10 but less than 14 hours	3

Cool-Down Breaks

If employees work outdoors, the employee handbook must additionally advise them of their right to take a paid cool-down rest break in the shade for a period of at least five minutes when they feel the need to do so to protect themselves from overheating. Employers in the agriculture, construction, landscaping, and oil and gas extraction industries, as well as those that are engaged in transportation of heavy materials, must advise their employees that they are required to take a minimum ten-minute break every two hours where the temperature is 95 degrees Fahrenheit or greater (see Section 9.4).

4.11 Lactation Accommodations

California employers must include in their employee handbooks a policy regarding lactation accommodations that includes:

- A statement about an employee's right to request a lactation accommodation.
- The process by which an employee may make a request for a lactation accommodation.
- The employer's obligation to respond to requests for lactation accommodations.
- A statement about an employee's right to file a complaint with the Labor Commissioner for any failure by the employer to provide lactation accommodations.

The policy additionally should state that employees will be provided with a room or place, other than a restroom, to express breast milk in private as needed. The policy should direct employees to take lactation breaks concurrently with meal and rest breaks already provided, and state that if additional lactation breaks are taken they will be unpaid.

4.12 Paid Holidays

An employee handbook should identify which, if any, holidays will be paid holidays and what requirements exist for an employee to be paid for a holiday. For example, paid holidays may be restricted to full-time employees who have completed their introductory period. The employee handbook may provide that, to be eligible for holiday pay, an employee must work the last scheduled day before the holiday and the first scheduled day after the holiday, unless the employee is taking a preapproved vacation on those days. The employee handbook should also provide that holiday pay does not count as "hours worked" for purposes of calculating an employee's entitlement to overtime during the week in which the holiday occurs. Moreover, the employee handbook should address the treatment of holiday pay for exempt employees, who typically are not paid extra for holidays but rather receive their usual salary for the workweek in which a holiday occurs.

4.13 Paid Vacation

An employee handbook should describe the employer's vacation policy in some detail, as disputes over vacation are common, and a clear and comprehensive vacation policy can help prevent such disputes. Elements of a vacation policy should include:

- *Eligibility.* Are all employees or only full-time employees provided vacation? Is there a waiting period for new hires until vacation begins to accrue?
- *Rate of accrual.* Will all employees accrue vacation at the same rate, or will employees with greater length of service accrue vacation at a higher rate? Will accrual be suspended when employees are on a leave of absence?
- *Maximum accrual cap.* Will accrual of vacation cease after reaching a certain point until some accrued vacation is used?
- *Pay in lieu of vacation.* Will employees be paid for accrued but unused vacation at the end of a year?
- *Increments of vacation.* What is the smallest increment of time in which employees will be allowed to take vacation?
- *Management approval.* Will employees be required to obtain management approval of their scheduling of vacation? This can help avoid unexpected absences due to unscheduled vacation days.

Some employers provide vacation to nonexempt employees but have no formal vacation policy for certain management, commission-paid, or professional employees. Such an approach is lawful, but it must be clearly explained in the employee handbook.

4.14 Paid Sick Leave

Paid sick leave policies must comply with California's paid sick leave law. Employees (including part-time and temporary employees) who have worked 30 or more days in California for the same employer within a year of their employment must accrue paid sick leave at the rate of one hour for every 30 hours worked beginning at the commencement of employment. Employees may be limited to using 40 hours (or five workdays, whichever is greater) of paid sick leave per year, and total accrual of paid sick time may be capped at 80 hours. These caps on use and accrual of paid sick leave are not automatic, however. They must be stated in your policy.

You may maintain a more generous sick leave policy if you wish, or you may combine sick leave and vacation into a paid time off (PTO) bank. Such policies will be compliant so long as they satisfy the law's accrual, use, and carry-over requirements and provide no less than 40 hours of paid sick leave annually. You may use a different accrual method, other than providing one hour for every 30 hours worked, provided that the accrual is on a regular basis so that an employee can accrue no less than 24 hours of accrued paid sick leave or PTO by the 120th day of employment, and no less than 40 hours of accrued sick leave or PTO by the 200th calendar day of employment, or in each calendar year or year of employment.

Paid sick leave starts to accrue when the employee commences employment, but employees may be required to wait until their 90th day of their employment to use accrued paid sick leave.

As an alternative to the accrual method, employers may "front-load" five paid sick days at the beginning of each year. Under this method, unused sick days do not carry over to the following year, as five new sick days are granted at the start of that year.

The paid sick leave policy should state that paid sick days may be used for the diagnosis, care, or treatment of an employee's existing health condition or for preventive care such as annual checkups. Paid sick leave may also be used for care of an employee's family members. These include spouses, registered domestic partners, children (regardless of age), parents (including stepparents and parents-in-law), grandparents, grandchildren, siblings, and a "designated person." Employees should be notified that they may identify such a "designated person" when they request to use paid sick leave, and an employee may be limited to one "designated person" per twelve-month period. The policy should also state that paid sick days also may be used by employees who are victims of domestic violence, sexual assault, or stalking. The statute for this policy does not limit these paid sick days to recovery from personal harm. In fact, other statutes providing time off for domestic violence, sexual assault, or stalking allow such time off for measures such as obtaining court injunctions or taking safety precautions.

Employees may decide the amount of leave they need to use, although employers may set a minimum increment of two hours. Employees should be required to provide advance notification of their need to use the leave as soon as practicable, but no specific amount of advance notice may be required. Employers may not require that employees produce a doctor's note when using paid sick leave.

The policy should state that accrued but unused sick days will carry over into the following year subject to the 80-hour accrual cap, but employees are not entitled to be paid for accrued but unused sick days upon resignation or termination of employment. If they are rehired within a year of their separation, however, any unused sick leave that was previously accrued and not paid at termination must be reinstated.

Whereas eligibility for other benefits such as vacation may be delayed until an employee has worked 90 days or six months, accrual of paid sick leave must start at the commencement of employment, so if a PTO policy is used, the PTO must start accruing upon commencement of employment.

In addition to California's paid sick leave requirement, numerous local jurisdictions in California have enacted their own paid sick leave ordinances. They include Los Angeles, Oakland, San Diego, and San Francisco (see Section 15.5). These ordinances differ in many respects from the California law, and when there is a conflict between state and local law, whichever law is more favorable to employees is the law that applies. If you have employees in local jurisdictions that have their own paid sick leave laws, these local laws should be referenced in your employee handbook.

Why You Should Consider Moving from PTO Back to Separate Vacation and Sick Leave

PTO became a popular concept because employees could decide when and how to use their paid time off. They did not have to call in sick when they were not sick so as not to lose their sick days, and they could use their vacation time for a serious illness or injury if needed. PTO became popular before California imposed mandatory sick leave on employers, however. Now that employees must receive at least five paid sick days per year, employers should consider moving away from PTO and back to separate vacation and sick leave accounts. There are at least two reasons for this.

One is that if paid sick leave is combined with vacation, the unused balance of all of it must be paid upon termination of employment. If paid sick leave is kept separate, only accrued vacation need be paid upon termination.

The second is that the paid sick leave law contains a strict anti-retaliation provision. If paid sick leave is combined with vacation, presumably all of it then becomes subject to that anti-retaliation provision. Thus, instead of five days for which an employee may provide little or no advance notice of the need for leave, under a combined PTO policy, *all* of the days could be taken with little or no advance notice and the employer would be restricted by the anti-retaliation provision from taking action against an employee who repeatedly took days off with little or no notice.

Where vacation and paid sick days are separate, you can put reasonable limits on an employee's use of vacation, such as requiring:

- That all vacation must be scheduled in advance and that the scheduling be approved by the supervisor. This prevents an employee from taking a vacation day off without advance notice.
- That vacation may not be taken during busy periods, such as the high tourist season for hospitality employers, the holiday shopping season for retail employers, and so on.
- That the number of employees on vacation at the same time in a department be limited.

There are some complications involved in transitioning from PTO back to separate vacation and paid sick leave, so if you intend to do so, you should consult with your employment counsel.

Consider whether it still makes sense to have a PTO policy versus separate vacation and sick leave policies. Taking into account mandatory paid sick leave, PTO represents the worst of both worlds. It all must be paid out at time of termination, yet controls cannot be placed on employees' usage of the time.

4.15 Family and Medical Leave Act/California Family Rights Act Leave

The California Family Rights Act (CFRA) differs significantly from the Family and Medical Leave Act (FMLA) in several respects. One key difference is in the minimum number of employees required for coverage. The FMLA applies to employers with 50 or more employees within a 75 mile radius. The CFRA applies to employers of five or more employees regardless of location. Employers of between five and 49 employees should have a CFRA policy in their employee handbook. Employers of 50 or more employees must have a policy that addresses both laws. The respective provisions of the FMLA and CFRA are covered in detail in Section 15.1.

Whether you have only a CFRA policy or you have both an FMLA and a CFRA policy, the policy should include:

- An explanation of the eligibility criteria for leave.
- A listing of the reasons leave may be taken.
- The definition of a "serious health condition."
- How leave may be taken, including when intermittent leave is available.
- How employees may continue their health benefits while on leave.
- How much advance notice is required for taking leave.
- What types of medical certifications are required at the beginning of leave, during leave, and upon the conclusion of leave.
- What will happen if the employee fails to return to work at the conclusion of leave.
- An explanation of when military-related leave (military caregiver leave and qualified exigency leave) is available.

Two additional topics should be addressed: how the 12 month period in which the maximum 12 weeks of leave is taken will be measured, and whether employees will be required or allowed to use paid leave while on FMLA/CFRA leave.

The 12-Month Measuring Period

Employers may choose one of the following methods for determining the 12-month measuring period in which the maximum of 12 weeks of FMLA/CFRA leave may be taken:

- The calendar year or the employer's fiscal year.
- The employee's anniversary year.
- The 12-month period measured forward from the first day of leave; for example, if an employee begins an FMLA/CFRA leave on July 1, their 12-month period would end on June 30 of the next year.
- The rolling 12-month period measured backward from the first day of leave; each time an employee uses FMLA/CFRA leave, the available amount of leave would be the balance of 12 weeks of leave that has not been used in the prior 12 months.

You may select any one of these four methods so long as the method is applied consistently to all employees, and you must provide notice to employees of which method you have selected. If you change the method you will use to measure available leave, you must provide 60 days' advance notice to employees, and you must ensure that the change does not result in employees losing any amount of their full leave entitlement. The 12-months rolling backward method is generally the most beneficial for employers because it accounts for all leave previously used by the employee in the 12 months preceding the current leave.

For FMLA leave taken to care for a covered military service member, the 12-month period must be calculated beginning on the first day the eligible employee takes FMLA leave to care for the service member and ending 12 months after that date.

Use of Paid Leave

Under both the FMLA and the CFRA, you may require or allow employees to choose to use accrued paid leave (such as vacation, sick leave, or PTO) while on FMLA/CFRA leave under certain circumstances.

Under the FMLA and CFRA, you may require employees to use accrued paid leave only when the leave would otherwise be unpaid. If paid leave is available (such as via workers' compensation, state disability, or state paid family leave), employees cannot be required to use accrued paid leave. An exception would be for the seven-day waiting period for state disability leave benefits under California law. You may require an employee to use accrued vacation or PTO during an otherwise unpaid portion of leave. You may require an employee to use accrued sick leave during any unpaid leave used for the employee's own serious health condition.

The FMLA/CFRA section in an employee handbook should therefore state that employees may request to use their accrued paid leave while on FMLA/CFRA leave. If you wish to require employees to use paid leave while on FMLA/CFRA leave that is not otherwise paid, the circumstances in which paid leave must be used should be specified.

Working During Leave

Your FMLA/CFRA policy should provide that while on a leave of absence, employees are prohibited from holding other employment, including self-employment, not held immediately before the start of the leave. In other words, an employee who has another job in addition to the employee's job with your company may continue working that job while on leave from your company if medically able to do so, but such an employee may not seek and hold other employment to replace the employee's job with your company while on leave. The policy should state that any violation may result in disciplinary action, up to and including immediate termination of employment.

4.16 Other Medical Leaves

The disability discrimination laws (Americans with Disabilities Act and Fair Employment and Housing Act) require that medical leave be provided as a reasonable accommodation for an employee's disability regardless of whether leave under the FMLA/CFRA is available. Such medical leaves may have to be granted when:

- The employer has fewer than five employees.
- The employee does not qualify for FMLA/CFRA leave.
- The employee has exhausted their FMLA/CFRA leave.

An employee handbook should therefore state that employees with a disability may be granted a medical leave if it amounts to a reasonable accommodation. A medical leave policy may require medical certification from the employee's physician as a condition for granting leave. Features that are not lawful and that should not be included are:

- Arbitrary limitations on the amount of leave that will be granted (such as 30 or 60 days, or a year); the only limit on the length of leave that the law allows is that the leave must be a reasonable accommodation and not constitute an undue hardship for the employer.
- A requirement that the employee return to work "100 percent healed" or without any restrictions; work restrictions may have to be accommodated so long as they do not impose an undue hardship on the employer.

4.17 Pregnancy Leave and Accommodations

Since California has a specific pregnancy disability leave law (see Section 15.4), a section on pregnancy leave and accommodations should be included in an employee handbook. It should state that pregnant employees may take a leave of absence of up to four months for disability relating to pregnancy, childbirth, or related medical conditions. Leave is available for such period of time, up to four months, that an employee is *disabled* by pregnancy or childbirth, so a statement from the employee's physician should be required that indicates that the employee is disabled on account of pregnancy or childbirth and when the employee is anticipated to be able to return to work.

With the enactment of the federal Pregnant Workers Fairness Act in 2023, both federal and California law requires employers to provide reasonable accommodations for pregnant employees. Examples of such accommodations should be stated in your policy and should include:

- Temporary modification of job duties;
- Temporary transfer to a lighter-duty position;
- Assistance with lifting and other manual work;
- Modified work schedule and time off as necessary for medical appointments;
- More frequent or longer rest breaks;
- More frequent restroom breaks;
- Modification of uniform requirements;
- Allowing the employee to sit and/or drink water while working;
- A closer parking space; and
- Leave to recover from childbirth.

Note that an essential job function may have to be eliminated temporarily as an accommodation for a pregnant employee, unlike for employees with other types of disabilities. A pregnant employee cannot be required to go onto a leave of absence if there are accommodations that could be made to allow them to continue working. Employees should be directed to notify HR or some other official in the event a reasonable accommodation for pregnancy is required.

4.18 Bereavement Leave

Employers of five or more employees must allow employees who have been employed for at least 30 days to take up to five days of bereavement leave for the death of a spouse, child, parent, sibling, grandparent, grandchild, domestic partner, or parent-in-law. The five days need not be taken consecutively, but they must be taken within three months of the date of the death of the family member. The leave need not be paid, but the employee must be allowed to use accrued vacation or sick leave while on bereavement leave. The employee may be required to produce proof of the family member's death, such as a death certificate, published obituary, or other written verification of death or memorial services from a government agency, religious institution, or funeral home.

4.19 Jury Duty Leave

California employers must provide unpaid leave for employees who are selected for jury service. Some employers elect to provide paid jury duty leave for some duration. The terms and conditions of such paid leave should be set forth in the employee handbook. Note that exempt employees must receive their regular weekly salary even though they miss partial days or partial weeks on account of jury duty.

4.20 Military Service Leaves

Federal and California laws provide for protected leaves of absence for military personnel, reservists, and members of the National Guard who are called to active duty (these laws are addressed in detail in Section 15.7). Mention of the availability of such leave and the expectations of employees who take such leaves should be included in an employee handbook.

4.21 Other Required Leaves of Absence

California law mandates that various other leaves of absence, some paid, others unpaid, be provided (further details on these leaves are found in Chapter 15). Applicable leaves should be set forth in an employee handbook:

- Employees required to testify in a court proceeding may take unpaid witness leave.
- Up to two hours of paid leave must be provided to employees who do not have sufficient time to vote in a public election outside of working hours.
- Victims of certain crimes and their immediate family members are entitled to unpaid leave to attend court proceedings regarding such crimes (see Section 15.11).
- Employees of employers with 25 or more employees who are victims, or whose family members are victims of "qualifying acts of violence" such as domestic violence, sexual assault, stalking, or any act, conduct or pattern of conduct that includes (i) bodily injury or death to another; (ii) brandishing, exhibiting, or drawing a firearm or other dangerous weapon; or (iii) a perceived or actual threat to use force against another to cause physical injury or death, may take unpaid leave for the following purposes:

  - To obtain or seek to obtain relief from a court, such as a restraining order or other injunctive relief;
  - To seek or obtain medical attention for, or to recover from, injuries;
  - To seek or obtain services from a domestic violence shelter or similar victim services organization;
  - To seek or obtain psychological counseling or mental health services;
  - To participate in safety planning;
  - To relocate or secure a new residence or enroll children in a new school;
  - To provide care to a family member who is recovering from injuries;
  - To seek or obtain civil or criminal legal services;
  - To prepare for or attend any civil, administrative or criminal legal proceeding; or
  - To seek, obtain or provide childcare or care to a dependent adult if necessary to ensure the safety of the child or dependent adult.
- Employees of employers with 25 or more employees may take up to 40 hours per year of unpaid leave (not exceeding eight hours per month) to attend school activities involving their children or their grandchildren or other children of whom they have custody.
- Employees who are volunteer firefighters, volunteer emergency rescue workers, or reserve police officers may take unpaid leave to perform emergency duty and may additionally take up to 14 days of unpaid leave per year to participate in training related to such activities.
- Employees of employers with 15 or more employees who have been employed for at least 90 days and who are members of the California Wing of the Civil Air Patrol may take up to 10 days of unpaid leave per year to participate in emergency Civil Air Patrol missions.
- Employees of employers with 25 or more employees and who are spouses or domestic partners of military personnel may take up to 10 days of unpaid leave when such spouses or domestic partners are on leave from active military duty.
- An employee who has been employed for at least 90 days is entitled to take paid leave for up to 30 business days per year for organ donation. Organ donors may take an additional 30 days of unpaid leave. Employees may be required to use up to two weeks of their accrued PTO, vacation, and/or sick leave for organ donor leave.
- An employee who has been employed for at least 90 days is entitled to take paid leave for up to five business days per year for bone marrow donation. Employees may be required to use up to five days of their accrued PTO, vacation, and/or sick leave for bone marrow donor leave.
- Employees who have a drug or alcohol addiction and who decide to enroll voluntarily in a rehabilitation program must be given unpaid time off to

participate in the program unless it would result in an undue hardship for the employer. You must make reasonable efforts to keep the fact that the employee enrolled in the program confidential. The employee may choose to use any available PTO, vacation, or paid sick leave for such leave.

- An employee who has been employed for at least 30 days is entitled to up to five days of unpaid reproductive loss leave in the event of a miscarriage, still-birth, unsuccessful assisted reproduction, failed surrogacy, or failed adoption. The employee may choose to use any available PTO, vacation, or paid sick leave for such leave.

4.22 Electronic Communications

Electronic communications are so pervasive in the workplace today that every employee handbook should contain a comprehensive electronic communications policy consisting of the following elements.

Mobile Devices

A policy prohibiting use of personal cell phones, smartphones, tablets, and other mobile electronic devices for personal calls and texting during working time except in an emergency should be considered. Such a policy should instruct employees to restrict use of their personal mobile devices to their meal and rest breaks. Before implementing such a policy, however, you should be prepared to enforce it consistently.

You may include a policy prohibiting employees from using cell phones or other devices to make unconsented audio or video recordings of customers or clients. You may also prohibit employees from taking photographs or making recordings of material constituting trade secrets and confidential business documents not related to wages or working conditions.

If employees are permitted to use personal or employer-owned mobile devices while working, they should be prohibited from using such handheld devices to make or receive calls or to write, send, or read any text-based communication, including text messages, instant messages, and emails while driving. Employees should be informed that if they are charged with traffic violations resulting from the use of mobile devices while driving, they will be solely responsible for all fines, penalties, and liabilities resulting from such actions.

Computers, Internet, and Email

A policy should address the use of all employer-owned computers, databases, and personal computers used for business, including laptops, tablets, or home computers that are connected to the employer's network on a regular or intermittent basis. The policy should state that all information that is temporarily or permanently stored, transmitted, or received with the aid of the employer's computer systems remains the sole and exclusive property of the employer. Employees should be informed that they shall have no expectation of privacy in connection with their access and use of the employer's computer systems, including internet access and company email, and that such use may be monitored without further notice at any time.

Employees should be prohibited from using the employer's computers or computer system for any unlawful purpose or in a manner that violates company policies, such as the policy against unlawful harassment or the confidentiality policy.

Employees should further be prohibited from removing any software or data from employer-owned computers upon termination of employment.

Finally, employees should be prohibited from soliciting personal business opportunities through the employer's computer system or via company email. They should also be prohibited from using employer-owned computers for gambling, streaming movies or videos, watching television programs, viewing pornography, playing electronic games, or trading stocks or other securities.

4.23 Confidentiality

Ideally, if employees have access to the employer's trade secrets or confidential business information, they should sign confidentiality agreements (see Section 11.5). A confidentiality policy in an employee handbook provides less protection for the employer, but it should be included if signed confidentiality agreements cannot be obtained from employees. Such a policy should begin with definitions of trade secrets and confidential information.

The policy should then state that all trade secrets and confidential information are the sole property of the employer, and that employees, except as required in the conduct of the employer's business, must not disclose or use for their own purposes or the purposes of any other person or entity any of the employer's trade secrets or confidential business information. The policy should further provide that all files, documents, and data relating to the employer's business are and will remain the sole property of the employer, must not be copied, and must be returned upon termination of employment.

Under California law, employers cannot prohibit employees from disclosing their own wages to coworkers or others. The same holds true under NLRB law, which extends further to cover discussion of working conditions as well as wages.

4.24 Social Media

An employee handbook should contain a social media policy covering employee use of online tools that allow the sharing of content and profiles, such as personal web pages, message boards, networks, and communities such as Facebook, X (formerly known as Twitter), LinkedIn, Pinterest, Instagram, Reddit, and blogs. The policy should provide that employees engaging in use of social media are subject to all the employer's policies and procedures, including those protecting trade secrets and confidential business information, prohibiting unlawful discrimination and harassment, and governing use of electronic communications. The policy should also prohibit the following:

- Using social media to post or to display comments about coworkers, supervisors, customers, vendors, suppliers, or members of management that are physically threatening or that constitute a violation of the employer's policies against discrimination, retaliation, or harassment on account of any protected category, class, status, act, or characteristic.
- Posting or disclosing the employer's trade secrets or confidential business information not related to employee wages or working conditions.
- Posting or displaying content that misrepresents, or constitutes an intentional public attack on, the quality of the employer's products or services in a manner that a reasonable person would perceive as calculated to harm the employer's business and that is unrelated to any employee concern involving wages or working conditions.
- Using social media while on working time, unless it is being used for company business and with prior authorization.

The NLRB has taken issue with numerous employers' social media policies in recent years. The law in this area continues to evolve, but, in general, to avoid an unfair labor practice charge, employer social policies should not:

- Be written broadly or vaguely such that they could be read as having a reasonable tendency to interfere with employees' exercise of their Section 7 right to engage in concerted activity over wages and working conditions (see Section 19.2);
- Prohibit social media content that is "discourteous" to management, "embarrassing" to the company, or critical of management;
- Prohibit employees from discussing their own pay, other employees' pay, their working conditions, or the financial performance of the company;
- Prohibit employees from using social media to communicate with other employees or to comment about company business, including prohibiting or discouraging employees from "friending" coworkers; or
- Prohibit employees from posting material on social media that portrays the employer in a negative light.

Note that the NLRB has held that a "savings clause," or disclaimer, that nothing in the social media policy is intended to interfere with employees' rights under the National Labor Relations Act will not protect a policy that otherwise contains unlawful provisions. It is important, therefore, to draft a social media policy precisely and in accordance with the latest rulings issued by the NLRB.

4.25 Other Rules of Conduct

Every employee handbook should contain basic rules of conduct for the workplace. Although these should be tailored to each employer's operation, a description of some common policies follows. A rigid structure of progressive discipline should be avoided. Rather, employees should be informed that violation of the conduct rules, as well as any other work-related misconduct, may lead to discipline ***up to and including immediate termination.*** This wording provides the employer with flexibility to apply the appropriate punishment for the offense involved.

A rigid structure of progressive discipline should be avoided. Rather, employees should be informed that violation of the conduct rules, as well as any other work-related misconduct, may lead to discipline *up to and including immediate termination.*

Absenteeism and Tardiness

Employees should be required to personally contact their supervisor if they are to be late for or absent from work, and they should be informed that leaving a voice mail message or sending a text message or email is not sufficient. Employees should also be prohibited from leaving work early without personally notifying their supervisor and obtaining the supervisor's permission.

Employees should be informed that if they fail to appear for work or to call in for more than three consecutive days, they will be considered to have abandoned their job and will be terminated.

Employees may also be informed that excessive absenteeism or tardiness will not be tolerated. Care must be used in terminating an employee for excessive absences or tardiness due to a health condition, however, as a reasonable accommodation in the form of time off or an adjusted work schedule may have to be provided if the health condition amounts to a disability. Care must also be used not to terminate an employee for poor attendance based on use of paid sick days. On the other hand, repeated absences or tardiness on account of car trouble, other transportation problems, incarceration, oversleeping, or other examples of personal irresponsibility need not be accommodated and may be the basis for discipline or discharge.

Finally, employees may be required to provide a medical excuse for absences due to illness unless they are on an approved leave of absence or have taken paid sick leave.

Dating and Sexual Relationships

An employee handbook should contain a policy addressing dating and sexual relationships between employees because of the potential for such relationships to pose conflicts of interest, disruption of work, perceptions of favoritism, or charges of sexual harassment. Managers and supervisors should be prohibited from engaging in dating or sexual relationships with subordinate employees. Although an employer may not lawfully prohibit dating or sexual relationships between peer employees, the policy should require that employees in such relationships behave in a professional manner at all times and avoid displays of affection at work and arguments in the workplace over relationship issues.

Drugs and Alcohol

Every employee handbook should contain a policy addressing drugs and alcohol. Employees should be prohibited from manufacturing, cultivating, distributing, dispensing, possessing, or using illegal drugs or marijuana, or other unauthorized, mind-altering, or intoxicating substances while on the employer's property (including parking areas and grounds), or while performing their work duties away from the employer's premises. This prohibition should include lawful controlled substances, such as prescription medications, that have been illegally or improperly obtained. Employees should be prohibited from having any such illegal or unauthorized controlled substances in their system, or being impaired by such substances, while at work. Employees should also be prohibited from being impaired by cannabis or tetrahydrocannabinol (THC)-containing products while on the employer's property, or while performing their work duties away from the employer's premises.

Employees should further be prohibited from distributing, dispensing, possessing, or using alcohol while at work or on duty. Employees should also be prohibited from allowing off-duty alcohol use to interfere with their ability to perform their job duties. If employees must occasionally consume alcohol in connection with their job duties, the policy should state that while moderate consumption is acceptable in the appropriate setting, overindulgence is not.

The drug and alcohol policy should describe when employees are subject to being tested. Pre-employment testing and reasonable suspicion testing are lawful in California, except testing for non-psychoactive THC metabolites. Until testing for only psychoactive THC (which potentially causes impairment) becomes readily available, California employers may not test job candidates or employees for marijuana unless the candidate or employee is in the building and construction trades, holds or would hold a position covered by the U.S. Department of Transportation's (DOT) drug testing requirements, or is otherwise required to be tested for drugs under federal, state, or local law.

Reasonable suspicion may arise from, among other factors, supervisory observation, coworker reports or complaints, performance decline, attendance or behavioral changes, results of drug searches or other detection methods, or involvement in a work-related injury or accident. Post-accident testing is allowed where drug or alcohol impairment could have contributed to the accident. Random testing is not generally allowed in California, except for employees who are covered by the DOT's drug testing regulations or who work in safety-sensitive positions in which serious injury to the employee or to coworkers might occur should an employee attempt to work while impaired by drugs.

The drug and alcohol policy should state that failure to cooperate fully with a drug or alcohol screening, or producing a positive result on any drug and alcohol test, will result in termination of employment.

fyi ▸ **Effect of California Ballot Initiative Legalizing Private Use of Marijuana on Workplace Substance Abuse Policies**

Proposition 64, adopted by California voters in November 2016, makes it lawful under state and local laws for adults to purchase, possess, and privately consume up to an ounce of marijuana. This law does not legalize the use or possession of marijuana at work, however. The text of the proposition specifically states that it does not prohibit or limit an employer's right to maintain a drug- and alcohol-free workplace

Fraud and Dishonesty

The employee handbook should contain a prohibition against employees providing false, dishonest, or misleading information on any employment application, medical history record, invoice, time card or time sheet, time entry, investigative questionnaire, workplace injury report, leave application, or any other business document. Employees likewise should be prohibited from making any dishonest or false statement to management or to any client, customer, or vendor concerning any matter within the scope of the employee's job duties. Employees who observe other employees engaging in fraud or dishonesty should be directed to report it to management.

Insubordination

The employee handbook should contain a policy against insubordination. Insubordination should be defined as including a failure to follow directions of the employee's supervisor or another member of management.

Personal Mail

An employee handbook should include a policy stating that all mail received at the employer's address is presumed to be related to business and will be opened. This is to avoid claims by employees that their privacy rights were violated by the employer's opening their personal mail. The policy should additionally provide that company postage meters and letterhead may not be used for personal correspondence.

Sleeping on the Job

An employee handbook may contain a policy prohibiting sleeping on the job. Automatically terminating an employee for sleeping on the job is likely to generate a claim of disability discrimination, however. An employee caught sleeping on the job should be questioned regarding the cause of the sleeping. If the employee attributes the sleeping to a medical condition such as sleep apnea or medication taken for depression or other medical condition, you will need to engage in the interactive process to determine whether a reasonable accommodation can be made (see Section 14.6). If the employee attributes the sleeping to nonmedical causes such as staying out too late the night before or working another job, the employee may be disciplined or terminated.

Smoking

Given California's law prohibiting smoking in closed work areas, an employee handbook should include a policy prohibiting smoking in all the employer's buildings and vehicles. This policy should apply to electronic cigarettes as well. If smoking is allowed in designated outdoor areas, those areas should be specified.

Solicitation and Distribution

An employee handbook should contain a policy prohibiting the solicitation by an employee of another employee for the support of any organization during the working time of either employee. In addition, the distribution of advertising materials, handbills, or other paper literature should be prohibited in all working areas at all times. Finally, nonemployees should not be allowed to come onto the employer's property at any time to solicit for any cause or distribute material or literature of any kind for any purpose.

Searches

There is no constitutional prohibition against searches of employees by private-sector employers. Employees must be informed in advance, however, that such searches may be performed. The employee handbook, therefore, should state that the employer reserves the right to inspect all clothing, purses, briefcases, backpacks, packages, lockers, work stations, and vehicles on the employer's property, and that failure to cooperate in such a search will result in disciplinary action up to and including termination.

Theft and Misappropriation

Theft or misappropriation of money or property from the employer, from coworkers, or from customers or clients should be strictly prohibited. The policy should state that employees found to have stolen or misappropriated money or property will be subject to immediate termination and will also be reported to law enforcement.

Workplace Violence Policy

Every employee handbook should contain a zero-tolerance policy prohibiting violence in the workplace. The policy should additionally prohibit fighting, threatening words or conduct, and the bringing of weapons of any type into the workplace.

4.26 Open Door Policy

Many employee handbooks contain an open-door policy in which employees are encouraged to bring concerns and grievances to their immediate supervisor first, and if they are not satisfactorily resolved there, to HR or to a higher company official. Policies that *require* employees to bring their concerns to HR or management, as opposed to merely encouraging it, will likely violate current NLRB rules.

CHAPTER 5

Employees or Independent Contractors?

The independent contractor relationship has become popular in recent years in California. Many businesses like it because they perceive it to be more flexible and to involve less of a commitment than an employment relationship. If a contractor's services are no longer needed, their contract can simply be terminated without worry about all the potential exposure that comes from terminating an employee. Also, contractors are not eligible for health insurance and other benefits, and contractors pay their own payroll taxes, so startups and other companies with limited resources often prefer contractors to employees.

Many contractors prefer the contracting arrangement too. As "self-employed" persons they can often deduct more of their business expenses on their tax returns than they could if they were employees, and contractors frequently have more flexibility than employees to work at home, work family-friendly schedules, or work for other companies. Just because a business and a worker would prefer to structure their relationship as an independent contractor relationship does not make it so, however. Under California law, as will be shown below, the test that must be satisfied for lawful classification of an independent contractor is difficult to meet. The intent of the parties is no longer a factor used in determining independent contractor status in most cases.

The intent of the parties is no longer a factor in determining independent contractor status in most cases.

There are two ways in which misclassified independent contractor relationships might bring substantial financial exposure to an employer. One is that contractors may change their minds, particularly after the relationship ends, and claim they really were employees in order to collect unemployment insurance or to attempt to recover unpaid overtime. The other is that even though the parties may be perfectly happy with a misclassified relationship, the state will not be, because the state loses revenue in the form of payroll taxes and unemployment insurance premiums when employees are misclassified as independent contractors. Misclassification of employees as independent contractors can be an expensive mistake. If you have independent contractors in California, therefore, you should determine whether those persons are correctly classified, or whether instead they should be treated as employees.

5.1 Determining the Proper Classification

In California there is a presumption that an employment relationship exists when one engages another to perform services. The party disputing that an employment relationship exists has the burden of proving that an independent contractor relationship exists instead.

Historically, different agencies used somewhat different tests to determine whether an employee or a contractor relationship existed. The California Supreme Court in *Dynamex Operations West, Inc. v. Superior Court* (2018), however, adopted a new legal standard for determining whether a person performing services is an employee or an independent contractor for purposes of the California Wage Orders, which govern minimum wage, overtime, days of rest, and meal and rest periods. The California legislature in turn, in Assembly Bill 5 (AB 5) enacted in 2019, extended the *Dynamex* test to cover all issues of California employment law, including the Labor Code (including workers' compensation law) and the Unemployment Insurance Code, with some exceptions for certain occupations and business relationships. The *Dynamex* case and AB 5 have redefined the test for classification of independent contractors for most occupations under California law.

The *Dynamex* Test

In *Dynamex*, the court adopted what is termed the "ABC" test for determining whether a worker is properly classified as an independent contractor. Under this test, a worker is presumed to be an employee under the Wage Orders unless the hiring entity establishes *all* of the following:

A. The worker is free from the control and direction of the hirer in connection with the performance of the work, both under the contract for the performance of such work and in fact;
B. The worker performs work that is outside the usual course of the hiring entity's business; and
C. The worker is customarily engaged in an independently established trade, occupation, or business of the same nature as the work performed for the hiring entity.

The "A" prong of this test is akin to the "right-to-control" factor used in other tests for independent contractor status. The "B" and "C" prongs are a significant change, however. Prong "B" examines whether workers are performing work that otherwise would be performed by an employee versus by an outside contractor. The *Dynamex* court gave the example of a retailer that hires a plumber or electrician to perform maintenance at its establishment. Such a worker would not typically be employed in the usual course of the retailer's business and therefore properly would be classified as an independent contractor. Conversely, a work-at-home seamstress engaged by a clothing manufacturer or a cake decorator hired by a bakery generally would not meet the standard because they perform work that is the essence of the hiring company's business. Under this prong it will be very difficult to classify as an independent contractor a worker who performs the same work as employees of the hiring entity.

Prong "C" of the test examines whether the worker has taken steps to create their own independent business. The *Dynamex* court maintained that a contractor does not necessarily have to incorporate a business or obtain licensure to meet this test. On the other hand, the court cautioned that a hiring company's merely not prohibiting or preventing a worker from engaging in such an independent business is insufficient to establish that a worker has made the decision to start an independent business. A worker who has no clients other than the hiring company will be difficult to classify as an independent contractor.

Employers therefore must use care in determining whether workers are properly classified as independent contractors. In some instances it will be relatively clear. An example is the person who operates a window-washing company that a retail business pays to come and wash its windows once every quarter. The window-washing company clearly is a separate business that performs window-washing work for a variety of other businesses. Its owner supplies all of the necessary equipment and carries the opportunity for a profit or a risk of loss. It is paid for the job and the retail company contracts for a specific result (clean windows). The customer does not exercise control over how the work is performed beyond perhaps specifying that window-washing work must not be done in a manner that interferes with the retail business. There would be little dispute that this is a properly classified independent contractor relationship.

Under the *Dynamex* test, a business cannot have employees and contractors working together performing the same work.

It is also clear under the *Dynamex* test that a business cannot have employees and contractors working together performing the same work. An example is an accountant who performs the same type of accounting work as is performed by employees of the business. They do not operate their own company but rather perform work for only one business. They work in the company's offices on a schedule set by the company that is similar to the work schedules of the company's employees. They work under the supervision of the company's controller. They submit an invoice at the end of each week listing the hours they worked during the week, and they are paid a flat amount per hour worked. This is an example of an arrangement that almost certainly would be found to constitute an employer–employee relationship regardless of any written contractor agreement to the contrary.

Sometimes employers misclassify temporary employees as independent contractors on account of the short-term nature of the relationship. Unless the contractor is retained to complete a discrete project and works on that project independently, hiring the person as a temporary employee is usually the better option. "Contractors" who are brought on board to fill in for employees on leave or to provide additional manpower during busy periods and who work alongside a company's regular employees are almost always misclassified.

5.2 Occupations and Business Relationships Excluded from the *Dynamex* Test

In AB 5, the California legislature decreed that a variety of occupations and business relationships would not be subject to the new *Dynamex* test but instead would remain subject to the old test set forth in *S.G. Borello & Sons, Inc. v. Department of Industrial Relations* (1989). In Assembly Bill 2257 (AB 2257), the legislature replaced AB 5 with a broader list of exclusions from the *Dynamex* test.

Under the *Borello* test, California courts and the California Labor Commissioner previously considered the following factors:

- Does the person to whom service is rendered have the right to control the manner and means of accomplishing the result desired?
- Is the person performing services engaged in an occupation or business distinct from that of the principal?
- Is the work performed a part of the regular business of the principal?
- Does the principal or the worker supply the instrumentalities, tools, and the place for the work performed?
- To what extent has the worker made an investment in the equipment or materials required for the performance of the work?
- Does the work performed require any special skills that the worker possesses?

- Is the work usually done under the direction of the principal or by a specialist without supervision?
- Does the worker have an opportunity for profit or carry risk for loss depending on their managerial skill?
- Are the services to be performed during a discrete period of time or on an ongoing basis?
- Is the worker paid based on time worked or based on the job?
- Can the relationship be terminated at will and without cause?
- Do the parties believe they have an employment relationship or a contractor relationship?

Exempt Occupations

Occupations that AB 2257 exempts from the *Dynamex* test and subjects to the *Borello* test are the following:

- Licensed insurance agents and brokers, and persons who provide underwriting inspections, premium audits, risk management, or loss control work for the insurance and financial services industries.
- Licensed physicians and surgeons, dentists, podiatrists, psychologists, and veterinarians.
- Licensed lawyers, architects, landscape architects, engineers, private investigators, and accountants.
- Licensed or registered securities brokers, broker-dealers, and investment advisers and their agents and representatives.
- Direct sales salespersons, such as real estate brokers and agents and yacht brokers.
- Manufactured housing salespersons.
- Commercial fishermen working on American vessels.
- Competition judges such as umpires and referees for amateur sports.

Exempt Professional Service Providers

AB 2257 also exempts from the *Dynamex* test and mandates that the *Borello* test applies to contracts for certain professional services. The professional services covered are those of:

- Marketing consultants who produce original and creative work;
- Human resources consultants whose work is predominantly intellectual and varied in character;
- Travel agents;

- Graphic designers;
- Grant writers;
- Fine artists;
- Internal Revenue Service (IRS) enrolled agents; and
- Payment processing agents through independent sales organizations.

The following professional services are covered by the *Borello* test where work is performed under a written contract that specifies the rate of pay and obligation to pay by a defined time, so long as the person is not replacing an employee who performed the same work for the hiring entity, the person does not perform services at the hiring entity's business, and the person is not restricted from working for entities other than the hiring entity:

- Still photographers, photojournalists, videographers, and photo editors (who may provide content to a digital content aggregator as an alternative to meeting the above standard);
- Freelance writers, editors, copy editors, translators, illustrators, and newspaper cartoonists; and
- Freelance content contributors, advisors, producers, narrators, or cartographers for a journal, book, periodical, evaluation, other publication or educational, academic, or instructional work in any format or media.

Licensed estheticians, electrologists, manicurists, barbers, and cosmetologists are subject to the *Borello* test, provided such persons (1) set their own rates, process their own payments, and are paid directly by their clients; (2) set their own hours and have sole discretion to decide the number of clients and which clients for whom they will perform services; (3) have their own book of business and schedule their own appointments; (4) maintain their own business license; and (5) issue a Form 1099 to the business owner from which they rent their business space.

Also subject to the *Borello* test are:

- Specialized performers hired by a performing arts company or organization to teach a master class for no more than one week. A "master class" is a specialized course for limited duration that is not regularly offered by the hiring entity and is taught by an expert in a recognized field of artistic endeavor who does not work for the hiring entity to teach on a regular basis;
- Real estate appraisers; and
- Registered professional foresters.

For a provider of professional services to be covered by the *Borello* test and not the *Dynamex* test, all of the following must apply:

- The person (which includes a corporation or limited liability company owned by the person) maintains a business location, which may be the person's residence, that is separate from where the person performs services. The person may choose to perform services at the location of the hiring entity, however.
- If the work is performed in a jurisdiction that requires a business license or business tax registration, the person has the required business license or business tax registration in addition to any required professional licenses.
- The person has the ability to set or negotiate their own rates for the services performed.
- Outside of project completion dates and reasonable business hours, the person has the ability to set their own hours.
- The person performs the same type of work for other hiring entities or holds themself out to other potential customers as able to perform the same type of work.
- The person customarily and regularly exercises discretion and independent judgment in the performance of the services.

Business-to-Business Contracts

Under AB 2257, if a business entity formed as a sole proprietorship, partnership, limited liability company, limited liability partnership, or corporation contracts to provide services to another such business, the determination of employee or independent contractor status of the business services provider is to be determined by the *Borello* test if the contracting business demonstrates that all of the following criteria are satisfied:

- The business service provider is free from the control and direction of the contracting business in connection with the performance of the work, both under the contract for the performance of the work and in fact.
- The business service provider is providing services directly to the contracting business rather than to customers of the contracting business. This requirement does not apply if the business service provider's employees are solely performing the services under the contract under the name of the business services provider and the business service provider regularly contracts with other businesses.
- The contract with the business service provider is in writing, and the contract specifies the payment amount, including any applicable rate of pay, as well as the due date for payment for services.
- If the work is performed in a jurisdiction that requires the business service provider to have a business license or business tax registration, the business service provider has the required business license or business tax registration.

- The business service provider maintains a business location that is separate from the business or work location of the contracting business.
- The business service provider is customarily engaged in an independently established business of the same nature as that involved in the work performed.
- The business service provider can contract with other businesses to provide the same or similar services and maintain a clientele without restrictions from the contracting business.
- The business service provider advertises and holds itself out to the public as available to provide the same or similar services.
- The business service provider provides its own tools, vehicles, and equipment to perform the services.
- The business service provider can negotiate its own rates.
- Consistent with the nature of the work, the business service provider can set its own hours and location of work.
- The business service provider is not performing the type of work for which a license from the Contractor's State License Board is required.

The business-to-business contracts exemption does not apply to an individual worker who performs labor or services for a contracting business, as opposed to a business entity.

Referral Agencies

Under AB 2257, if a business entity formed as a sole proprietorship, partnership, limited liability company, limited liability partnership, or corporation provides certain services to clients through a referral agency, the *Borello* test and not the *Dynamex* test applies to the relationship between the referral agency and the service provider if the following conditions are met:

- The service provider is free from the control and direction of the referral agency in connection with the performance of the work for the client, both as a matter of contract and in fact.
- If the work for the client is performed in a jurisdiction that requires the service provider to have a business license or business tax registration, the service provider must certify to the referring agency that it has the required business license or business tax registration.
- If there is an applicable professional licensure, permit, certification, or registration administered or recognized by the state for the type of work being performed, the service provider must certify to the referring agency that it has the required professional licensure, permit, certification, or registration.

- If the work for the client requires the service provider to hold a state contractor's license, the service provider has the required contractor's license.
- The service provider delivers services to the client under service provider's name, rather than under the name of the referral agency.
- The service provider provides its own tools and supplies to perform the services.
- The service provider is customarily engaged in the same type of business as that involved in the work performed for the client.
- The service provider maintains a clientele without any restrictions from the referral agency and the service provider is free to seek work elsewhere, including through a competing agency.
- The service provider sets its own hours and terms of work and is free to accept or reject clients and contracts.
- The service provider sets its own rates for services performed, without deduction by the referral agency.
- The service provider is not penalized in any form for rejecting clients or contracts.

The services covered under this exemption include, but are not limited to, graphic design, web design, photography, tutoring, consulting, youth sports coaching, caddying, wedding or event planning, minor home repair, moving, home cleaning, errands, furniture assembly, animal services, dog walking, dog grooming, picture hanging, pool cleaning, yard cleanup, and interpreting services. It does not apply to businesses that provide janitorial, delivery, courier, transportation, trucking, agricultural labor, retail, logging, in-home care, or construction services other than minor home repair.

The referral agencies exemption does not apply to an individual worker, as opposed to a business entity, who performs services for a client through a referral agency. The determination whether such an individual is an employee of a referral agency is determined by the *Dynamex* test.

Other Exempted Occupations and Businesses

Other occupations and businesses that AB 2257 exempts from the *Dynamex* test include licensed real estate brokers and agents, home inspectors, licensed repossession agencies, licensed contractors and subcontractors in the construction industry, professional speakers, and motor clubs and persons performing services to motor club members through third-party entities.

AB 2257 also exempts musicians from the *Dynamex* test where certain conditions are met. Musicians who are potentially exempt include recording artists, vocalists, songwriters, lyricists, composers, record producers and directors, musical engineers, and similar persons who are engaged in creative work in the music industry.

AB 2257 further exempts from the *Dynamex* test the relationship between a data aggregator and persons who are paid to provide feedback to data aggregators under certain conditions.

5.3 The Consequences of Misclassifying Employees as Contractors

The most common way in which an employer gets into trouble in California for having employees misclassified as independent contractors is when a contractor's assignment ends and they go to the Employment Development Department (EDD) to apply for unemployment benefits. That agency will not have any record of the person having been employed, or the employer will respond to the EDD's unemployment claim notice that the person claiming benefits was an independent contractor. The EDD will then begin an investigation of the arrangement involving the claimant, and in many cases it will commence a broader audit of the employer to determine how many workers have been classified as independent contractors and whether they have been properly classified. Such audits typically go back three years. Thus, many workers who are satisfied with being considered a contractor may nonetheless have their status challenged by the EDD.

If the EDD finds one or more contractors to be misclassified, it will assess the employer for back unemployment and state disability taxes, state income tax not withheld, and penalties and interest. In addition, the EDD often shares its audit results with the IRS, which may conduct a further audit for assessment of unpaid Federal Insurance Contributions Act (FICA) taxes and federal income taxes not withheld, along with penalties and interest. A misclassified contractor might also file a claim with the Labor Commissioner or a lawsuit for unpaid minimum wages, overtime, premiums for missed meal and rest breaks, and/or unreimbursed business expenses, plus interest and penalties. When multiple contractors are allegedly misclassified, these claims may be pursued on a class action basis, and penalties under the Private Attorneys General Act (PAGA) may also be pursued. These are often the most difficult and expensive claims to defend. If the contractor was paid by the hour and worked more than eight hours per day or 40 hours per week, overtime due will be relatively easy to calculate, but if the contractor was paid on a weekly, monthly, or other basis, and no record of hours worked was maintained, the worker's estimate of hours worked is likely to be significantly inflated. Add to the amount of overtime claimed two hours of premium pay per day for missed meal and rest breaks (these are not typically taken by those classified as contractors), plus reimbursement for mileage and personal cell phone use when applicable, plus waiting time penalties, PAGA penalties, interest and (in court cases) the claimant's attorneys' fees and litigation costs, and whatever savings may have been realized from classifying the worker as a contractor will likely be dwarfed by the cost of noncompliance with the applicable wage and hour and tax laws.

Finally, an employer found to have willfully misclassified an employee as an independent contractor may be liable for additional civil penalties of between $5,000 and $15,000 for each violation, and civil penalties of between $10,000 to $25,000 for a pattern and practice of violations. Such an employer will also be required to prominently display a notice (signed by an officer of the company) on its website for one year admitting to violating the law. If the employer does not have a website, the notice must be displayed in an area that is accessible to all employees and the general public. Outside consultants (excluding attorneys) who advise an employer to willingly misclassify employees as independent contractors may be personally liable for these monetary penalties as well.

The most common way in which an employer gets into trouble in California for having employees misclassified as independent contractors is when a contractor's assignment ends and they go to the EDD to apply for unemployment benefits.

5.4 Minimize Your Exposure for Misclassified Independent Contractors

Many businesses, aware of the risks or not, nonetheless retain independent contractors to perform a variety of functions. There are alternatives, however, that minimize the risk of legal exposure.

First, if the goal is to avoid the commitment to an employment relationship and the cost of providing benefits to a short-term worker, consider procuring temporary employees from a staffing firm. This option provides greater flexibility and can be cheaper than hiring employees directly for short-term assignments, and the obligation to pay employment taxes will lie with the staffing firm. Be aware, however, that other liabilities may still exist for temporary employees provided by a staffing agency. When the employer terminates the assignment, the temporary employee may sue both the employer and the staffing agency for discrimination or wrongful termination, alleging that the employer and staffing agency were in fact joint employers. Also, under California law, an employer may be sued for a staffing agency's failure to comply with California's wage and hour laws. An employer that contracts with a staffing agency should have a written contract with the agency that clearly sets out each party's obligation to indemnify the other in the event an employee supplied by the agency should file a claim.

Second, if use of a staffing firm is not practical, treat workers hired temporarily to flex the workforce or for specific projects as temporary employees. Temporary employees are eligible for health insurance coverage under the Patient Protection and Affordable Care Act (ACA) if they work 30 or more hours per week, but they need not be eligible for other benefits such as paid holidays, paid vacation and the like. Temporary employees will accrue California paid sick leave (see Section 15.5), but they need not be allowed to use it until they have been employed for at least 90 days. You should have temporary employees acknowledge their status in writing (including their ineligibility for certain employee benefits), and that they are being hired only for a specific period or project, but that employment is at will and can be terminated at any time by either party.

5.5 Freelance Worker Protection Act

California law places requirements on the use of bona fide independent contractors who are individuals (whether or not incorporated) performing professional services under contracts worth more than $250. The professional services covered by this law include marketing, human resources administration, travel agent services, graphic design, grant writing, fine artists, IRS enrolled agents, payment processing agents, photographers, videographers, photo editors, digital content aggregators, writers, editors, and translators, among others. This law does not cover an individual hiring services for the personal benefit of themselves, their family members, or their homestead.

For covered contractors ("freelance workers"), the law requires a written contract, and that a copy of the contract be given to the freelance worker. The contract must include, at a minimum:

- The name and mailing address of each party.
- An itemized list of all services to be provided by the freelance worker, including the value of those services and the rate and method of compensation.
- The date on which the hiring party shall pay the contracted compensation or the mechanism by which the date shall be determined.
- The date by which a freelance worker shall submit a list of services rendered under the contract to the hiring party to meet the hiring party's internal processing deadlines for purposes of timely payment of compensation.

Under this law, the hiring party must pay the freelance worker by the due date specified in the contract, and if no due date is specified, within 30 days of completion of the work, the hiring party may not require the freelance worker to accept less compensation or provide more goods and services than are set forth in the contract.

5.6 Other Issues Involving Independent Contractors

Independent contractors may sue and be sued for sexual and other forms of harassment in California, so they should be provided a copy of the company's policy against harassment at the beginning of the contracting relationship. They should be informed to whom in the company they should direct complaints of harassment.

Bona fide independent contractors are also covered by California's Unruh Civil Rights Act, which prohibits business establishments from intentionally discriminating against individuals with whom they do business based on sex, gender identity and expression, race, color, religion, ancestry, national origin, disability, medical condition, genetic information, marital status, or sexual orientation. A business should be mindful of these prohibitions when selecting and terminating independent contractors.

CHAPTER 6

The Hiring Process

The process of hiring new employees has become more complex with the proliferation of laws protecting applicant and employee privacy and requiring various disclosures. Still, employers have considerable latitude to screen job applicants. Some employers unfortunately feel that if they ask an applicant much more than "How quickly can you start?" they will be sued. In fact, however, wrongful failure-to-hire lawsuits are rare compared to wrongful termination lawsuits. You must be mindful of the various laws affecting hiring, but you should not be intimidated by them. Many wrongful termination lawsuits are filed by employees who never should have been hired in the first place. You should take the time to scrutinize new hires carefully; doing so will save a much greater amount of time spent on defending a lawsuit brought by a bad hire.

6.1 The Importance of a Current Job Description

In many organizations, job descriptions are outdated, yet the HR staff is often too busy to undertake a comprehensive review and updating of all job descriptions. Current job descriptions are important for identifying the essential functions of the job to determine whether an applicant with a disability can perform it and for finding a reasonable accommodation for a disabled employee or applicant. They also provide a means of defending against claims of discriminatory hiring or promotion. They can additionally provide helpful evidence of the actual duties of a position should a dispute later arise over whether the position was correctly classified as exempt from overtime.

When recruiting for a position, therefore, first review the job description to see if it is current and accurate. The supervisor or department manager for the position should review the job description as well. It should describe the job as it currently exists, not as it existed at one time or as it ideally might be. Ensure that the job description describes the level of education and amount of experience (if any) required for the job. The job description should accurately describe the manual and mechanical functions of the job (for example, the ability to lift, walk, sit, bend, reach, manipulate controls, assemble objects) as well as the job's intellectual requirements (for example, the ability to read and understand blueprints or manuals, the ability to perform basic mathematical calculations). It should also describe the intangible requirements of the job—such as the ability to work as a team, meet deadlines, achieve quotas, work independently under limited supervision, or work effectively with customers or the public. Make any necessary changes to the job description before proceeding with the recruitment process for the position.

6.2 Where to Recruit

Recruiting for new employees should be done through a variety of sources, including internal job postings, the company's website, internet-based job boards, the California Employment Development Department (EDD), employment agencies, and colleges and universities or trade schools. Though posting a job opening internally may produce referrals to qualified recruits, internal referrals should not be the only source of candidates. Considering only current employees or their friends or relatives for open positions can limit diversity and lead to internal conflicts between employees based on their outside relationships.

6.3 Staffing Agencies and "Temp-to-Hire" Employees

Some employers prefer to obtain new employees through staffing agencies that provide "temp-to-hire" personnel. This option leaves much of the screening and selection to the agency and provides an opportunity to try the employee out for a time as a temporary worker before making the commitment for a full-time hire. Although many agencies do an excellent job of providing workers well-suited to the job, you should keep the following points in mind:

- An agency might not use the same screening criteria as its client company; some additional screening, therefore, might be necessary to ensure a candidate is a good fit.
- Using temporary employees from an agency will not generally insulate an employer from potential liability to those employees for wrongful termination, harassment, discrimination, and the like, especially if the employer's personnel were involved in the events that led to litigation. Both the agency and the employer in these cases typically will be alleged to be joint employers.
- If temporary employees are maintained in temporary status too long, they could claim to be qualified for benefits provided to the company's regular employees, especially if the eligibility criteria for such benefits are not well-defined. If long-term temporary employees are utilized, ensure that it is made clear to them in a written document that they are not eligible for benefits.

- If you are considering converting a temporary employee to a regular full-time employee, put the employee through the same screening process you use for new hires.

6.4 Requirement That Pay Scale Be Published

Employers of 15 or more employees must include the pay scale for the position in any job posting. The pay scale is the salary or hourly wage range that the employer reasonably expects to pay for the position. Employers that use third parties to publish job openings must provide the third party with the pay scale for the position so it can be included on the third party's job posting. The Labor Commissioner may impose a penalty of between $100 and $10,000 for each violation of this requirement.

6.5 The Employment Application

All applicants should be required to complete an employment application before being interviewed. Résumés should not be accepted in lieu of applications because résumés are selective in the information they provide. A good employment application is much more comprehensive. Such an application should contain the following elements:

- A section for the applicant to list all prior employers, along with dates of employment, positions held, names of supervisors, and reasons for leaving.
- A question asking if the applicant is legally authorized to work in the United States.
- A question asking if the applicant has reliable transportation to work.
- A question asking if the applicant has been fired or asked to resign from any prior jobs.
- An authorization to check references.
- An acknowledgment that any job offer will be contingent on passing a background check and pre-employment drug screen.
- An acknowledgment that any employment offered will be employment at will.
- A certification that all information provided is true and correct and that if any material information is falsified or omitted, the candidate will not be eligible for employment or, if hired, will be subject to immediate termination.

Applications of candidates who were considered but not hired must be retained for at least two years. Unsolicited résumés need not be retained.

When was the last time you read a résumé that listed the jobs from which the applicant was fired? Many résumés are fiction. Applications are autobiographies. Read the autobiography.

6.6 Criminal Record Inquiries

Under California's "Ban the Box" law, inquiries about an applicant's criminal record may not be lawfully made until a conditional offer of employment has been extended. This restriction applies to all public and private-sector employers of five or more employees. The only exceptions are for jobs where a state or local agency must conduct a criminal background check or where the employer is required by any state, federal, or local law to conduct criminal background checks for employment purposes or to restrict employment based on criminal history.

Employment applications therefore may not contain questions about the applicant's criminal convictions or arrests for which the applicant is out on bail. Also, applicants must not be asked during job interviews whether they have any criminal convictions.

Once a conditional offer of employment has been extended, the applicant may be asked to disclose prior criminal convictions. The following need not be disclosed and must not be considered:

- Arrests that did not result in conviction.
- Convictions that have been expunged, sealed, or dismissed, or any conviction for which the applicant has received a full pardon or a certificate of rehabilitation.
- Referrals to, or participation in, any pre-trial or post-trial diversion program (convictions may be considered until a diversion program is completed and charges are dismissed or expunged, and a diversion program may be offered by the applicant as evidence of rehabilitation or mitigating circumstances).
- Non-felony convictions for marijuana possession that are more than two years old.
- Convictions or other adjudications by juvenile courts.

You may ask about arrests for which the applicant is out on bail or released on personal recognizance pending trial.

> An applicant who lies about their criminal record should not be hired. A dishonest criminal is not a good hire.

Subject to the aforementioned exceptions, the applicant should be asked to disclose in writing all criminal convictions, and to certify that all information provided on the criminal history form is true and complete. The criminal history form should include a written warning that in the event of falsification or omission of any material information, the applicant will not be hired or, if hired, will be subject to immediate termination. The applicant should also be advised that a background check will be conducted (if applicable), but the background check disclosure and consent language must appear on a separate document (see Section 6.14). Finally, the applicant should be advised that the offer of employment is contingent upon the outcomes of the criminal history inquiry, background check (if conducted), and pre-employment drug test (if administered).

You should not automatically exclude applicants who disclose criminal convictions. If the applicant discloses any criminal convictions, or criminal convictions are reported in the results of the background check you conduct, for each conviction you must perform an Initial Individualized Assessment. This is a reasoned, evidence-based determination of whether the applicant's conviction history has a direct and adverse relationship with the specific duties of the job that justifies denying the applicant the position. This assessment must consider:

- The nature and gravity of the offense or conduct;
- The time that has passed since the offense or conduct and completion of the sentence; and
- The nature of the job held or sought.

With respect to the nature and gravity of the offense or conduct, you should consider:

- The specific personal conduct of the applicant that resulted in the conviction;
- Whether the harm was to property or people;
- The degree of the harm (e.g., amount of loss in theft);
- The permanence of the harm;
- The context in which the offense occurred;
- Whether a disability, including but not limited to a past drug addiction or mental impairment, contributed to the offense or conduct, and if so, whether the likelihood of harm arising from similar conduct could be sufficiently

mitigated or eliminated by a reasonable accommodation, or whether the disability has been mitigated or eliminated by treatment or otherwise;
- Whether trauma, domestic or dating violence, sexual assault, stalking, human trafficking, duress, or other similar factors contributed to the offense or conduct; and
- The age of the applicant when the conduct occurred.

With respect to the time that has passed since the offense or conduct and completion of the sentence, you should consider:

- The amount of time that has passed since the conduct underlying the conviction, which may significantly predate the conviction itself; and
- When the conviction led to incarceration, the amount of time that has passed since the applicant's release from incarceration.

With respect to the nature of the job held or sought, you should consider:

- The specific duties of the job;
- Whether the context in which the conviction occurred is likely to arise in the workplace; and
- Whether the type or degree of harm that resulted from the conviction is likely to occur in the workplace.

For example, a convicted sex offender could lawfully be excluded from a playground monitoring job, but not from a manufacturing job not involving unsupervised interaction with the public. A convicted embezzler could be excluded from an accounts payable position but not from a customer service job that does not involve access to company finances.

Note that an applicant's possession of a benefit, privilege, or right required for the performance of a job by a licensing, regulatory, or government agency or board indicates that the applicant's conviction history is not being directly and adversely related to the specific duties of that job. For example, if a candidate for a construction manager's job has a contractor's license that post-dates a criminal conviction, the job offer should not be withdrawn based on that conviction.

An applicant who lies about their criminal record should not be hired. A dishonest criminal is not a good hire. You should use care, though, before jumping to the conclusion that an applicant lied on the application when a background check shows a criminal conviction. It is possible that the conviction was later dismissed or expunged, or that the applicant and the person convicted are different persons. An applicant or employee who has denied having a criminal conviction but whose background check indicates such a conviction should be given a chance to explain the discrepancy before being declared ineligible for hire or terminated.

If, after making an Initial Individualized Assessment, you preliminarily decide to withdraw a job offer based on one or more criminal convictions, you must notify the applicant in writing of your preliminary decision. You may, but you are not required to, explain your reasoning for making your preliminary decision. You must identify the conviction(s) at issue, include a copy of any documentation of the conviction record (including the applicant's self-disclosure, the background check report, public records, internet search results, or news articles), and allow the applicant to submit evidence challenging the accuracy of the conviction record, offer evidence of rehabilitation or mitigating circumstances, or both, before your preliminary decision becomes final. Evidence of rehabilitation or mitigating circumstances may include:

- The length and consistency of employment history before and after the offense or conduct;
- The facts or circumstances surrounding the offense or conduct;
- The applicant's current or former participation in self-improvement efforts, including but not limited to school, job training, counseling, community service, or rehabilitation programs, including in-custody programs;
- Whether trauma, domestic or dating violence, sexual assault, stalking, human trafficking, duress, or other similar factors contributed to the offense or conduct;
- The age of the applicant when the conduct occurred;
- Whether a disability, including but not limited to a past drug addiction or mental impairment, contributed to the offense or conduct, and, if so, whether the likelihood of harm arising from similar conduct could be sufficiently mitigated or eliminated by a reasonable accommodation, or whether the disability has been mitigated or eliminated by treatment or otherwise;
- The likelihood that similar conduct will recur;
- Whether the applicant is bonded under a federal, state, or local bonding program.
- The fact that the applicant is seeking employment; and
- Successful completion, or compliance with the terms and conditions, of probation or parole.

The applicant may submit any of the following documentation demonstrating rehabilitation or mitigating circumstances:

- Certificates or other documentation of participation in, enrollment in, or completion of an and rehabilitation efforts such as educational, vocational, or training, counseling, community service, or rehabilitation programs, including in-custody programs.

- Letters from current or former teachers, counselors, supervisors, co-workers, parole or probation officers, or others who know the applicant.
- Police reports, protective orders, and/or documentation from healthcare providers, counselors, case managers, or victim advocates who can attest to the applicant's status as a survivor of domestic or dating violence, sexual assault, stalking, or comparable offenses.
- Documentation confirming the existence of a disability.
- Any other document demonstrating rehabilitation or mitigating circumstances.

You may not require the applicant to provide any of the foregoing, or to provide any specific type of evidence of rehabilitation or mitigating circumstances. It must be voluntary on the applicant's part.

The applicant must be given five business days from the receipt of your notice to submit a response. If the applicant indicates that they are challenging the accuracy of conviction record, the applicant must be given an additional five business days to respond.

Upon your receipt of any information submitted by the applicant, you must conduct a reassessment. In evaluating the evidence of rehabilitation or mitigating circumstances submitted you may consider:

- When the conviction led to incarceration, the applicant's conduct during incarceration, including participation in work and educational or rehabilitative programming and other prosocial conduct;
- The applicant's employment history since the conviction or completion of sentence;
- The applicant's community service and engagement since the conviction or completion of sentence, including but not limited to volunteer work for a community organization, engagement with a religious group or organization, participation in a support or recovery group, and other types of civic participation; and
- The applicant's other rehabilitative efforts since the completion of sentence or conviction or mitigating factors not captured in the other factors above.

If your decision is still to reject the applicant, you must notify the applicant in writing of your decision. You may, but you are not required to, provide an explanation of your decision. You must also notify the applicant of any internal appeal rights within your organization, and of the applicant's right to contest the decision by filing a complaint with the California Civil Rights Department (CRD). You are not required to provide any internal appeal rights, nor are you required to provide the address, phone number, or email address of the CRD.

Local "Ban the Box" Ordinances

California's "Ban the Box" law does not override local ordinances that are stricter or that provide more protection for applicants or employees. Therefore, if you do business in a jurisdiction that has a "Ban the Box" ordinance, you must comply with that ordinance unless the state law is more beneficial to applicants or employees.

San Francisco's "Fair Chance Ordinance"

Private-sector employers having five or more full-time or part-time employees and located in or doing business in San Francisco, as well as city contractors and subcontractors, are prohibited from inquiring about an applicant's criminal history until after a conditional offer of employment has been made. Even then, employers may not ask about convictions that are more than seven years old, juvenile convictions, convictions that have been expunged or judicially dismissed, convictions of infractions that do not amount to a felony or misdemeanor, or convictions for conduct that has been decriminalized such as recreational use of marijuana. Employers must state in postings for jobs in San Francisco that qualified applicants with criminal histories will be considered. Employers also must post a notice in four languages (English, Spanish, Chinese, and Tagalog) regarding the ordinance and give a copy of the ordinance to an applicant before asking about criminal history or running a background check that might reveal a criminal history. Upon lawfully obtaining information regarding an applicant's criminal history, an employer is required to conduct an individualized assessment to determine whether the criminal history is directly related to the job.

Los Angeles's "Fair Chance Initiative for Hiring" Ordinance

The Los Angeles ordinance covers employers of 10 or more employees that are located in or do business in the city. Covered employers must not include questions regarding criminal convictions on employment applications and must post notices stating that qualified applicants with criminal convictions will be considered. An inquiry about criminal convictions may not be made until a conditional offer of employment has been extended. Where a candidate discloses one or more criminal convictions, you must conduct a *written assessment* on a form provided by the city (available at https://bca.lacity.org/fair-chance) that analyzes the specific aspects of the conviction(s) and the risks posed in the job at issue. You must consider:

- The nature and gravity of the offense or conduct;
- The time that has passed since the offense, conduct and/or completion of the sentence;

- The nature of the job held or sought;
- The applicant's age at the time of the last criminal activity; and
- Activities since the criminal activity, such as work experience, job training, etc.

Next, you must undertake the fair chance process before deciding not to hire the applicant. You must notify the applicant in writing that you are considering withdrawing the employment offer and include a copy of the written assessment. You then must wait at least five business days to give the applicant a chance to challenge the accuracy of the criminal record and submit other evidence to be considered in your assessment. The applicant may provide:

- Evidence of rehabilitation or mitigating factors;
- Facts or circumstances of the conviction;
- Number of offenses or convictions;
- Evidence of similar work with no incidents of criminal conduct; and
- Length/consistency of employment before and after offenses.

If the applicant provides information for you to consider, you must conduct another written reassessment. If you stick with your decision to withdraw the offer of employment, you must notify the applicant in writing and include a copy of the written reassessment. The only exceptions to this ordinance are where the job requires use or possession of a firearm or where the law prohibits hiring of an applicant with a criminal record.

6.7 Megan's List

California state government maintains a website containing names, photographs, and other information regarding registered sex offenders living in the state; this list has become known as "Megan's List." California law prohibits use of information found on that list for employment and other specified purposes. Employers, therefore, should not review Megan's List to determine if job applicants or employees appear on it.

This law does not prohibit an employer from taking a sex offense conviction into account in determining whether to hire or retain a person with such a conviction, however. In the hiring process, an employer may inquire about criminal convictions, and an applicant would be bound to disclose convictions for sex offenses as well as other convictions. If such a conviction were related in any way to the job, the applicant could be rejected on account of it. If an applicant failed to disclose a conviction for a sex offense on a job application, and it surfaced during a background check, the employer could reject the applicant or fire the employee, if hired, for providing false information on the application.

6.8 Interviewing Job Candidates

Some employers are reluctant to ask probing questions during a job interview, but they should not be. Obvious questions that should not be asked include "Where is your accent from?"; "Are you planning to start a family?"; and "When are you planning to retire?" Instead of "Will your family obligations affect your job?" ask an applicant: "Are you able to work overtime as required?" and "Are you able to travel on business?" Focus interview questions on the applicant's ability to meet the requirements of the job, not on personal or family factors that are at best marginally relevant to job performance.

There are numerous probing questions that are perfectly legal and should be asked, such as the following examples:

- Have you ever been fired or asked to resign from a job?
- What do you think of your current supervisor?
- How do you think your supervisor will respond if we call them to provide a reference for you?
- What part of your current job do you most dislike?
- What do you find most attractive about our company or organization?
- What do you find least attractive about our company or organization?
- What are your career aspirations?
- Do you work better on a team or by yourself?
- What is your biggest challenge in terms of using technology?
- Do you currently use illegal drugs (other than marijuana)?

It is important during an interview not to over-sell the job. California's Labor Code prohibits an employer from causing a person to change their residence by misrepresenting the terms or conditions of the employment offered. Although the statute was designed to protect migrant farm workers, it has been applied to other types of employees as well, including executives. Employees who believe they were lied to regarding the terms of employment might also sue for intentional or negligent misrepresentation. Use care, therefore, not to overstate a job's earning or bonus potential. Similarly, gratuitous statements about a job's long-term potential should be avoided so as not to contradict the at-will nature of the employment.

6.9 Salary History

California law prohibits employers from seeking salary history information, orally or in writing, personally or through an agent (such as a recruiting or staffing firm), about an applicant for employment. Salary history information includes information regarding benefits as well as compensation.

In addition, an employer may not rely on the salary history information of an applicant as a factor in determining whether to offer employment to an applicant or what salary to offer an applicant. An applicant is not prohibited from disclosing their salary history information to a prospective employer so long as the disclosure is voluntary and without prompting. If the applicant voluntarily discloses their salary history information, you may consider or rely on that information in determining the salary for that applicant. In the event you do so, you should retain any document (such as a résumé or email communication) in which salary history information was disclosed. This prohibition only applies to applicants for employment and not to current employees. You may consider salary history of internal candidates for promotion or transfer. Also, you may ask an applicant what is their salary *expectation*.

Employers of 15 or more employees must provide a pay scale in all job postings. Employers of fewer than 15 employees must provide the pay scale for a job to an applicant applying for that job upon the applicant's request. Such a pay scale must be a good faith estimate of the actual salary or hourly wage range that the employer reasonably expects to pay upon hire. All forms of compensation must be included, such as overtime, bonuses, employee benefits, and expense reimbursements.

6.10 The Use of Social Media to Screen Applicants

California law prohibits employers from asking applicants or employees for their personal email or social media account *passwords*, but there is no prohibition against asking applicants for their personal email addresses or to reveal social media websites where they have profiles. Social media that focus on professional qualifications, such as LinkedIn, can sometimes be useful in locating qualified candidates and reviewing their backgrounds. Social media that are more focused on personal interests, such as Facebook, Instagram, Pinterest, and X (formerly known as Twitter), should be used with caution as screening tools, if at all. An applicant might reveal a personal quality on such a website, such as an illness, sexual orientation, pregnancy, or plans for a family that, if discovered by the hiring manager, could be the basis for a discrimination claim should the candidate not be hired.

6.11 The Use of Automated-Decision Systems in Hiring

An Automated-Decision System (ADS) is defined as a "computational process that makes a decision or facilitates human decision making" with respect to employment matters, including hiring. It may be derived from artificial intelligence (AI), machine learning, algorithms, statistics, and/or other data processing techniques. Examples include the use of AI in résumé screening, making predictive assessments about applicants or employees, and analyzing applicant or employment data from third parties.

It is unlawful for an employer to use an ADS that discriminates against an applicant, employee, or class of applicants or employees on a prohibited basis. While anti-bias testing of an ADS is not strictly required, such testing or lack of testing will be relevant to a claim of ADS-based discrimination.

Employers that use AI in screening or other assessments of employment applicants should ensure that the applications used have been tested for inherent bias based on the protected classifications under California law.

6.12 Testing of Candidates

Some employers wish to subject job candidates to aptitude, honesty, or personality testing before making a job offer. Such testing is generally lawful, but with the following qualifications:

- Tests should not be used that are designed to detect or diagnose medical or mental disorders.
- If tests are meant to measure aptitude for a job, they must be validated. This means that they must be shown to measure what they purport to measure, and they must measure a skill or attribute that is required to perform the job.
- The candidate must not be required to pay for the cost of the test.

6.13 Polygraph Testing

Although public-sector employers may lawfully polygraph job applicants, California law prohibits private-sector employers from requiring a polygraph test as a condition of employment or continued employment. Before a private-sector employer may *request* that an applicant or employee take a polygraph test, it must provide the person with a written notice stating that the person is not required to take the test. Employers in California are also subject to the federal Employee Polygraph Protection Act (EPPA). EPPA prohibits employers from requiring or requesting an applicant to take a polygraph, except for applicants for positions with armored car, guard and alarm companies, and pharmaceutical manufacturers and distributors.

6.14 Pre-Employment Drug Testing

Employers in California may lawfully require job candidates to undergo pre-employment drug testing, either before or after an offer of employment has been extended. Some employees must be given a pre-employment drug test as a matter of law, such as those employees covered by U.S. Department of Transportation drug testing regulations. Employers that are not legally required to conduct pre-employment drug testing should consider doing so nonetheless. Employees who use illegal drugs are more likely to be involved in accidents and incur workers' compensation claims, have attendance problems, and pose a greater theft risk than employees who are drug-free.

You may not test job candidates for marijuana unless they are candidates for a position covered by DOT testing. You may test all job candidates for illegal drugs other than marijuana.

Candidates who fail the pre-employment drug test should not be hired. You should not make exceptions for otherwise qualified candidates who fail the drug test because doing so will produce potential liability for discrimination if exceptions are not made for other applicants or employees who fail a drug test.

You are not required to hire candidates who have a prescription for medical marijuana, and who claim to have a need to use marijuana before or during working time. The California Supreme Court has determined that an employer need not "reasonably accommodate" medical marijuana use.

6.15 Background Checks

Employers may conduct background checks on candidates to review their employment history, educational history, criminal record (where permitted), driving record, credit record (where permitted), and other aspects of their backgrounds.

Limits on Use of Consumer Credit Reports

California law prohibits employers under most circumstances from using consumer credit reports for employment purposes. The only exceptions are for the following positions:

- Managers who are exempt from overtime under the executive exemption.
- Sworn law enforcement officers.
- Positions for which the information in the report is required by law to be disclosed.
- Positions that require regular access (other than routine solicitation of credit card applications in a retail store) to *all* of the following information of any one person: (a) bank or credit card account info, (b) Social Security number, and (c) date of birth.
- Positions in which the employee is a signatory on a company bank or credit card account, is authorized to transfer money for the employer, or is authorized to enter financial contracts for the employer.
- Positions involving access to trade secrets.

- Positions that involve regular access to cash totaling $10,000 or more of the employer or a customer during the workday.

An employer may obtain a consumer report to verify a job candidate's income and employment history whether or not the candidate falls within one of these exceptions, so long as credit information is not obtained in such a report on candidates who do not fall within one of the above exceptions. Also, the requirements of the federal Fair Credit Reporting Act (FCRA) and California's Investigative Consumer Reporting Agencies Act (ICRAA) must be met with respect to any consumer report obtained on an applicant or employee, whether or not credit information is sought.

FCRA/ICRAA Requirements

The FCRA and the ICRAA are similar in some respects and different in others. Under both laws, the following step-by-step process must be followed any time a consumer report is obtained.

First, provide a written disclosure to the person on whom the report is obtained before the report is obtained. The disclosure must state that an investigative consumer report may be obtained and must identify the reason for the report (for example, pre-employment background check), the scope of the report, and the source of the report (including the name, address, telephone number, and website address of the reporting agency). The disclosure must also include a statement that the report may contain information on the person's character, general reputation, personal characteristics, and mode of living. This disclosure must be separate from any other document and it may not contain any other information such as written consent, a liability waiver, or the provisions of state background laws. A separate document must be provided setting forth the candidate's rights under ICRAA, and it must include a box to check if the person wants a copy of the report.

Second, obtain a signed authorization of the candidate for the report to be obtained. Providing such an authorization may be made a condition of hire or continued employment.

Third, certify to the reporting agency that all required disclosures have been made, that the candidate's authorization has been obtained, and that the information provided will be used for lawful purposes.

Fourth, if the candidate has requested a copy of the report, send them a copy free of charge within three days of receiving it. If the candidate did not request a copy of the report and it contains negative information about the candidate, before taking adverse action based on information contained in the report, give the candidate a copy of the report, a statement of rights under the FCRA, and a notice of your intent to take adverse action against the candidate on account of information contained in the report. You must then provide the candidate with a reasonable period of time to challenge the accuracy of negative information in the report.

Finally, after allowing a reasonable period of time to elapse, provide the candidate with notice of taking adverse action (for example, withdrawal of an offer of employment) if the negative information in the report played a role in the decision to take adverse action. Such notice must include the name, address, phone number, and website address of the agency that provided the report; a statement that the agency that provided the report did not make the decision to take adverse action and cannot give specific reasons for the decision; and notice of the candidate's right to dispute the accuracy or completeness of any information in the report and to obtain an additional free report from the agency if such a report is requested within 60 days.

The ICRAA (but not the FCRA) limits consumer reporting agencies to providing criminal convictions and civil lawsuits that are no more than 7 years old, and bankruptcies that are no more than 10 years old.

California law also regulates background investigations conducted by the employer without the assistance of a reporting agency if the investigation involves a review of public records such as court records or Department of Motor Vehicles (DMV) records. The employer must provide the candidate with copies of all records reviewed within seven days of receipt of the records unless the candidate has waived the right to receive these documents (such a waiver may be given by checking a box on the employment application). A copy of any public record containing negative information about the candidate must be provided to the candidate if adverse action is taken against the candidate on account of such negative information. Employers are not subject to the seven-year limit on discovering criminal convictions and other negative public records that applies to consumer reporting agencies.

Reasons to Withdraw a Job Offer

A conditional offer of a job may be withdrawn as a result of negative information discovered during the background check, such as prior firings not reported in response to questions on the employment application or during the interview, poor references from prior employers, or bad credit (for those positions exempt from California's prohibition on credit checks). A private-sector employer may reject a candidate on account of a prior bankruptcy (such an employer may not fire an employee for filing bankruptcy, however). A public-sector employer may not reject an applicant or fire an employee on account of a bankruptcy filing.

Sometimes a background check will reveal unfavorable nonwork-related information about a candidate, such as a relationship with a current or former employee or involvement in an activity such as pornography. The law regarding rejection of an applicant for lawful off-duty conduct is sometimes misunderstood. California

Labor Code Section 96(k) prohibits an employer from suspending, demoting, or terminating an employee for lawful off-duty conduct. It does not apply to applicants for employment. Nonetheless, be mindful of prohibitions against discrimination on such bases as political activity or beliefs, religious beliefs or expression, sexual orientation, or association with a person with a disability or of another race.

6.16 Reference Checks

Telephone reference checks should be conducted on all candidates. Federal and state laws regulating background checks conducted for employment purposes do not apply to telephone reference checks. California Civil Code Section 47(c) establishes a qualified privilege for accurate information provided by former employers without malice, meaning that a candidate cannot sue a former employer for defamation for providing truthful information in response to a reference check. Employers may state whether or not they would rehire a former employee and, if not, whether the decision not to rehire is based on a determination that the former employee engaged in sexual harassment.

Nonetheless, out of fear of being sued, many employers are reluctant to provide reference information beyond confirming dates of employment and position(s) held. If met with such a response, have the hiring manager call their counterpart at the prior employer to attempt to obtain a reference. If no qualitative information is provided, ask if the candidate is eligible for rehire. If the answer is no, you probably have all the information you really need.

6.17 Medical Examinations and Inquiries

Applicants may not be asked about their medical condition or any physical or mental disability before being given a conditional job offer. This includes questions about prior work-related injuries and workers' compensation claims. Applicants may lawfully be asked about their ability to perform the essential functions of the job during the interview process.

Once a conditional offer of employment has been made, a candidate may be required to undergo a pre-employment physical or mental examination provided (a) the exam is related to the job and consistent with business necessity, and (b) all new hires in the same job classification are required to undergo the same examination. A conditional job offer may be withdrawn only if the examination reveals that the candidate cannot perform the essential functions of the job. A mere fear that an applicant may aggravate a prior injury and file a workers' compensation claim is not a lawful basis for withdrawing a job offer.

The employer must bear the total cost of any pre-employment testing or examinations it requires candidates to undergo.

6.18 Onboarding Documents

The law requires that new hires be provided with several documents. They include:

- Internal Revenue Service (IRS) W-4 tax withholding form;
- EDD Employee's Withholding Allowance Certificate (Form DE 4);
- EDD State Disability Insurance pamphlet (Form DE 2515);
- EDD Paid Family Leave pamphlet (Form DE 2511);
- California Civil Rights Department sexual harassment information pamphlet (Form CRD-185 or equivalent);
- California Civil Rights Division Notice to Survivors of Violence and Family Members of Victims Right to Leave and Reasonable Accommodations (Form CRD E20N-ENG);
- Workplace Know Your Rights Act notice;
- Workers' compensation information pamphlet;
- Notice of Consolidated Omnibus Budget Reconciliation Act (COBRA) rights; and
- Notice of rights of victims of domestic violence, sexual assault, and stalking (employers of 25 or more employees).

In addition, the employer must file a Report of New Employees (Form DE 34) with the EDD online (at https://eddservices.edd.ca.gov) within 20 days of the start date of any new or rehired employee.

Form I-9

Federal law requires that all employers verify a new employee's eligibility to work in the United States. To be eligible, the employee must be a U.S. citizen, be a permanent ("green card") resident, or have an employment authorization card issued by U.S. Citizenship and Immigration Services. All new hires must complete Form I-9 within three business days of starting to work.

The employee must produce documents for inspection by a representative of the employer. The employee may produce one "List A" document establishing both identity and authorization to work, or one document from "List B" establishing identity and one document from "List C" establishing authorization to work (see Table 6.1). All documents produced must be unexpired. Employees who are missing a required document under List A, List B, or List C may submit a receipt for the replacement of such document if the document was lost, stolen or damaged. The receipt is valid for 90 days from the date of hire. The employee must submit a replacement document within that 90 day period in order to continue to be authorized to work.

Table 6.1 Acceptable I-9 Documents

List A Documents	Identity and employment authorization	• U.S. Passport or U.S. Passport Card. • Permanent Resident Card or Alien Registration Receipt Card (Form I-551). • Foreign passport that contains a temporary I-551 stamp or temporary I-551 printed notation on a machine-readable immigrant visa. • Employment Authorization Document that contains a photograph (Form I-776). • For a non-immigrant alien authorized to work for a specific employer because of their status: › Foreign passport; and › Form I-94 or Form I-94A that has the following: » The same name as the passport; and » An endorsement of the alien's nonimmigrant status as long as that period of endorsement has not yet expired and the proposed employment is not in conflict with any restrictions or limitations identified on the form. • Passport from the Federated States of Micronesia (FSM) or the Republic of the Marshall Islands (RMI) with Form I-94 or Form I-94A indicating nonimmigrant admission under the Compact of Free Association Between the United States and the FSM or RMI.
List B Documents	Identity only	• Driver's license or ID card issued by state or outlying possession of the United States provided it contains a photograph or information such as name, date of birth, gender, height, eye color, and address. • ID card issued by federal, state, or local government agencies or entities provided it contains a photograph or information such as name, date of birth, gender, height, eye color, and address. • School ID card with photograph. • Voter's registration card. • U.S. military card or draft record. • Military dependent's ID card. • U.S. Coast Guard Merchant Mariner Card. • Native American tribal document. • Driver's license issued by a Canadian government authority. **For persons under age 18 who are unable to present a document listed above:** • School record or report card. • Clinic, doctor, or hospital record. • Day-care or nursery school record.
List C Documents	Employment authorization only	• A Social Security Account Number card unless the card includes one of the following restrictions: › NOT VALID FOR EMPLOYMENT. › VALID FOR WORK ONLY WITH INS AUTHORIZATION. › VALID FOR WORK ONLY WITH DHS AUTHORIZATION. • Certification of report of birth issued by Department of State (Forms DS-1350, FS-545, FS-240). • Original or certified copy of birth certificate issued by a state, county, municipal authority, or territory of the United States bearing an official seal. • Native American tribal document. • U.S. Citizen ID Card (Form I-197). • Identification Card for Use of Resident Citizen in the United States (Form I-179). • Employment authorization document issued by the Department of Homeland Security.

A qualified E-Verify employer (see the following section) may examine an employee's I-9 documents remotely by following this procedure within three business days of the employee's hire:

- Examine copies (front and back, if the document is two-sided) of Form I-9 documents or an acceptable receipt to ensure that the documentation presented reasonably appears to be genuine;
- Conduct a live video interaction with the employee presenting the document(s) to ensure that the documentation reasonably appears to be genuine and related to the individual. The employee must first transmit a copy of the document(s) to the employer (per the first step above) and then present the same document(s) during the live video interaction;
- Indicate on the Form I-9, by completing the corresponding box, that an alternative procedure was used to examine documentation to complete Section 2 or for reverification, as applicable;
- Retain a clear and legible copy of the documentation (front and back, if the documentation is two-sided); and
- Create an E-Verify case if the employee is a new hire.

An employer choosing to use this alternative method of examining Form I-9 documents must do so consistently for all employees at that worksite. An employer may, however, choose to use this alternative method only for remote new hires and use the traditional in-person review method for other employees.

The employee may not be required to produce more than one document from each list. Documents produced must appear to be genuine and to relate to the employee. If the documents appear to be genuine, the employer is not required or allowed to investigate them further.

Forms I-9 must be retained as long as the employee is employed, and then for three years from date of hire or one year from date of termination, whichever is longer. Forms I-9 should be stored in a location other than employees' personnel files, as they must be produced for inspection in the event of an audit by U.S. Immigration and Customs Enforcement or the U.S. Department of Labor.

E-Verify

E-Verify is a U.S. government web-based program that compares the information on the Form I-9 with information in government databases to verify an employee's eligibility to work. Use of E-Verify is mandatory for federal contractors and subcontractors and voluntary for other California employers. An employer that is not a federal contractor is prohibited from using E-Verify to determine the lawful work status of existing employees, however.

Wage Theft Prevention Act Notice

Each new nonexempt employee must also be given a written notice containing the following information on their first day of work:

- Basis of pay (for example, hourly, piece rate, commission);
- Rates of pay (including overtime);
- Any allowances claimed for meals or lodging;
- How paid sick days accrue or number of paid sick days provided;
- Employer's regular paydays;
- Legal name of employer and any doing business as (DBA) names used;
- Address and telephone number of employer's main office; and
- Name, address, and telephone number of workers' compensation insurance carrier and workers' compensation insurance policy number.

Employees must be notified in writing within seven days of the change in any of this information. A separate written notice is not required, however, if the change is reflected on another document such as a pay statement (indicating a new hourly rate) or on a new workers' compensation poster listing a new carrier or policy number. Employees who are exempt from overtime and employees covered by a collective bargaining agreement that (a) specifies employees' wages, hours, and working conditions; (b) provides an overtime premium wage; and (c) provides a regular hourly wage of at least 30 percent more than the state minimum wage for employees need not be given the notice.

Commission-Paid Employees

Employees who are paid on commission must be given a written agreement upon hire setting forth how the commission will be computed and paid. The document must be signed by both the employee and a representative of the employer, the employee must be given a copy of it, and the employee must sign a receipt for the copy, which the employer must retain.

This document should address the following matters:

- How will the commission be computed, and at what rates? Will the commission be computed on revenue or on profit? If on profit, how will profit be calculated?
- When will a commission be earned? On booking of the sale, delivery of the product, or payment by the customer?
- If there is a draw, will it be applied to future commissions?
- Will chargebacks for returned items be applied against future commissions?

- To which commissions will the employee be entitled upon termination of employment?

Employee Handbook, At-Will Agreement, and Arbitration Agreement

New hires should also receive a copy of the employee handbook on their first day (employee handbooks are discussed in more detail in Chapter 4). Employees should be required to sign an acknowledgment that they received a copy of the employee handbook. That acknowledgment also may include an acknowledgment that the employment relationship is at-will. Employees should be offered a separate arbitration agreement during the onboarding process (see Section 3.10).

6.19 "Stay or Pay" Agreements

Employers may not require employees or prospective employees as a condition of employment to sign an agreement requiring a payment of a debt, penalty, fee, or cost to the employer upon the termination of employment. Examples include a replacement hire fee, a retraining fee, lost profits, or reimbursement for immigration or visa-related costs. There are exceptions for tuition reimbursement agreements and retention bonuses that meet certain criteria, as follows.

Tuition Reimbursement Agreements

Agreements for reimbursement of an employer's payment of the cost of an academic degree program for an employee are allowed, provided:

- The agreement is offered separate from any contract of employment.
- The degree being sought is not required as a condition of employment.
- The repayment amount is stated in the agreement and it does not exceed the costs advanced by the employer for the degree program.
- The repayment obligation is prorated over the required employment period and does not include an accelerated repayment schedule if the employee leaves.
- Repayment is not required if the employee is terminated, unless terminated for misconduct connected with work.

Retention Bonuses

Retention bonuses offered *at the outset of employment* and not tied to any specific job performance are also allowed, provided:

- The agreement is offered separate from the primary contract of employment.
- The employee is notified of their right to consult an attorney and is given at least five business days to do so.

- The repayment obligation for early termination of employment is prorated based on the remaining term of any retention period, not to exceed two years, and is not subject to interest accrual.
- The employee has the option to defer receipt of the bonus until the end of the retention period.
- Separation from employment was at the sole election of the employee, or at the election of the employer for misconduct connected with work.

CHAPTER 7

Paying Employees Correctly

Paying California employees correctly is often a daunting task. This is because California has many statutes, wage orders, opinion letters, and court cases that not only set different standards for California than are in effect under the federal Fair Labor Standards Act (FLSA) but that additionally lack clarity and certainty in some instances.

7.1 Sources of California Wage and Hour Laws

There are two principal sources of wage and hour law in California—the California Labor Code and the wage orders issued by the former Industrial Welfare Commission (IWC). Twelve of these wage orders cover specific industries. Others (such as Wage Orders 4, 14, 15, 16, and 17) cover occupations. The wage orders are outlined in Table 7.1. Although the IWC is no longer in operation, the Division of Labor Standards Enforcement (DLSE) continues to enforce the wage orders.

Table 7.1 Industrial Welfare Commission Wage Orders

No. 1	Manufacturing Industry
No. 2	Personal Services Industry (includes beauty and nail salons, health clubs, and mortuaries)
No. 3	Canning, Freezing, and Preserving Industry
No. 4	Professional, Technical, Clerical, Mechanical, and Similar Occupations (includes accountants, bookkeepers, mechanics, doctors, nurses, lawyers, and journalists; applies to businesses such as banks, insurance companies, newspapers, and utilities)
No. 5	Public Housekeeping Industry (includes restaurants, hotels, apartment houses, hospitals, private schools and colleges that provide dormitories, cleaning and groundskeeping companies, and veterinary hospitals)
No. 6	Laundry, Linen Supply, Dry Cleaning, and Dyeing Industry
No. 7	Mercantile Industry (includes wholesale, retail, and rental businesses)
No. 8	Industries Handling Products After Harvest
No. 9	Transportation Industry (includes storing and warehousing of products or property and the parking, rental, maintenance, or cleaning of vehicles)
No. 10	Amusement and Recreation Industry (includes theaters, amusement parks, golf courses, gymnasiums, bowling alleys, and race tracks)

No. 11	Broadcasting Industry
No. 12	Motion Picture Industry
No. 13	Industries Preparing Agricultural Products for Market, on the Farm
No. 14	Agricultural Occupations
No. 15	Household Occupations (includes companions, butlers, chauffeurs, and housekeepers)
No. 16	Occupations in the On-Site Construction, Drilling, Logging, and Mining Industries
No. 17	Miscellaneous Employees

It is important to determine which of the wage orders covers your organization and your employees, as the wage orders differ in some respects. For example, Wage Orders 4 and 7 contain an inside salesperson exemption from overtime, but the other wage orders do not. Look first to determine whether your business is covered by an industry wage order. If your business does fall under an industry wage order then all occupations within that industry typically will be covered by that wage order. If your business does not fall under an industry wage order, look to the occupation of the employee involved (for a detailed listing of the types of businesses and employees that fall under each wage order, see *Which IWC Order?* at https://www.dir.ca.gov/dlse/WhichIWCOrderClassifications.pdf).

The California Labor Commissioner issues opinion letters in which provisions of the Labor Code or the wage orders are applied to specific factual scenarios. The opinion letters are not binding on the courts, but sometimes courts find them to be persuasive authority (the opinion letters may be found at https://www.dir.ca.gov/dlse/DLSE_OpinionLetters.htm). In addition, the Labor Commissioner has issued an *Enforcement Policies and Interpretations Manual* that is updated from time to time. It is not binding on the courts, but deputy labor commissioners typically follow it in enforcement proceedings (this manual may be found at https://www.dir.ca.gov/dlse/DLSEManual/dlse_enfcmanual.pdf).

There is no blanket exemption from California wage and hour laws for employees covered by a collective bargaining agreement. Rather, certain sections of the Labor Code provide limited exemptions from those respective sections to employees covered by a collective bargaining agreement when specified criteria are met (see Section 19.6).

Finally, California's Supreme Court and appellate courts are issuing rulings on wage and hour issues with greater frequency than in the past. These rulings often result in shifting interpretations of the law. Therefore, employers should remain up-to-date on developments in California's wage and hour laws.

7.2 Coverage of California Wage and Hour Laws

California's Labor Code and IWC wage orders cover private-sector employees who work in California, regardless of where their employer is based. Employees who are based in other states but assigned to work for full days or weeks in California generally must be paid under California's wage and hour laws while working in California. California wage and hour laws do not apply to employees regularly working in other states for a California-based employer.

Most state, county, municipal, and other governmental employees are not covered by California's wage and hour laws but rather fall under the FLSA. Employees of public school districts in California are covered by the minimum wage provision of the IWC wage orders.

7.3 Equal Pay

Both federal and California law have long required that men and women be paid equally for equal work. California's law was recently amended, however, to prohibit pay disparities based on race and ethnicity as well as sex, and an earlier amendment made it easier for employees to bring lawsuits alleging pay inequity.

California law prohibits employers from paying employees of one sex, race, or ethnicity less than employees of the opposite sex or a different race or ethnicity for "substantially similar work," when viewed as "a composite of skill, effort, and responsibility, and performed under similar working conditions." There is an exception for situations in which the employer can show that the wage differential is based on a seniority system, a merit system, a system that measures earnings by quality or quantity of production, or a bona fide factor other than sex, race, or ethnicity such as education, training, or experience.

Should an employer attempt to justify a pay differential as being based on a bona fide factor other than sex, race, or ethnicity, it must demonstrate that the factor (1) is not derived from a differential in compensation based on sex, race, or ethnicity; (2) is job-related with respect to the position in question; and (3) is consistent with business necessity. "Business necessity" is defined as an overriding legitimate business purpose such that the factor relied upon effectively fulfills the business purpose it is supposed to serve. This exception will not apply if the employee can show that an alternative practice exists that would serve the same business purpose without producing the wage differential.

Prior salary cannot justify a wage differential based on sex, race, or ethnicity. In other words, a new hire cannot be paid less than their peers for substantially similar work that meets the test stated above simply because they earned less in a previous job and would be willing to take less for the new job. It is important, therefore, that you establish a pay rate (or pay range) before recruiting for an open position and then pay that rate (or a rate in the range) to the employee hired for the position.

There is no requirement under California law that the comparison of wage rates be limited to employees in the same facility. Employees may contend that jobs across the organization, even at other locations, involve "substantially similar work." It is not yet clear whether comparison to jobs outside of California is permissible.

Freedom of Speech Regarding Wages

California law bars employers from prohibiting employees from disclosing their wages to others, discussing their wages, or inquiring about the wages of another employee. However, an employer is not required to disclose another employee's wages, and an employee is not required to disclose their own wages in response to a coworker's inquiry.

Pay Data Reporting

To help identify pay disparities based on sex, race, or ethnicity, every private employer of 100 or more employees must submit specific pay data to the California Civil Rights Department (CRD) on or before the second Wednesday of May of each year.

The report must include the number of employees in California by sex, race, and ethnicity for each of the following job categories:

- Executive or senior level officials and managers;
- First or mid-level officials and managers;
- Professionals;
- Technicians;
- Sales workers;
- Administrative support workers;
- Craft workers;
- Operatives;
- Laborers and helpers; and
- Service workers.

The employer may choose a single pay period between October 1 and December 31 of the previous calendar year and provide a "snapshot" of the information above for that pay period.

The report must also include the number of employees by sex, race, and ethnicity whose earnings fall within each of the pay bands used by the U.S. Bureau of Labor Statistics in its Occupational Employment Statistics Survey. You must calculate the total earnings shown on the IRS Form W-2 for each employee in the "snapshot" pay period for the entire reporting year, regardless of whether the employee worked the full calendar year. You must also include:

- For each job category above, for each combination of sex, race, and ethnicity, the median and mean hourly rates;
- The total number of hours worked by each employee counted in each pay band during the reporting year;
- Your North American Industry Classification System (NAICS) code; and
- You may, but are not required to, provide clarifying remarks. Such clarifying remarks might explain that certain employees are paid based on seniority, on a merit system, or on a system measuring earnings by quality or quantity of work performed, such as a commission system. You might also highlight bona fide job-related factors other than sex, race, and ethnicity, such as education, training, and experience.

Employers with multiple establishments must provide a report containing this data for each establishment in California. An "establishment" is an "economic unit producing goods or services." Employers that obtain workers through labor contractors must submit a separate pay data report to the CRD covering the workers hired through labor contractors during the prior year. All data must be submitted in a format that will allow the CRD to search and sort the information using readily available software.

One of the purposes of this law is to encourage employers to conduct examinations of their own pay data to determine if inequities exist. Such an examination should be conducted with the assistance of legal counsel, however, so that the examination will be covered by the attorney-client privilege.

Recordkeeping Requirement

Employers must maintain records of job titles and wage rate or salary history for each employee during their employment plus three years after termination of employment. The Labor Commissioner may inspect these records to determine if there is a pattern of wage differentials.

7.4 Minimum Wage

The California state minimum wage is $16.90 per hour during 2026. The minimum wage will increase every year on January 1 by the greater of 3.5 percent or the percentage increase in the U.S. Consumer Price Index for Urban Wage Earners and Clerical Wage Earners (U.S. CPI-W) for the prior July 1 to June 30, rounded to the nearest ten cents. If the CPI-W is negative, there will be no increase in the minimum wage on the next January 1.

Minimum wage need not be paid in a variety of limited situations, including to salaried exempt employees (although the minimum weekly salary must be paid);

outside salespersons (that is, those employees who spend more than half their working time away from their employer's place of business selling tangible or intangible items or obtaining orders or contracts for products, services, or use of facilities); to a parent, child, or spouse of the employer; to employees subject to approved deductions for meals and lodging; to certain employees subject to a lower minimum wage under the California Labor Code; or to apprentices regularly indentured under the California Division of Apprenticeship Standards.

Minimum Wage for Fast Food Workers

A minimum wage for fast food workers of $20.00 per hour went into effect on April 1, 2024. It applies to employees of limited-service restaurants that are part of a national fast food chain consisting of more than 60 such restaurants. A new Fast Food Council has been created within the state Labor Commissioner's Office, and it is authorized to increase the minimum wage for fast food workers annually effective January 1 of each year.

Minimum Wage for Health Care Workers

The minimum wage for most health care workers in California increased effective October 16, 2024. Covered health care facilities include hospitals, certain licensed skilled nursing facilities, licensed home health care agencies, medical and psychological clinics, urgent care facilities, physician groups, ambulatory surgery centers, and mental health clinics including county mental health facilities. The law does not only apply to physicians, nurses and other caregivers, but also to janitors, housekeepers, groundskeepers, guards, clerical workers, food service workers, billing personnel, schedulers, call center workers, and laundry workers. The minimum wage also applies to independent contractors and contract employees who work on the premises of a health care facility. It does not apply to waste collection workers, workers providing medical transportation services, and outside salespersons. The minimum wages are as follows:

- **Hospital or Integrated Health System** with 10,000 or more full-time equivalent employees, including skilled nursing facilities operated by these entities: $24.00 per hour July 1, 2025 – June 30, 2026; $25.00 per hour from July 1, 2026 – December 31, 2027; adjusted for inflation after January 1, 2028.
- **Dialysis Clinics:** $24.00 per hour July 1, 2025 – June 30, 2026; $25.00 per hour from July 1, 2026 – December 31, 2027; adjusted for inflation after January 1, 2028.
- **"Safety Net" Hospitals**: $18.63 per hour July 1, 2025 – June 30, 2026; $19.28 per hour July 1, 2026 – June 30, 2027; $19.95 per hour July 1, 2027 – June 30, 2028; $20.65 per hour July 1, 2028 – June 30, 2029; $21.37 per

hour July 1, 2029 – June 30, 2030; $22.12 per hour July 1, 2030 – June 30, 2031; $22.89 per hour July 1, 2031 – June 30, 2032; $25.00 per hour July 1, 2033 – December 31, 2034; adjusted for inflation as of January 1, 2035.

- **Covered Health Care Facilities Run by Large Counties** (more than 5 million people as of January 1, 2023): $23.00 per hour January 1, 2025 – June 30, 2025; $24.00 per hour July 1, 2025 – June 30, 2026; $25.00 per hour July 1, 2026 – December 31, 2027; adjusted for inflation as of January 1, 2028.
- **Covered Health Care Facilities Run by Medium-Sized Counties** (250,000 to 5 million people as of January 1, 2023): $21.00 per hour January 1, 2025 – June 30, 2026; $23.00 per hour July 1, 2026 – June 30, 2028; $25.00 per hour July 1, 2028 – December 31, 2029; adjusted for inflation as of January 1, 2030.
- **Covered Health Care Facilities Run by Small Counties** (less than 250,000 people as of January 1, 2023): $18.63 per hour July 1, 2025 – June 30, 2026; $19.28 per hour July 1, 2026 – June 30, 2027; $19.95 per hour July 1, 2027 – June 30, 2028; $20.65 per hour July 1, 2028 – June 30, 2029; $21.37 per hour July 1, 2029 – June 30, 2030; $22.12 per hour July 1, 2030 – June 30, 2031; $22.89 per hour July 1, 2031 – June 30, 2032; $23.69 per hour July 1, 2032 – June 30, 2033; $25.00 per hour July 1, 2033 – December 31, 2034; adjusted for inflation as of January 1, 2035.
- **Clinics**: $21.00 per hour through June 30, 2026; $22.00 per hour July 1, 2026 – June 30, 2027; $25.00 per hour July 1, 2027 – December 31, 2028; adjusted for inflation as of January 1, 2029.
- **Other Health Care Facilities** (not covered above): $21.00 per hour through June 30, 2026; $23.00 per hour July 1, 2026 – June 30, 2028; $25.00 per hour July 1, 2028 – December 31, 2029; adjusted for inflation as of January 1, 2030.

Minimum Wage for Federal Contractors

Under Executive Order 14026, President Biden increased the minimum wage to be paid by certain federal contractors to $17.75 per hour. President Trump rescinded that order, however, causing the minimum wage for federal contractors to revert to $13.30, as established by President Obama in 2014.

Local Minimum Wage Laws in California

Several local jurisdictions in California have enacted their own minimum wage ordinances, requiring that a higher wage than the state minimum be paid for work performed within their geographical boundaries.

City of Los Angeles: The minimum wage in the City of Los Angeles is $17.87 per hour. It will increase annually on July 1 based on the CPI-W for the Los Angeles area published by the Bureau of Labor Statistics. It applies to employees who perform at least two hours of work per week in the city.

In addition, the City of Los Angeles requires that a higher minimum wage be paid to employees of hotels in the city having 60 or more rooms. The minimum wage is adjusted every July 1. The current minimum wage for such hotel workers is $22.50 per hour.

County of Los Angeles: The minimum wage in the County of Los Angeles is $17.81 per hour. This minimum wage is applicable to employees who perform at least two hours of work per week in the unincorporated areas of the county. Unincorporated areas are places within the county that fall outside the boundaries of a city such as Los Angeles, Santa Monica, Long Beach, and Burbank. The minimum wage will increase annually on July 1 based on the CPI-W for the Los Angeles area published by the Bureau of Labor Statistics.

Oakland: The City of Oakland's minimum wage is $17.34 per hour. It will increase annually on January 1 based on yearly increases in the CPI-W in the San Francisco-Oakland area. The minimum wage applies to employees who work two or more hours per week in the city. Oakland also imposes a minimum wage for employees of hotels with 50 or more rooms. Effective January 1, 2026 it is $18.85 per hour for employees with health benefits and $25.14 per hour for employees without health benefits.

San Diego: The minimum wage in the City of San Diego is $17.75 per hour for employees of private employers who work within the city boundaries for at least two hours in a workweek. The minimum wage increases on January 1 of each year according to increases in the CPI-W U.S. City Average or to match increases in the state minimum wage, whichever is greater.

San Francisco: The minimum wage in the City of San Francisco is $19.18 per hour. It increases annually on July 1 according to increases in the CPI-W for the San Francisco-Oakland area. The minimum wage must be paid for all hours worked in the city.

Other Cities: A growing number of smaller California cities have established minimum wages that exceed the state minimum, including Berkeley, Long Beach, Pasadena, Sacramento, San Jose, Santa Clara, Santa Monica and West Hollywood. You should check the city government website for each city in California in which your employees work to determine whether a higher local minimum wage applies generally as well as the specific conditions under which the local minimum wage is applicable.

Subminimum Wage

California law permits employers to pay "learners" with no prior experience in the occupation 85 percent of the state minimum wage, rounded to the nearest nickel, for their first 160 hours of work. Thus, an employer may pay a learner a subminimum wage of $14.37 per hour in 2026.

Most local minimum wage ordinances (including those in the city and county of Los Angeles, Oakland, San Diego, and San Francisco) expressly state that the higher minimum applies only to employees who are entitled to be paid the state minimum wage under California law, thus allowing a subminimum wage for learners. If you have employees subject to a local minimum wage ordinance in California and you wish to pay a subminimum wage to learners, however, you should verify that payment of a subminimum wage is permissible in that jurisdiction.

Living Wage

Some local jurisdictions in California have enacted a higher "living wage" applicable in certain industries (such as large hotels), in certain geographical areas, or for employers with contracts to provide goods or services to the local government entity.

Prevailing Wage

Prevailing wages must be paid on public works projects financed by state funds. The prevailing wage rate is the basic hourly rate paid on public works projects to a majority of workers engaged in a particular craft, classification, or type of work within the locality and in the nearest labor market area (if a majority of such workers are paid at a single rate). If there is no single rate paid to a majority, then the rate being paid to the greater number of workers is deemed prevailing. California's prevailing wage laws ensure that the ability to secure a public works contract is not based on paying lower wage rates than a competitor. All bidders are required to use the same wage rates when bidding on a public works project. The director of the Department of Industrial Relations issues prevailing wage determinations for each craft, classification, or type of worker in each geographical area on February 22 and August 22 of each year that take effect ten days later.

7.5 Piece-Rate Employees

The IWC wage orders define "hours worked" as the time during which an employee is *under the control of the employer*, and includes the time the employee "is suffered or permitted to work," whether or not required to do so. This is a broader definition than under federal law. The notion that employees must be paid at least minimum wage for all hours worked is simple when applied to employees paid a stated hourly wage. It becomes more complicated, however, when applied to employees paid on a piece-rate basis.

Under federal law, whether the minimum wage is met is determined by dividing an employee's total compensation earned in a workweek by the total hours worked during the workweek. If the result equals or exceeds the minimum wage, the test is satisfied. Not so under California law. California courts have held that piece rates compensate employees only for the time they spend performing piece-rate work. Such employees must additionally be compensated for nonproductive time such as waiting time between jobs and training time. They also must be paid separately for their rest and recovery breaks.

Piece-rate employees therefore must either be paid a separate wage (at least minimum wage) for nonproductive working time spent performing other than piece-rate work, or be paid an hourly rate (at least minimum wage) for all hours worked plus an incentive to reward productivity (with overtime if applicable). Piece-rate employees must be paid for their rest breaks (and cool-down breaks, if taken; see Section 9.4) at the average hourly rate earned during the workweek, taking into account all earnings except overtime and pay for rest and cool-down breaks. A piece-rate employee's earnings for nonproductive time and for rest and cool-down breaks must be stated separately on each wage statement (see Section 7.26).

7.6 Unpaid Interns and Volunteers

Unpaid interns once were common in many businesses, as students or new graduates were willing to work without pay in order to gain on-the-job experience. In recent years, however, many of these interns have sued to recover minimum wages, overtime, and penalties, alleging that they really were employees.

For many years, the U.S. Department of Labor (DOL) applied a six-part test to determine whether an intern in a for-profit business is actually an employee who must be paid wages. The criteria were as follows:

- The internship, even though it includes actual operation of the facilities of the employer, is similar to training that would be given in an educational environment.
- The internship experience is for the benefit of the intern.
- The intern does not displace regular employees, but works under close supervision of existing staff.
- The employer that provides the training derives no immediate advantage from the activities of the intern; on occasion its operations may actually be impeded.
- The intern is not necessarily entitled to a job at the conclusion of the internship.
- The employer and the intern understand that the intern is not entitled to wages for the time spent in the internship.

The DOL took the position that each of these criteria must be met for an unpaid internship to be lawful. California's Labor Commissioner has adopted the same test. Several federal appellate courts, however, refused to follow the DOL's test, holding that the correct test is whether the intern or the employer is the primary beneficiary of the relationship. These courts noted that lower courts may consider the DOL's criteria in applying this "primary beneficiary" test but that each of the DOL's criteria need not be satisfied. The DOL has since announced that it will now apply the "primary beneficiary" test applied by the federal courts.

The new DOL test based on the federal court decisions noted above is not necessarily binding in California, however, so until a California court or the Labor Commissioner adopts a new test, California employers should apply the DOL criteria in determining whether interns must be paid. As the DOL noted in its explanation of its criteria, the more an internship is structured around a classroom or academic experience, the more likely the intern will be determined not to be entitled to pay. On the other hand, where interns are engaged in the operations of the employer or are performing productive work such as filing, clerical work, or customer assistance, even if they are also learning a skill or improved work habits, they are more likely to be found entitled to be paid wages.

Those who volunteer their services to religious, charitable, or similar nonprofit organizations for public service, religious, or humanitarian objectives need not be paid wages so long as the volunteer has no expectation of being paid. There are two exceptions. One is that an employee of a religious, charitable, or similar nonprofit organization may not donate services to that organization that are within the scope of their usual job duties. The other exception is where a religious, charitable, or similar nonprofit organization operates a commercial enterprise that serves the public, such as a thrift store or restaurant, or where a nonprofit provides personal services to businesses. Unpaid volunteers may not be used in these enterprises.

If you utilize unpaid interns or volunteers, you should have them sign a written agreement acknowledging that they have no expectation of being paid.

7.7 Travel Time

Unlike under federal law, in which travel time outside the normal workday ordinarily need not be paid, California law requires that nonexempt employees be paid for all travel time beyond their normal commute (including travel outside the normal workday) until they arrive at their destination and can use the time effectively for their own purposes. For example, a nonexempt employee who travels to another city outside of normal working hours must be paid for the time traveling by air or other conveyance, plus local travel time, until the employee checks into a hotel or is otherwise free to eat, sleep, or engage in recreation. Points to consider regarding travel time include the following:

- Employees may be paid a lower hourly rate (at or above the applicable minimum wage) for travel time, although when using different rates of pay, employers must pay any overtime premium at a blended rate (taking into consideration all rates of pay during the pay period).
- Employees' work schedules may be adjusted to reduce or eliminate overtime due to travel time. An employee who normally starts work at 8 a.m. may be scheduled to start at noon on a day when travel is planned, for example.
- Exempt employees need not be paid extra if they are required to travel outside their normal workdays.

7.8 Commuting Time

Commuting time between an employee's home and place of work is ordinarily not compensable. There are some exceptions, however:

- When an employer provides the employee a company vehicle for transportation, this alone does not mean that the employee's commute to the regular place of work in the vehicle, including refueling, is compensable working time. However, when certain restrictions are placed on the employee's use of the company vehicle or on the nature of the travel (such as prohibiting personal errands, prohibiting personal use of a cell phone while requiring it to remain turned on to answer calls from the office, prohibiting taking passengers, or the requirement that the employee drive the vehicle directly from home to their job and back), the travel time may have to be compensated as hours worked.
- When employees are required to travel to a different worksite on a temporary basis or in the employer's vehicle, the employees must generally be paid for the travel time. When use of the employer's transportation is optional, however, employees who use the employer's transportation generally need not be paid for time spent traveling.
- When employees are required to report to work at, or return home from, a location more distant than their usual place of work, they must be paid for the additional time over and above their normal commute.
- When employees are required to drive a company vehicle, and they report to their first assignment at the beginning of their workdays, they generally must be paid for the travel time between home and their first assignment.

7.9 Preparation and Concluding Time

Time spent changing clothes, washing up, or preparing for or concluding work is compensable. If the work requires the wearing of protective clothing or gear, employees must be paid for the time spent putting on and taking off the clothing or gear. California does ***not*** apply the ***de minimis*** rule applied under federal law for small amounts of work that employees perform before clocking in and after clocking out. Therefore, employees must be paid for time spent on tasks such as opening a store or facility before clocking in and closing the store or facility after clocking out. Therefore, if employees are required to unlock the building, boot up a computer, or check emails before starting their shift they must be paid for that time. Likewise, if employees must shut down a computer system, activate a security system, or walk coworkers to their cars after a shift they must be paid for the time. In addition, employees must be compensated for time spent waiting for, and undergoing, security or bag checks at the end of their shift.

7.10 Education and Training Time

Time spent in training or meetings required by the employer or required for employees to be able to perform their current job duties must be paid. Examples would include training on a new accounting system, new computer software, or new company protocols or procedures. If training or meetings occur during employees' lunch hours, employees must be paid for the time spent in training even if lunch is provided by the employer, and they must additionally be provided with either an unpaid meal break of at least 30 minutes before or after the meeting or training (but within the first 5 hours of work) or an hour's pay as a premium for the missed meal break (see Section 9.1).

Employees need not be paid for education or training time that is voluntary on the part of the employee and that meets all of the following criteria:

- The training occurs outside of normal working hours;
- The training is not related to the employee's current job but rather is geared toward qualifying the employee for a new job or a promotion; and
- No production work is performed.

Thus, employees who take night or weekend classes to obtain a degree or certification to qualify them for a new and different occupation, or in the hope that the additional credential will lead to future career advancement, need not be paid for time spent in such classes.

7.11 Sleeping Time

Under federal law, employees who are required to be on duty for 24 hours or more may agree with their employers to exclude bona fide meal periods and up to 8 hours of sleeping time from hours worked. An employee called to work during sleeping time must be paid for time worked. If the employee cannot get at least 5 hours of sleep during sleeping time, the entire period of sleeping time must be counted as hours worked.

The federal sleeping time rule does not generally apply under California law, however. It applies only to ambulance drivers and attendants. Whether sleeping time need be paid to other employees depends on the governing wage order. Wage Order 5, covering the public housekeeping industry, states that, with respect to the definition of "hours worked," in the case of an employee who is required to reside on-premises "that time spent carrying out assigned duties shall be counted as hours worked." Sleeping and other nonworking time of these employees need not be paid. Wage Order 5 also states that, with respect to the health care industry, hours worked should be interpreted in accordance with the provisions of the FLSA. "Health care industry" is defined as hospitals, skilled nursing facilities, intermediate care and residential care facilities, convalescent care institutions, home health agencies, clinics operating 24 hours per day, and clinics performing surgery, urgent care, radiology, anesthesiology, pathology, neurology, or dialysis. As the federal sleeping time rule is found in the regulations defining hours worked under the FLSA, it would be applicable to those health care employers mentioned in the wage order.

Wage Order 15, which covers domestic employees, states, among other things, that a live-in employee must have at least 12 consecutive hours free of duty during each workday of 24 hours and that the total span of hours for a day of work may be no more than 12. Such an employee need not be paid for nonworking time. "Personal attendants," who are employed in a private household to supervise, feed, or dress a child or person who by reason of advanced age, physical disability, or mental deficiency needs supervision, are not covered by this provision of the wage order.

Employees covered by other wage orders, and personal attendants covered by Wage Order 15, must be paid for time they spend sleeping if they are required to remain on the employer's premises.

7.12 Reporting Pay

An employee who reports for their regular shift and is given less than half the scheduled hours of work must be paid at least half the number of scheduled hours, but never less than two hours nor more than four hours of pay (or actual time worked if more than four hours). For example, an employee who is scheduled to work eight hours but is sent home after three hours must be paid for four hours. An employee who is scheduled to work eight hours but is sent home after five hours must be paid for five hours. Reporting pay need not be provided when:

- Work cannot start or continue due to threats to employees or property, or when recommended by civil authorities;
- There is a failure in the public utility system that affects the employer (a power outage, for example); or

- The interruption in work is caused by a natural disaster or other cause not within the employer's control.

An employee who is called back to work again after completing a workday must be paid for at least two hours or the actual time worked, whichever is greater.

An employee who is called into work for a prescheduled amount of time on a scheduled day off must be paid for at least half the scheduled time, or for the actual time worked, whichever is greater. For example, if an employee is scheduled to attend a one-hour mandatory staff meeting on their day off and they attend that meeting, they only need be paid for one hour because the meeting was prescheduled.

By contrast, an employee who is called into work on a scheduled day off must be paid for at least two hours, or for the actual time worked, whichever is greater. An employee who is called in to be fired on a day they are not scheduled to work must therefore be paid for at least two hours on that day, and such pay must be included in the employee's final paycheck.

Employees who are scheduled for "call-in" or "on-call" shifts where they must call in to the employer at a specific time to determine if they will be required to work a scheduled shift on that day (or early the next day), and who must appear at work if directed to do so, must be paid reporting pay if they are told not to come to work. Employees need not be paid simply for calling in or checking email or a website to obtain their work schedule, however.

7.13 Split-Shift Pay

A split shift is defined as two distinct work periods separated by more than a one-hour break of nonworking time other than a bona fide meal period. An employee who voluntarily takes an extended meal break would not work a split shift. Regular overnight shifts do not qualify as split shifts, moreover.

Employees who work a split shift must be paid a split-shift premium of at least one hour at the applicable minimum wage unless they receive a higher hourly wage where the difference between that wage and the minimum wage at least offsets the split-shift premium on a given workday. In other words, any additional amounts paid by the employer above the minimum wage obligation can be used to offset the split-shift premium. For example, assuming a minimum wage of $16.90 per hour, if employees are paid at least $19.02 per hour, they need not be paid a split-shift premium because the excess of their hourly rate over the minimum wage ($2.12) multiplied by eight hours equals $16.96, which exceeds one hour of pay at minimum wage.

7.14 Shift-Differential Pay

Whereas some employers offer a premium rate for second or third shift work to incentivize employees to work those shifts, there is no legal requirement under California or federal law that a shift differential be paid.

7.15 On-Call Pay

In determining whether employees are required to be paid while on call, the relevant question is whether they are *engaged to be waiting* or *waiting to be engaged.* In the former instance, they are required to remain at or near the employer's premises, and they are substantially limited in their ability to use the time for their own purposes. These employees must be paid for the time they spend waiting to go to work. A classic example would be firefighters on duty waiting for a call.

In the latter instance, the employees are free to leave the employer's premises and free to an extent to go about their own business, but they must be able to go to work in response to a call within a certain period of time if necessary. They may be required to carry a cell phone or pager and leave it on. However, in determining whether the employees are predominantly free to engage in personal activities, the courts will analyze a variety of factors, such as the frequency of calls to work, geographical limitations, and to what extent employees actually engage in personal activities during the on-call time. If waiting to be engaged, these employees need not be paid for the time they are not actually working. If they are called to work, they must be paid for a minimum of two hours or actual time spent working, including their travel time to and from the job, whichever is greater.

In determining whether employees are required to be paid while on call, the relevant question is whether they are *engaged to be waiting* or *waiting to be engaged.*

7.16 Time Clock Rounding

Historically, rounding employees' time entries to the nearest tenth or quarter of an hour has been considered lawful in California, provided the rounding system was used in such a manner that it did not result, over a period of time, in a failure to compensate employees properly for all time actually worked. Given the availability of technology that can capture time worked by most employees to fractions of a minute, courts have become more hostile to time clock rounding. Rounding therefore should be avoided where precise time measurements are available.

Note that rounding of meal period time punches is *not* permitted. Time punches for meal periods must reflect the actual number of minutes taken.

7.17 Uniforms, Tools, and Equipment

Uniforms are apparel or accessories of a distinctive design or color. If employees are required to wear uniforms, the employer must provide and maintain them. Clothing that is standard in the industry yet generic in nature and can be worn from one job to the next is not considered a uniform that the employer must provide. Examples include white nurses' uniforms, and white shirts, black pants, and slip-resistant shoes worn by many bartenders and food servers.

Unless uniforms can be laundered and tumble-dried or drip-dried at home with other laundry, the employer must clean and maintain the uniforms, or reimburse employees for the cost of cleaning and maintaining the uniforms.

When tools or equipment are required for the performance of the job, the employer must provide and maintain such tools and equipment. Employees who are paid at least twice the state minimum wage may be required to furnish their own hand tools or equipment customarily required by the trade or craft. This rule does not apply to personal protective equipment and safety devices required by Occupational Safety and Health Administration regulations, however. The employer is always responsible for providing such equipment and devices.

Employers may require a reasonable deposit from employees to secure the return of uniforms, tools, or equipment. There are strict rules requiring the holding of such a deposit: the employer and employee must have a written agreement describing how the money will be maintained. The money must be deposited into a savings account in a bank authorized to do business in California, and it may be withdrawn only upon the signature of both the employer and employee. Moreover, the money in this account may not be commingled with other funds of the employer. The money must be returned to the employee with accrued interest upon the employee's return of the employer's property. Because of the difficulty of complying with these requirements, the deposit method is not recommended. Alternatively, the employer may obtain from the employee a written authorization to deduct a specified amount from the employee's final paycheck for the cost of any such uniforms, tools, or equipment that were not returned to the employer upon termination of employment. The employee may not be charged for reasonable wear and tear, and the deductions may not reduce the employee's pay below the minimum wage.

7.18 Meal and Lodging Allowances

An employer may take credit against the minimum wage for meals and lodging furnished to nonexempt employees provided a written agreement exists between the employer and employee. Effective January 1, 2026, the allowable credits are provided in Table 7.2.

Even if the employer does not take a credit against minimum wage, it may not charge rent in excess of the below amounts when employees are required as a condition of employment to occupy quarters owned or controlled by the employer. A resident manager of an apartment building may be charged up to ⅔ of the ordinary rental value of the apartment so long as the charge is not used as a credit against minimum wage.

Table 7.2 Meal and Lodging Credits

Meal or Lodging Provided	Credit Allowed Employers Toward Minimum Wage
Room occupied alone	$79.46 per week
Room shared	$65.59 per week
Apartment—⅔ of the ordinary rental value, and in no event more than	$954.43 per month
Apartment where both members of a couple are employed by the employer, ⅔ of the ordinary rental value, and in no event more than	$1,411.85 per month
Breakfast	$6.10
Lunch	$8.42
Dinner	$11.28

7.19 Tips and Service Charges

There is no "tip credit" in California. Rather, tips are considered the property of the employee who earned them, and the employer may not take them or credit them against wages owed the employee. Tips charged to a credit card must be paid to the employee no later than the next regular payday after the patron charged the tip. The employer may not pass along any credit card processing fees to the employee.

Tip pooling is lawful, and tipped employees may be required to pool their tips to provide an equitable share of the tips for all tipped employees or to provide for tips for all employees who contribute to a patron's service, such as bartenders, bussers, and even kitchen staff and dishwashers. No manager or supervisor may lawfully receive a share of pooled tips.

A California appellate court has held that a "service charge" might also be considered a gratuity that must be paid only to the employees providing service, with no portion being retained by the employer. Accordingly, the term "service charge" should not be used. A percentage of the bill paid to the employees performing the service should be called a gratuity even if it is mandatory (if it is mandatory the customer should be notified in advance). Any additional surcharge that is retained by the employer should be designated a "management fee" or "administrative fee" and it should be stated that such fee will not be paid to employees.

7.20 Commissions

A commission is defined as compensation for selling goods or services that is based on the amount or value of the goods or services sold. It is commonly a percentage of revenue or profit on a sale, but it may also be a flat amount per item sold. Bonuses or incentives based on a percentage of the profit of the company or of a particular store or department do not qualify as commissions.

Commission-paid employees must be provided with a written commission agreement that describes the method by which commissions are computed and paid. An employer must give the employee a signed copy of the agreement, and it must obtain a signed receipt from the employee for the copy of the commission agreement.

The commission agreement should be clear as to how the commission is calculated. If it is based on the profit on a sale, the elements of both revenue and cost of the sale that will be used to compute profit must be clearly identified.

The commission agreement should also be clear regarding when the commission will be deemed earned. The employer has some latitude to determine when the commission is earned, which will determine which commissions a terminating employee will be entitled to receive, such as the following examples:

- Commission is earned upon booking the sale;
- Commission is earned upon delivery of the product; or
- Commission is earned upon employer's receipt of payment from the customer.

The most beneficial option for the employer is the last one, but custom and practice in the industry often influence when a commission will be deemed earned. Also, California courts and the Labor Commissioner will not enforce a commission agreement that provides for earned commissions to be forfeited upon termination of employment; they typically view a commission as being earned when all of the employee's work necessary to effect the sale is complete. If a commission is not deemed earned based on the booking of a sale alone, but it requires certain additional conditions to be satisfied, such commission may be withheld upon termination if such conditions are not satisfied. However, if a commission will not be deemed earned until the product is delivered or payment is received, for example, the employee must play an active role in delivering the product or securing payment from the customer. These conditions for earning the commission should be clearly described in the commission agreement.

The commission agreement may provide for chargebacks against commissions paid if the customer fails to pay for or returns an item, or if an adjustment in the purchase price is made after the sale. Chargebacks must be limited to the employee's own sales. It is unlawful to "pool" chargebacks and distribute them pro rata to employees.

If draws are to be paid to commissioned employees, they should also be stated in the commission agreement, and they should be specified as repayable draws or non-repayable or guaranteed draws. For example, if at the time of separation commissions are not sufficient to meet outstanding draws, the agreement should specify whether the draws are recoverable as debts following separation from employment. Otherwise, the periodic draws will be treated as part of the employee's regular compensation.

Under California law, commissions are deemed to compensate commission-paid employees only for time spent *selling* the employer's goods or services. A California appellate court has held that an employer may not pay employees on a 100 percent commission basis without accounting separately for paid rest breaks. The rationale of that decision could logically be extended to cover other nonselling duties such as attending meetings or training sessions, stocking or straightening merchandise, and reconciling point-of-sale terminals at the end of the day. The only exception would be for outside salespersons (see Section 8.15) who are exempt from the minimum-wage requirement.

Nonexempt commissioned employees therefore should either be paid a separate wage (at least minimum wage) for their non-selling working time and paid rest breaks, or be paid an hourly rate (at least minimum wage) for all hours worked plus commission (with overtime if applicable). A mere draw against commissions that amounts to at least minimum wage for all hours worked will not be sufficient because it will not separately compensate commissioned employees for nonselling time and rest breaks.

Commissions must be paid to employees at least twice monthly except for employees of automobile and truck dealerships who may be paid commissions on a monthly basis.

7.21 Vacation

Vacation is not required by law to be provided to employees, but if an employer elects to provide vacation, it is deemed to be a form of wages under California law. As wages, it vests incrementally as labor is performed, and it cannot be taken away once it is vested. "Use it or lose it" vacation policies are therefore not lawful in California, and unused vacation must be paid out upon termination of employment.

Because vacation is not required to be offered at all, there is no requirement that any specific amount of vacation be provided. An employer may prescribe that no vacation may be earned during the first 90 days or 6 months of employment. Such a policy is advisable when there is significant turnover among newer employees, to avoid having to pay accrued vacation to short-term employees when they leave. Earning of vacation must be proportional, however; it must not be accelerated. For example, a policy that employees earn no vacation during their first 6 months, 1 week of vacation in their second 6 months, and 2 weeks of vacation per year thereafter would be a proportional basis of earning vacation. A policy that employees earn no vacation during their first 6 months, 2 weeks during their second 6 months, and 2 weeks per year thereafter would not be proportional.

Employers may prevent employees from accruing large amounts of vacation three ways:

- Pay employees for their accrued but unused vacation at the end of each year.
- Require that employees use some of their vacation during planned plant shutdowns.
- Cap the accrual of vacation such that once an employee reaches the cap, no more vacation will accrue until vacation is used to draw the accrued balance down below the cap. The minimum permissible cap is 1–1½ times the annual accrual. If an employee accrues 10 days of vacation per year, the minimum accrual cap is 15 days.

Employers may place reasonable restrictions on the use of vacation. Employees may be required to schedule vacation in advance (to prevent the taking of vacation days without prior warning), or they may be prevented from taking vacation during certain times of the year. The Labor Commissioner does not permit a requirement that employees use all of their vacation in the same year it accrues, however.

Some employers combine vacation and sick leave into "paid time off" or "PTO." In that situation, all of the PTO becomes subject to the accrual and vesting rules that apply to vacation. Although unused sick days do not need to be paid out upon termination, if PTO covers both sick pay and vacation, all accrued but unused PTO must be paid out upon termination.

fyi **Why Separating Vacation and Paid Sick Days Is the Best Approach**

Although combining sick leave and vacation into PTO has become common, it is no longer the best approach given state and local requirements that employees be provided paid sick days. If paid sick days are combined with vacation, all such PTO days carry the same rights for employees as paid sick days. That is, an employer cannot require advance notice of taking PTO days, require management approval of their use, or impose "blackout periods" during busy periods. Each PTO day may be taken upon minimal notice, which can be quite disruptive to an organization's operations. If paid sick days are separated from vacation, by contrast, management can place reasonable conditions and restrictions on the use of vacation days.

Paid holidays that are taken at the employee's discretion ("floating holidays" or "personal days") are considered the equivalent of vacation and, if unused, must be paid upon the employee's termination. By contrast, paid national holidays, such as Christmas and Thanksgiving Day, do not accrue until the arrival of the holiday. Future national holidays, therefore, need not be paid out when an employee terminates.

Vacation must be paid out at the rate of pay in effect at the employee's termination, not at the rate in effect when the vacation was earned. Moreover, the statute of limitations (four years when a written vacation policy is concerned) on an employer's failure to pay accrued vacation at termination does not begin to run until the failure to pay has occurred. For example, all accrued but unused vacation must be paid at the time of termination, regardless of when that vacation accrued. In such a case, the four-year statute of limitations begins to run at the time of termination. The employee may recover the value of *all* accrued but unused vacation regardless of when it accrued, plus interest and waiting time penalties.

Vacation must be paid out at the rate of pay in effect at the employee's termination, not at the rate in effect when the vacation was earned.

An employer may avoid the obligation to pay accrued but unused vacation at termination by paying vacation through a vacation trust covered by the Employee Retirement Income Security Act (ERISA). Three requirements must be met for such a trust to preempt California law:

- An actual plan subject to ERISA must be established. There must be a plan document that establishes the trust, and all of ERISA's notice requirements apply.
- Vacation must be paid out from the assets in the plan, not from the employer's general operating account.
- There must be some investment and management of the assets in the plan.

7.22 Reimbursement of Expenses

You must reimburse employees for all expenses they necessarily incur in the direct consequence of the discharge of their duties. Thus, if you require an employee to travel on business, you must pay for all travel costs. You must also reimburse employees for the business use of their personal vehicles. Reimbursement at the Internal Revenue Service (IRS) mileage rate then in effect (which may be found at https://www.irs.gov/Tax-Professionals/Standard-Mileage-Rates) will presumptively satisfy this obligation, or a fixed monthly auto allowance may be provided.

Employees who are required to use their personal cell phones for business-related calls, emails, or text messages are entitled to be reimbursed for a portion of their monthly phone charges. This includes employees who have unlimited calling plans in which the business use will not increase the employee's regular expenses. Employers should therefore consider doing one of the following:

- Pay an allowance to employees who use their personal phones for business that amounts to a fair reimbursement for business use.
- Provide company-owned phones to employees for business use.
- Institute a policy that employees are not allowed to use their personal phones for business purposes.

Employers must reimburse the expenses incurred by employees who work at home. Such expenses include internet access, telephone service (if used for work), and use of a telephone headset, computer, and necessary peripherals. There is no prescribed amount that must be reimbursed for these items. Rather, employees should be reimbursed an amount that reflects the employee's business use of the items utilized.

Employers also must reimburse all costs incurred by food-handling restaurant employees in obtaining their food handler cards, including training and testing. Employees must be paid for the time they spend training for and taking the food handler test, and they must be relieved of all of their regular duties while training and testing. Moreover, employers may not require food-handling employees to have a food handler card as a condition of hire.

7.23 Paydays

Employers are required to designate specific regular paydays and provide written notice to employees of the designated paydays. Generally, employees are required to be paid at least twice per month. Wages earned between the 1st and 15th of the month must be paid between the 16th and 26th days of the month. Wages earned between the 16th and last day of the month must be paid between the 1st and 10th day of the following month. Employees may also be paid weekly or biweekly so long as they are paid no later than seven calendar days following the end of the pay period. Premium wages for unscheduled overtime may be paid no later than the next regular pay period.

Commissions must be paid as soon as they are reasonably calculable. Commissions of salespersons outside of the retail automotive industry must be paid at least twice per month. Commissions earned by salespersons at automobile and other vehicle dealerships may be paid once monthly. Bonuses paid at quarterly or other intervals must be paid on the next regular payday after the bonus is calculated.

Agricultural and domestic service workers who are boarded and lodged by the employer may be paid once per month on designated paydays that are not more than 31 days apart provided they are paid all wages due up to the payday. Employees of farm labor contractors must be paid on a weekly basis, however, to include all wages earned up to and including the fourth day before the weekly payday.

Employees of temporary service agencies must be paid weekly, with wages earned during any calendar week being payable not later than the regular payday of the following week. Wages of day laborers and striker replacements provided by temporary services agencies must generally be paid each day.

Wages coming due on a legal holiday may be paid on the next business day if an employer observes that holiday by closing its business. Wages coming due on a weekend may be paid on the nearest business day to the weekend day.

7.24 Form of Wage Payment

Wages must be paid in cash, or by a check or money order payable in cash, without discount, at a bank or other business within the state. If an employer uses an out-of-state bank for its payroll, paychecks must show on their face the name and address of an in-state bank or other institution where the check may be redeemed for cash without a fee or discount.

Wages may be direct deposited into a bank or other financial institution located within California if the employee provides written authorization. An employer cannot mandate that wages be direct deposited, however.

Payroll debit cards may be issued for payment of wages, provided:

- The employee authorizes payment in this manner;
- There is no fee to use the debit card at least one time per pay period at a California bank; and
- The funds are immediately available.

Sufficient funds to cover a paycheck must remain in the employer's payroll account for at least 30 days after the paycheck is issued. If a paycheck is presented within such 30 days and is dishonored, waiting time penalties in the amount of the employee's wages will continue to accrue for up to 30 working days or until the check is honored, whichever is sooner, unless the employer can establish that the shortfall of funds to cover the paycheck was unintentional. Civil penalties payable to the state may also be assessed for a dishonored paycheck.

7.25 Deductions from Wages

Deductions may only be made from employee wages if required by law (for example, deductions for FICA, state disability insurance (SDI), and state and federal income taxes), or as authorized in writing by an employee for the benefit of the employee such as health or other insurance plan premiums. Employers may also deduct for contributions to a defined contribution retirement plan—such as a 401(k) plan—unless the employee opts out in writing. An employer generally may not take deductions from wages for its own benefit.

Debts Owed the Employer

An employer may lawfully agree in writing with an employee that amounts loaned or advanced to the employee will be repaid in installments via payroll deductions. Should the employee quit or be terminated before the loan or advance is fully repaid, though, the employer may not deduct the outstanding balance from the employee's final paycheck. Employees should be required to sign a promissory note in exchange for any loan or advance, therefore, which should state that if any balance on the note is outstanding when the employee's employment terminates, such balance will be due and payable within a specified number of days (for example, 10 or 30 days) from the date of termination. The note should additionally specify that if a lawsuit is filed to enforce its provisions, the prevailing party will recover its court costs and reasonable attorneys' fees. A terminating employee should be reminded that the likely cost of not paying the amount due will be substantially greater than the amount due should a lawsuit be filed and the employer prevail.

A negative vacation balance is a form of debt owed the employer. Such a negative balance must not be deducted from the employee's final paycheck. The fact that a negative vacation balance may never be recovered from a final paycheck should cause employers to think carefully about whether to allow employees to carry negative vacation accruals.

Overpayment of Wages

An employer generally may not deduct prior wage overpayments from an employee's current wages without the employee's written consent. Should the employee fail to consent, an employer may sue the employee to recover the overpayment.

Losses to the Business

The wage orders authorize a deduction from wages for cash shortage, breakage, or loss of equipment resulting from an employee's dishonest or willful act, or an employee's gross negligence. Such a deduction may be taken from regular wages or the final paycheck so long as the employee's earnings do not fall below the minimum wage. Two important caveats must be borne in mind before taking such a deduction, however:

- The authorization for such a deduction is found in Section 8 of the wage orders, but Section 1 of the wage orders states that Sections 3 through 12 do not apply to employees subject to the executive, administrative, and professional exemptions from overtime and that no part of the wage orders applies to outside salespersons. Given that wage deductions not authorized by the employee for the employee's own benefit are lawful only if allowed or required by law and that no law appears to authorize deductions against white-collar

exempt employees and outside salespersons, deductions should not be taken against those employees. Such a deduction would also be inconsistent with the "salary basis" for compensation that is necessary for the white-collar exemptions to apply (see Section 8.10).
- The employer has the burden of proving that the employee committed a dishonest or willful act or was grossly negligent. Absent a signed confession or video surveillance evidence, this may be difficult to prove. If the employer is unsuccessful in proving a dishonest, willful, or grossly negligent act, a court or the Labor Commissioner will order that the deducted amounts be repaid, and in the case of a terminated employee, may order that waiting time penalties of up to 30 working days be awarded.

Employers may not charge employees for losses due to their ordinary negligence. Nor may employers charge an employee for other costs of doing business. An employee may not lawfully be required to pay the wages and benefits of their assistants, as clerical assistance is considered a cost of doing business. This rule, however, does not preclude awarding employees an incentive bonus based on the profitability of the company or of a particular store or facility, so long as the bonus is in addition to the employees' usual wages or salary.

Garnishments

Wage garnishments must be honored, with wages being deducted subject to legal limits until the amount of the judgment is satisfied. The employer may also deduct a fee of $1.50 for each payment made pursuant to a garnishment order. A garnishment order for other than child or spousal support may not exceed the lesser of the following amounts:

- 20 percent of weekly disposable earnings; or
- 40 percent of the amount by which weekly disposable earnings exceed 40 times the state or applicable local hourly minimum wage, whichever is greater.

"Disposable earnings" are what is left after deductions required by law, not including health plan or other insurance, or 401(k) contributions.

When a garnishment is for child or spousal support, the limits are the following:

- 50 percent of weekly disposable earnings when the employee is supporting a spouse or dependent child other than the spouse or child who is the subject of the withholding order; or

- 60 percent of weekly disposable earnings when the employee is not supporting a spouse or dependent child other than the spouse or child who is the subject of the withholding order.

These limits are increased by five percent if the garnishment applies to a period that is more than 12 weeks before thc workweek for which wages are subject to garnishment. Local child support agencies, as well as courts, may issue wage garnishments for child or spousal support. If the garnishment order is issued by a local child support agency, the employer must provide a copy to the employee within 10 days of receipt. If the employee is no longer employed, the employer must so notify the local child support agency. Orders for child or spousal support have precedence over other garnishments. If an employer fails to withhold wages pursuant to a valid withholding order for child or spousal support, the employer is liable to the children, spouse, or both for whose benefit the order was issued for all amounts of support that were not withheld.

7.26 Wage Statements

With every payment of wages an employer must provide to each employee a statement setting forth the following information:

- Gross wages earned;
- Total hours worked by the employee, unless the employee is paid solely based on salary and is exempt from overtime;
- The number of piece-rate units earned and any applicable piece rate if the employee is paid on a piece-rate basis;
- All deductions;
- Net wages earned;
- Inclusive dates for which the employee is paid;
- The name of the employee and the last four digits of the employee's Social Security number or an ID number other than the Social Security number;
- The name and address of the legal entity that is the employer, and if the employer is a farm labor contractor, the name and address of the legal entity that secured the services of the employer;
- All applicable hourly rates in effect during the pay period and the number of hours the employee worked at each hourly rate, and if the employer is a temporary services employer, the rate of pay and total hours worked for each temporary services assignment; and
- The amount of the employee's paid sick leave accrual (see Section 15.5).

These records must be maintained for at least three years at the place of employment or at a central location within California, but employers should keep them for at least four years, as the statute of limitations for some wage claims is four years.

Electronic Wage Statements

The required wage statement may be provided to employees electronically where:

- The employee may elect to receive paper wage statements at any time;
- The electronic statement contains all of the above information and is available on a secure website no later than payday;
- Access to the website is controlled by use of a unique employee identification number or user name and a confidential personal identification number (PIN) or password. The website must be protected by a firewall and must be accessible at all times except when offline for maintenance;
- Employees are able to access their records through their own personal computers or via company-provided computers. If employees do not use computers in their work, computer terminals must be made available for accessing payroll information;
- Employees are able to print their wage statement at work on printers in close proximity to the computer used to access the statement;
- Employees are not charged any fee for accessing or printing their wage statements;
- Wage statements must be maintained electronically for three years and be available to employees during that time; or
- Former employees are provided paper copies of their wage statements upon request (see Section 10.3).

7.27 Final Paycheck

You must provide an employee whose employment is terminated a final paycheck on the last day of work that includes compensation for all hours worked through the termination date plus the cash value of all accrued but unused vacation or PTO. It is not lawful in California to require a terminated employee to wait until the next regular payday to be paid unless the employee continues to be paid through that payday.

An employee who resigns without advance notice must be provided a final paycheck within 72 hours of the time of resignation. An employee who provides at least 72 hours' notice of resignation must be provided a final paycheck on the last day of work. An employee who quits without notice should be notified by phone, letter, or email that the final paycheck is ready to be picked up at the employer's place of business. A final paycheck should *not* be mailed to an employee who quits without notice unless the employee requests in writing that the paycheck be mailed and provides a mailing address.

The deadline for providing a final paycheck to a quitting employee also applies to an employee who retires. Such an employee must be given their final paycheck on the last day of work if 72 or more hours' notice of retirement was provided.

You need not include bonuses or commissions in a terminating employee's final paycheck if they are not capable of being calculated until sometime later. Such bonuses or commissions must be paid at the usual time, or as soon as reasonably calculable, whichever is sooner. For example, if an employee who is paid an hourly wage plus a commission based on their own sales is terminated, and the amount of their sales is known and calculable on their termination date, they must be paid for their hours worked and their commissions earned through their termination date. If instead they are paid a bonus calculated monthly based on the performance of their department, they must be paid for their hours worked upon termination and for their bonus when it is calculated following the end of the month.

Expense reimbursements are not required to be paid in the final paycheck but may be processed as usual.

The employee's final wage statement (see Section 7.26) may be provided with the final paycheck, or it may be provided no later than the employer's next regular payday.

If a final paycheck containing all amounts due is not provided on a timely basis, the employer may be assessed a "waiting time penalty" amounting to a day's pay for every day of delay up to a maximum of 30 working days. Note that this is a daily rate running for up to 30 days, which generally exceeds a calendar month of pay. Therefore, 30 working days means 6 weeks of pay for an employee who works 5 days per week. A former employee may recover costs and attorneys' fees for the successful pursuit of waiting time penalties in court. Therefore, if a final paycheck is provided a day or two late because it was not possible to calculate the amount due less deductions in time for the employee's termination, the employee should be paid through the date on which the final check is provided, thus negating any claim for waiting time penalties.

Waiting time penalties will not be imposed when there is a good faith dispute regarding whether wages are owed, pending resolution of such dispute. An employer must pay all nondisputed wages on a timely basis, however. You are prohibited from requiring an employee to sign a release of wages that are concededly due, and such a release will not be enforceable. Following a resolution of a dispute over wages, the employee should be asked to sign an acknowledgment that all wages due have been paid. If the amount of wages actually owed is reasonably disputed or unknown, you may require a release of claims for the wages paid in the settlement. By contrast, if you discover a clear error in computing an employee's wages, and the amount of the underpayment resulting from the error is known, upon repayment of such wages (which are concededly due), you may require an acknowledgment that such wages have been paid, but not a release of claims.

Do not send a final paycheck via certified mail to an employee who quits without notice unless the employee requests in writing that you do so. Otherwise, the final check is likely to remain at the post office unclaimed for several weeks until it is returned to the employer, raising the possibility of exposure to waiting time penalties for failure to timely provide the final paycheck.

7.28 Final Pay for a Deceased Employee

In the event of the death of an employee, the question arises of how to pay the final wages due the employee. If the employee has a surviving spouse or registered domestic partner, that person or the guardian or conservator of that person may present the employer with an affidavit or declaration under penalty of perjury as described in California Probate Code Section 13601.

Upon receipt of such an affidavit or declaration, and confirmation of the identity of the declarant, the employer must pay that person final wages due the deceased employee (including accrued vacation) up to a maximum of $20,875.00 net. On April 1, 2028, and at each three-year interval ending on April 1 thereafter, this dollar amount will be adjusted by the Judicial Council of California based on the change in the United States city average of the Consumer Price Index for All Urban Consumers, as published by the Bureau of Labor Statistics, from the December that is 40 months before the adjustment to the December immediately preceding the adjustment, with each adjusted amount rounded to the nearest $25.00. If more than $20,875.00 net (or the then-applicable amount) in wages is owed the deceased employee, the excess should be paid upon demand by the executor of the estate upon presentation of proof of appointment.

Payment of final wages in this matter will protect the employer against claims by other beneficiaries of the estate. Payment of final wages due a deceased employee should not be paid to others, such as parents, children, siblings, or significant others of the deceased employee, as other beneficiaries of the estate may have superior claims.

Wages due a deceased employee that are not claimed within three years must be paid to the state controller.

CHAPTER 8

Overtime

California has unique overtime rules, and there are numerous differences between California and federal law regarding overtime. One principal difference is that, in California, overtime must be calculated on a daily as well as a weekly basis. The basic overtime requirements are as follows:

One and one-half times the regular rate for:

- More than 40 hours per workweek.
- More than 8 hours per workday.
- The first 8 hours on the seventh consecutive workday in a single workweek.

Two times the regular rate for:

- More than 12 hours per workday.
- More than 8 hours on the seventh consecutive workday in a single workweek.

Daily overtime must be paid when an employee works more than 8 hours in a day. Weekly overtime is not due until employees have worked more than 40 straight-time hours in a week. Overtime does not "pyramid" in California such that daily *and* weekly overtime must be paid for the same hours, however. This is avoided by designating as *straight time* all nonovertime hours worked in a workweek up to a maximum of 40. Alternatively, you may pay the greater of the daily or weekly overtime due. For example:

- An employee works 10 hours on Monday, Tuesday, and Wednesday; 6 hours on Thursday; and 8 hours on Friday (44 hours total). There will be 2 hours of overtime due for Monday, Tuesday, and Wednesday, respectively (because the employee worked more than 8 hours per day), but no additional overtime is due because the employee did not work more than 40 hours of straight-time during the workweek. Alternatively, because daily overtime ($2 \times 3 = 6$ hours) exceeds weekly overtime (4 hours), you pay only the greater of the two, which is daily overtime (6 hours).

- An employee works 8 hours on Monday, Tuesday, and Wednesday; 10 hours on Thursday and Friday; and 8 hours on Saturday (52 hours total). There will be 2 hours of overtime due for Thursday and Friday, respectively, plus 8 hours of overtime due for Saturday (because the employee worked more than 40 straight-time hours during the week). Alternatively, because the total weekly overtime (12 hours) exceeds daily overtime (4 hours), you need pay only the greater of the two, which is weekly overtime (12 hours).

In determining whether weekly overtime is due, hours paid but not worked (such as vacation, sick days, or holidays) are not counted.

8.1 Workday

The concept of the workday is important because daily overtime need be paid only for more than 8 hours in a single workday. A workday is any period of 24 consecutive hours starting at the same time every day. The most common workday begins and ends at midnight each day, but other workdays are also permissible as long as all employees in a single group or classification of employees have the same workday. A different workday would be desirable for employees who work an overnight shift, for example. Otherwise, these employees would start and end work on different workdays, potentially creating liability for a split-shift premium. This may be avoided by designating a different workday for night-shift employees that starts at 2:00 p.m., for example, and ends at 1:59 p.m. the following calendar day.

8.2 Workweek

A workweek is any seven consecutive 24-hour periods that start on the same day. Different groups or classifications of employees may have different workweeks. The default workweek runs from midnight Sunday to 11:59 p.m. on Saturday. The workweek is important in determining whether more than 40 hours have been worked in a given workweek. It is also key in determining whether overtime is due on the seventh consecutive day of work. If an employee works seven consecutive days in a single workweek, overtime at 1½ times the regular rate must be paid for the first 8 hours on the seventh day, and twice the regular rate must be paid for more than 8 hours on the seventh day. If the seventh consecutive day falls in a different workweek, however, the seventh-day overtime premium will not be due. This overtime rule applies regardless of how many hours the employee has worked during the prior six days. For example:

- The workweek runs from midnight Monday to 11:59 p.m. Sunday. An employee works 6 hours each day Monday through Sunday. Therefore, six hours of overtime will be due for work on the seventh consecutive workday in the workweek.

- The workweek runs from midnight Sunday to 11:59 p.m. Saturday. An employee works 6 hours each day Monday through Sunday. No overtime will be due because the employee worked 36 hours in the first workweek and 6 hours in the second workweek.

8.3 Regular Rate

The "regular rate" is the rate used to determine the amount of overtime due. The regular rate includes hourly pay, bonuses, commissions, piece rates, shift differentials, and meal and lodging allowances. The following items are not included in calculating the regular rate:

- Gifts;
- Purely discretionary bonuses (e.g., holiday bonus);
- Tips;
- Hours paid but not worked;
- Expense reimbursements;
- Contributions to 401(k) or profit-sharing plans;
- Overtime premiums; and
- Premiums for split shifts or missed meal or rest breaks.

The regular rate is calculated differently based upon whether the employee's compensation includes (1) productivity bonuses, piece rates, or commissions; (2) flat sum bonuses; or (3) salary.

Productivity Bonuses, Commissions, or Piece Rates

A productivity bonus (also known as an incentive bonus) is one that may vary based on the performance of the employee or the employee's team, department, or location. Where an employee is paid productivity bonuses, commissions, or piece rates in addition to hourly pay, the overtime premium amounts to one-half of the regular rate for regular overtime and the full regular rate for all double time. For example:

Total Hours Worked:	45
Hourly Rate:	$18.00
Productivity Bonus, Piece-Rate Pay or Commission:	$425.00
Regular Rate:	$25.44 ($18.00/hour × 45 hours = $810.00) + commissions ($425.00) = $1,235/45 = $27.44

Overtime Due:	\$27.44 × 0.5 × 5 hours OT = \$68.60
Total Compensation Due:	\$810.00 + \$425.00 + \$68.60 = \$1,303.60

In the alternative, the overtime due for hourly pay and commissions may be calculated separately, as follows:

Hourly Overtime:	\$135.00 (\$18.00 × 1.5 = \$27.00 × 5)
Commission Overtime:	\$23.60 (\$425/45 = \$9.44 × 0.5 × 5)
Total Compensation Due:	\$720.00 straight time wages
	+ \$425.00 commissions
	+ \$135.00 hourly overtime
	+ \$23.60 commission overtime
	= \$1,303.60

Flat Sum Bonuses

In contrast to a productivity bonus, which is designed to be an incentive to increase productivity during all hours of work, a flat sum bonus is designed to incentivize the employee to remain in the employ of the employer or to work on a particular day, and it does not vary according to the productivity of the employee or their work unit. Examples of such bonuses include a fixed-amount "stay-on" bonus if the employee remains employed until the end of the season or a flat sum bonus (such as \$50.00) for working on a weekend day.

The regular rate where a flat sum bonus is paid is calculated by dividing the bonus by the number of non-overtime hours worked during the period covered by the bonus. This amount is multiplied by 1.5 and then multiplied again by the number of overtime hours worked during the period covered by the bonus (the amount is multiplied by 2 if double-time pay is due). For example:

Total Hours Worked:	45
Hourly Rate:	\$18.00
Flat Sum Bonus for Weekend Work:	\$50.00
Hourly Overtime:	\$135.00 (\$18.00 × 1.5 = \$27.00 × 5)
Flat Sum Bonus Overtime:	\$9.38 (\$50.00/40 = \$1.25 × 1.5 × 5)
Total Compensation Due:	\$720.00 straight time wages
	+ \$50.00 flat sum bonus
	+ \$135.00 hourly overtime
	+ \$9.38 flat sum bonus overtime
	= \$914.38

Salaried Employees

For salaried employees, California law requires that the regular rate be determined by dividing the salary by 40 hours. The regular rate is then multiplied by 1.5 times or 2 times, as appropriate, and then multiplied by the number of hours of overtime worked at the applicable overtime premium during the workweek to determine the amount of overtime due. For example:

Total Hours Worked:	45
Salary:	$1,400.00
Salary Overtime:	$262.50 ($1,400/40 = $35.00 × 1.5 × 5)
Total Compensation Due:	$1,400.00 salary
	+ $262.50 salary overtime
	= $1,662.50

The "fluctuating workweek pay plan" is not permitted under California law. Under that payment method, nonexempt employees are paid a salary to cover all hours worked and then are paid an additional 0.5 of the regular rate (determined by dividing the salary by total hours worked) for overtime hours worked. Instead, as shown in the above example, in California if a nonexempt employee is paid a salary, the salary must be divided by 40 to determine the regular rate.

Moreover, "Belo contracts," written contracts under which a pre-arranged amount of overtime is paid on a daily or weekly basis to a nonexempt employee, are not valid in California. This is because premium pay for overtime is intended to be a sort of penalty against the employer for requiring employees to work overtime and a "Belo contract" actually encourages the working of overtime because a certain amount of overtime per week is already paid under the contract.

Multiple Pay Rates

Where an employee is paid at two or more rates during a workweek (for example, their usual hourly rate plus a lesser rate for travel time outside the usual workday), the regular rate is determined by use of a weighted average. Total earnings received under all rates during the workweek are divided by total hours worked under all rates to calculate the regular rate.

For example: If an employee works a total of 50 hours, consisting of 40 hours at the employee's ordinary rate of $25.00 per hour and 10 hours at the travel rate of $16.50, the blended regular rate and overtime would be calculated as follows:

$25.00 × 40 hours =	$1,000.00
$16.50 × 10 hours =	$165.00

Total Hourly Pay:	$1,165.00
Blended Regular Rate:	$1,165.00/50 = $23.30
Overtime Premium:	$116.50 ($23.30 × 0.5 × 10)
Total Compensation:	$1,165.00 hourly pay
	+ $116.50 overtime pay
	= $1,281.50

It is important to note that overtime is paid at one-half the regular rate because all hours worked are used in the fraction to calculate the regular rate. The base hourly portion of the compensation ($1,165.00) has already been paid, leaving only the premium due.

8.4 Payment of Overtime on Bonuses or Commissions

When incentive bonuses or commission are paid immediately following the pay period in which they were earned, overtime is computed as set forth in the preceding section. The bonus or commission is merely one of the forms of compensation used to calculate the regular rate for that pay period.

When an incentive bonus or commission paid to a nonexempt employee is not able to be computed and paid in the next pay period (such as is the case with monthly or quarterly bonuses), an overtime premium must be added to the commission or bonus when it is paid if the employee worked overtime during the period in which the commission or bonus was earned. To calculate this premium, first determine the regular rate on the commissions or bonus by dividing the amount of commissions or bonus earned during the commission or bonus period by the total number of hours worked during the bonus period. That regular rate on the bonus or commissions is then multiplied by ½, and then multiplied by the number of overtime hours worked during the period. For example:

> An employee is paid an incentive bonus of $2,000.00 covering two two-week pay periods in which they worked 45 hours per week. Divide $2,000.00 by total hours worked (180) to determine the regular rate on the bonus which is $11.11. Multiply $11.11 by 0.5 to arrive at $5.56. Multiply that number by total overtime hours worked (20) to equal $111.20, which is the overtime premium applicable to the bonus. The total bonus including the overtime premium is $2,111.20.

The regular rate on the bonus is multiplied by 0.5 rather than by 1.5 because the bonus was earned during ***all*** hours worked, straight time and overtime. The employee has already been compensated at the regular rate on the bonus for overtime hours worked. What is left to be paid is the overtime premium (that is, the additional 0.5) for the overtime hours worked during the bonus period.

8.5 Overtime May Be Mandatory

Employees may be required to work overtime. Absent any restrictions on hours worked, California law does not regulate the number of overtime hours an adult employee may be assigned. An employer may require all production employees to work on Saturdays during the busy season, for example, so long as the applicable overtime premium is paid. Some restrictions do exist, however. For example, under several wage orders, nonexempt employees may not be required to work more than 72 hours in a workweek, but they may do so voluntarily. Some wage orders impose other restrictions on working hours, such as requiring a certain amount of time off in specified situations. Additionally, the Labor Code imposes restrictions on hours worked by registered pharmacists. The Labor Code also imposes general restrictions on working time as to days (not hours) worked, such as requiring one day's rest in seven days of work (see Section 9.7).

8.6 Unauthorized Overtime

Employees must be paid for overtime hours worked as long as the employer has "constructive notice" of the hours worked, even if the employees were not authorized to do so, and even if they worked overtime against their employer's direction. Employees may be disciplined or terminated for working unauthorized overtime, but they must be paid for the hours they worked.

8.7 Makeup Time

A nonexempt employee may request in writing to make up hours missed due to a personal obligation (such as a doctor's appointment or a meeting at a child's school) by working more than 8 hours (but no more than 11) on another day or on other days during the same workweek in which the time was lost without the need to be paid overtime. The employer may not solicit or encourage employees to use makeup time but may inform employees of their right to do so. For example:

- An employee asks to leave 3 hours early on Tuesday for a doctor's appointment and to make up the time by starting work 1 hour early on Wednesday, Thursday, and Friday. This is permissible, and the employee does not need to be paid overtime for working more than 8 hours on Wednesday, Thursday, and Friday.
- The employer requires an employee to work 9 hours per day on Monday, Tuesday, and Wednesday and tells the employee to take off work 3 hours early on Friday. This is not makeup time. Overtime would be due for the extra

hour worked on Monday, Tuesday, and Wednesday because the extra time was required by the employer, not requested by the employee.

If an employee needs to use makeup time each week over a series of consecutive weeks, a new written request must be submitted every four weeks.

8.8 Overtime for Domestic Workers

Special overtime rules apply to domestic workers. "Personal attendants" are persons employed to work in private households to supervise, feed, or dress a child or to care for a person who on account of advanced age or a physical or mental disability requires supervision. A personal attendant may not spend more than 20 percent of their total weekly hours worked on other household duties such as preparing meals or housecleaning. A personal attendant employed by a private household must be paid overtime at the rate of time-and-a-half for more than 45 hours worked in a week or more than 9 hours worked in a day. A personal attendant employed by a third-party employer must be paid overtime under federal law for all hours worked over 40 in a workweek.

Wage Order 15 governs other household occupations such as butlers, chauffeurs, cooks, gardeners, and housekeepers who are employed in private households. It imposes different overtime requirements for live-in employees and non-live-in employees.

Live-in domestic workers who are not personal attendants must be paid overtime at time-and-a-half for time worked in excess of 9 hours per day for the first five days in a workweek, and for the first 9 hours on the sixth and seventh days in a workweek. Time worked in excess of 9 hours on the sixth and seventh days in a workweek must be paid at double time. Live-in domestic workers also must have at least 12 consecutive hours free of duty during each workday of 24 hours, plus 3 hours (which need not be consecutive) free of duty during the 12-hour span of work. They must be paid overtime at time-and-a-half if required or permitted to work during any of their off-duty periods. Live-in employees also must not be required to work more than five days in a workweek without 24 hours off unless an emergency occurs.

Non-live-in employees are subject to California's normal overtime rules, that is, time-and-a-half for more than 8 hours per workday or 40 hours per workweek and for up to 8 hours on the seventh consecutive day in a workweek, and double time for more than 12 hours in a day or more than 8 hours on the seventh consecutive day in a workweek.

8.9 Alternative Workweeks

Alternative workweeks are popular in California. One common version is the "4/10" in which employees work four 10-hour days and receive an extra day off each week.

Another version is the "9/80" in which employees work four 9-hour days and one 8-hour day (typically Friday) and have every other Friday off. In the health care industry, employees may work a "3/12" schedule consisting of three 12-hour days. The benefit to the employer is that overtime need not be paid for hours worked up to ten in one workday in an alternative workweek (up to 12 hours in the health care industry).

An employer may implement an alternative workweek by completing a series of steps required under California law. You should review the alternative workweek provisions of the applicable IWC wage order because the requirements for an employer to adopt an alternative workweek differ slightly among wage orders. The alternative workweek is not available under Wage Orders 14 and 15.

Generally, the first step is to determine the work unit where the alternative workweek will apply. This can be an entire facility or a department, shift, or job classification. It may involve just one employee if there is only one employee in a particular job classification. Exempt employees are not included in the election process, although they may also work an alternative workweek if the nonexempt employees in their facility, department, or office select one.

Next, you must present a written proposal or agreement to the affected employees that describes a regularly scheduled alternative workweek. The proposal must specify the number of days and hours that will be worked under the proposed alternative workweek. An employer may also propose a menu of schedule options from which employees can choose. Wage Orders 1, 2, 3, 6, 7, 8, 11, 12, and 13 require that employees be provided two consecutive days off in an alternative workweek.

You must make a written disclosure to all affected employees that includes a description of the effect, if any, of the proposed alternative workweek on employees' wages, hours, and benefits (note that you may not reduce the hourly rate of pay of any employee as the result of the adoption or repeal of an alternative workweek). The disclosure must also provide notice of the time and place of meetings to be held with employees to discuss the effects of the alternative workweek. If at least five percent of the affected employees primarily speak a language other than English, this disclosure must be provided in such language(s) in addition to in English. Meetings of employees must be held at least 14 days before the secret ballot voting. The written disclosure must be mailed to employees who do not attend the meetings.

The secret ballot election must be conducted at the worksite during regular working hours, and the employer must bear the costs of holding the election. An employer may not intimidate or coerce employees to vote either in favor of or against the proposed alternative workweek. Should any affected employee complain about the manner in which the investigation was conducted, the Labor Commissioner, after an investigation, may order the employer to select a neutral third party to conduct the election.

The alternative workweek must be adopted by a vote of at least two-thirds of the affected nonexempt employees in the work unit. If a sufficient number of employees vote in favor of the alternative workweek, the new workweek schedule may be implemented after a waiting period of 30 days. You must report the results of the election within 30 days to the Office of Policy, Research, and Legislation of the California Department of Industrial Relations. That agency lists all employers having properly adopted alternative workweeks on its website.

If you require an employee to work fewer hours than would normally be scheduled under an alternative workweek, you must pay overtime after eight hours in a workday under the normal rules. You must attempt to reasonably accommodate an employee whose religious belief or observance conflicts with an alternative workweek schedule. You must also attempt to find a work schedule of up to eight hours per workday to accommodate an employee who is unable to work the schedule adopted under the alternative workweek. You are permitted, but not required, to provide a work schedule of up to eight hours per workday to accommodate an employee hired after the election who is unable to work the alternative workweek schedule.

An alternative workweek adopted by a secret ballot election may be repealed by the affected employees in a similar manner. Upon a petition signed by at least one-third of the affected employees, a new secret ballot election must be held, and a two-thirds vote of affected employees is required to repeal the alternative workweek schedule. Such an election may not be held sooner than 12 months after the same group of employees voted in an election to adopt or repeal an alternative workweek. If the alternative workweek is repealed, the employer must comply within 60 days. An employer may also eliminate an alternative workweek arrangement on its own initiative simply by providing reasonable prior notice to employees.

Overtime Under Alternative Workweek Schedules

Overtime at 1½ times the employee's regular rate must be paid for work in excess of the alternative workweek schedule, up to 12 hours per day. Double time must be paid for hours worked beyond 12 in one day. An employee working a 4/10 schedule, for example, would have to be paid overtime at time-and-a-half for hours worked beyond 10 and at double time for hours worked past 12. Employees may work a 12-hour schedule but they must be paid overtime at time-and-a-half for more than 10 hours except in the health care industry. Health care employees may be scheduled for 12 hours before overtime must be paid.

Employees who are required to work on scheduled days off must be paid at time-and-a-half for all hours worked up to 8 hours and double time thereafter.

If an employer, whose employees have adopted an alternative workweek, requires an employee to work fewer hours than those that are regularly scheduled under the alternative workweek schedule, overtime at the rate of 1½ the employee's regular rate must be paid for all hours worked more than 8 hours in a day.

8.10 White-Collar Overtime Exemptions Generally

California's "white-collar" exemptions for executive, administrative, and professional employees differ from the federal law exemptions in some notable ways. In most respects, California's exemptions are generally more favorable to employees so they are more important where California employees are concerned.

In determining whether an employee is exempt, you should focus on the employee's actual job duties, not merely on the job title. The terms "executive," "administrator," and "professional" are used widely, yet the holders of such titles do not necessarily meet the requirements for the white-collar exemptions. It is the employer's burden to show that an overtime exemption applies, so if the case for treating an employee as exempt is not compelling, it may be safer to treat the employee as nonexempt.

The Salary Requirement

For any of the white-collar exemptions to apply, the employee must be paid on a salary basis. Under California law the salary must be at least twice the state minimum wage for a 40-hour week. Beginning January 1, 2026 the minimum salary is $70,304.00 annually, $5,858.67 per month, or $1,352.00 per week.

In order to qualify for the white-collar exemption in the health care industry in California, employees must be paid a monthly salary equivalent to at least 200 percent of the applicable minimum wage or 150 percent of the health care worker minimum wage, whichever is greater.

Note that the "highly compensated employee" exemption from overtime under federal law (which potentially applies where an employee is paid at least $107,432.00 annually) does not apply in California, and there is no counterpart under California law.

A commission-only pay arrangement will not qualify as a salary, as the employee will likely earn a different amount in each workweek. This problem cannot be solved by paying a recoverable draw to ensure that commission-paid employees earn at least the minimum salary threshold because draws are not considered wages. The only way that commissioned employees will satisfy the salary test for the white-collar overtime exemptions is if they are paid a guaranteed salary that is at least the applicable minimum salary plus a commission over and above their salary.

> As the minimum wage continues to rise, be sure that all salaried exempt employees are being paid a salary that is equivalent to at least twice the current state minimum wage for a 40-hour week.

To be exempt, an employee must be paid a regular salary for every week in which work is performed. The salary must not be reduced on account of the quality or quantity of work performed. It must not be prorated for part-time work, nor may the salary be reduced if the employer fails to provide a full week of work. Just as an exempt employee does not have to be paid overtime for working more than 8 hours in a day or 40 hours in a week, likewise such an employee may not be docked for working fewer than 8 hours in a day or 40 in a week. There are three exceptions to this basic rule:

- A new or terminating exempt employee need be paid only for days of the workweek actually worked.
- Whole days may be unpaid (deducted from the weekly salary in daily increments) if they are taken for vacation, approved leave, religious holidays, or personal reasons other than sickness or accident. If the employee performs any work in a day, even if at home, the day must be paid, however.
- Whole days taken off due to sickness or accident may be unpaid (deducted from the weekly salary in daily increments) if the employer has a bona fide sick pay policy and there are no accrued but unused sick days remaining.

Different rules apply to an employer's right to deduct an employee's paid leave balances, which can be done in partial-day increments. Partial-day absences due to sickness or accident may be charged to sick leave or paid-time-off (PTO) balances. Partial-day absences from the regular schedule due to personal reasons other than sickness or accident may be charged to vacation or PTO balances. By contrast, an employee's salary may never be docked in less than full-day increments. Therefore, once these paid-leave balances are exhausted, you are prohibited from deducting the employee's salary for partial-day absences due to personal reasons or illness.

Under the salary-basis rules, a salaried exempt employee's pay may not be deducted for time spent on jury duty, providing testimony as a witness in court, or temporary military leave for periods less than one week. A salaried exempt employee's pay may not be deducted for penalties assessed against the employee for misconduct or rule violations. The federal law provision allowing deductions from salary for safety violations does not apply in California.

Finally, a salaried employee's hours and pay may be reduced in a furlough situation without losing the exemption. For example, an employer could reduce its salaried employees' work schedules to four days per week and cut their salaries by 20 percent, so long as the reduced work schedules are maintained on an ongoing basis. Note that reduced salaries must still exceed the minimum salary threshold for the overtime exemption to apply. An employer may not, moreover, declare work schedule reductions on an ad hoc or intermittent basis:

- The employer, facing a diminished demand for its products, places all salaried employees on a reduced four-day workweek and reduces their salaries by 20 percent until demand for its products improves again. This type of furlough will not disturb the salary basis of payment as long as the circumstances fairly suggest that the reduction was the result of significant economic difficulties.
- The employer, facing only a fluctuating demand for its products, declares on Friday that all salaried employees will work only four days in the following week and be paid 80 percent of their usual salaries, and that it anticipates that a full workweek will be restored in the next succeeding week but will not know for certain until the next Friday. This is not a permissible type of furlough, and salaried employees will lose the exemption for all weeks in which they are not paid their full salaries.

The "Primarily Engaged in" Requirement

Each of the white-collar exemptions requires that the employee be *primarily engaged in* performing the duties that meet the test for the exemption. This means that more than one-half of the employee's working time must be spent performing exempt work. This test differs from the federal test, which requires only that the "primary duty" of the employee falls within the exempt duties. Thus, a manager of a restaurant or retail store who spends most of their time serving customers but who also provides supervision to hourly employees while working alongside them might qualify as exempt under federal law but likely would not qualify under California law.

Requirement of Exercising Discretion and Independent Judgment

To qualify for one of the white-collar exemptions, an employee must customarily and regularly exercise discretion and independent judgment in performing their work duties. This means that the employee compares and evaluates possible courses of action and makes a decision after the various possibilities have been considered. The employee must have the authority to make an independent choice, free from immediate direction or supervision, and with respect to matters of significance. This is distinguished from simply using skill in applying techniques, procedures, or specific standards. The test is not satisfied by the kinds of decisions made normally by clerical employees or employees who repair malfunctioning equipment. Rather, it is satisfied when the decisions are made by persons who formulate or participate in the formulation of important employer policies within their area of responsibility or who exercise authority within a wide range to commit their employer in substantial respects financially or otherwise. The test does not require, however, that an employee make final decisions with unlimited authority and with a complete absence of review. Under this test, the fact that higher company officials may review and occasionally modify or reverse a decision or recommendation does not mean that the employee who made the decision lacked discretion and independent judgment to make the decision or recommendation.

8.11 The Executive Exemption

To fall under the executive exemption, assuming the minimum salary requirement is met, an employee's duties must involve all of the following:

- Managing the enterprise or one of its departments or operating units;
- Customarily and regularly directing the work of two or more employees;
- Having the authority to hire and fire employees or to make recommendations as to hiring, firing, or promotion of employees that will be given particular weight;
- Customarily and regularly exercising discretion and independent judgment; and
- Primarily engaging in the duties that meet the test of the exemption.

Examples of management work include interviewing and hiring employees, setting and adjusting their rates of pay and hours of work, directing the work of employees, evaluating and disciplining employees, handling their complaints and grievances, planning work, and scheduling and assigning work to employees. Management work also includes:

- Determining the type of materials, supplies, machinery, equipment, or tools to be used;
- Determining which merchandise will be bought, stocked, and sold;
- Providing for the safety of employees and security of property;
- Planning and administering budgets; and
- Handling legal and compliance issues.

The requirement that two or more employees be managed may be met by two or more full-time equivalents; management of four part-time employees who together work at least 80 hours per week would qualify, for example. A manager who directs only two full-time employees, though, may not spend enough time on management duties to qualify for the exemption given the requirement that more than half of an exempt employee's working time be spent performing exempt duties. A supervisor who spends most of their time performing production work, such as a lead or a foreman, would not qualify for the exemption. Also, an assistant manager who supervises two or more employees only in the manager's absence would not qualify for the exemption.

The authority to hire and fire employees need not be final. That a manager must obtain approval for hiring or termination decisions from a higher manager or HR is permissible so long as the employee's recommendations are taken seriously. A manager must use discretion and independent judgment in performing management duties to qualify for the exemption.

A manager who is required to follow rigid and detailed procedures in an operations or procedures manual, for example, may not exercise sufficient discretion and independent judgment to qualify for the exemption.

8.12 The Administrative Exemption

To qualify for the administrative exemption, assuming the minimum salary requirement is met, an employee's duties must involve each of the following:

- Performing office or nonmanual work directly related to management policies or general business operations of the employer or the employer's customers (or performing administrative functions in an educational institution or school system);
- Customarily and regularly exercising discretion and independent judgment;
- Regularly and directly assisting a proprietor or another executive or administrative exempt employee; performing, under only general supervision, work along specialized or technical lines requiring special training, experience, or knowledge; or executing, under general supervision, special assignments and tasks; and
- Primarily engaging in duties that meet the test for the exemption.

To qualify for this exemption, an employee must perform work directly related to the running or servicing of a business, versus performing production work, or routine sales work in a retail or service establishment. One way to characterize the administrative exemption is to say that it covers employees who manage aspects of the business but whose duties do not primarily involve supervision of other employees. Administrative exempt employees might include controllers, HR managers, purchasing managers, marketing directors, safety managers, credit managers, tax managers, benefits administrators, and IT administrators. Employees who advise their employer's clients, such as financial consultants or HR consultants, may also qualify for the exemption.

An employee must also exercise discretion and independent judgment about matters of significance to qualify for this exemption. Factors to consider in determining whether this test is met include:

- Whether the employee has authority to formulate, affect, interpret, or implement management policies or operating practices;
- Whether the employee has authority to commit the employer in matters that have significant financial impact;
- Whether the employee has authority to negotiate and bind the company in significant matters;
- Whether the employee provides consultation or expert advice to management; and
- Whether the employee represents the company in handling complaints, arbitrating disputes, or resolving grievances.

Mere use of skill or knowledge alone will not be sufficient to meet the test for this exemption. An accounting employee may have substantial skill and experience in accounting, but unless they have authority to make or change policy or commit their employer in significant financial matters, as would a controller in most companies, they would not qualify for the exemption. Also, an employee will not be found to exercise discretion and independent judgment in matters of significance merely because the employer may experience a financial loss if the employee fails to perform the job properly (for example, a bank teller).

Clerical employees who perform administrative functions will not qualify for the exemption. This includes most secretaries, clerks, and administrative assistants. Executive assistants who assist a business owner or a senior executive of a large business may qualify for the exemption if they have been delegated authority regarding matters of significance.

The administrative exemption is often the most difficult exemption to apply accurately because its criteria are somewhat less tangible than those for the other exemptions. For many employees who may be covered by the administrative exemption, a fact-specific inquiry regarding their actual job duties is essential. An employee with the title of "manager" may not, in fact, perform enough management work and may not exercise enough discretion to qualify for the exemption at one company, whereas at another company the same person may have the same title yet qualify for the exemption because they are more involved in management of the business and exercise more discretion than at their former company. Moreover, job descriptions must be kept current and must accurately reflect the nature of the employee's work if the exemption is applied. The exemption may be difficult to defend if the job description does not reflect enough exempt duties even though the employee may in fact perform a sufficient amount of exempt work to qualify for the exemption.

8.13 The Professional Exemption

Three types of professional exemptions are recognized in California: *licensed* professionals, *learned* professionals, and *artistic* professionals.

Licensed Professionals

The wage orders recognize certain licensed professionals as exempt:

- Lawyers;
- Physicians;
- Dentists;
- Optometrists;
- Architects;
- Engineers;
- Teachers; and
- Accountants.

Note that an employee must actually be licensed in one of these professions to qualify. A law clerk who has graduated from law school but has not yet passed the bar exam or an accountant who has a degree in accounting but has not yet been licensed as a Certified Public Accountant (CPA) would not qualify as a "licensed professional." Only licensed engineers qualify. Electrical engineers, for example, who do not hold a license, would not qualify under this exemption (but they might qualify under the learned professional exemption).

In addition, to be exempt, a licensed professional must customarily and regularly exercise discretion and independent judgment and, with the exception of physicians, they must be paid a salary that meets the applicable minimum salary standard. The latter requirement precludes paying lawyers or accountants by the hour if they are to be exempt from overtime. Licensed physicians or surgeons may be paid hourly without losing the exemption provided they are paid at least $107.17 per hour in 2026. The Department of Industrial Relations (DIR) Labor Research and Statistics Office adjusts this amount in October of every year to become effective on January 1 of the next year (the update can be found at https://www.dir.ca.gov/OPRL/Physicians.htm).

Registered pharmacists and most registered nurses are not eligible for this exemption, although they might qualify for the administrative or executive exemption if their job duties meet the test for one of those exemptions. Certified nurse practitioners, certified nurse anesthetists, and certified nurse midwives qualify for the exemption if they spend more than half their working time performing duties for which their advanced certification is required.

To be exempt, a teacher must be state-certified or must teach at an accredited college or university. Teachers in trade or technical schools, or uncertified teachers in private schools, do not fall within this exemption.

Learned Professionals

The learned professional exemption covers employees who meet the following criteria:

- Earn the applicable minimum required salary;
- Customarily and regularly exercise discretion and independent judgment;
- Spend more than half their working time performing work requiring knowledge of an advanced type in a field of science or learning customarily acquired by a prolonged course of specialized intellectual instruction or study (including work that is an essential part of or necessarily incident to such work), as distinguished from a general academic education or an apprenticeship, or from training in the performance of routine mental, manual, or physical processes; and
- Are engaged in work that is predominantly intellectual and varied in character (as opposed to routine mental, manual, mechanical, or physical work) and that is of such character that the output produced or the result accomplished cannot be standardized in relation to a given period of time.

A "prolonged course of specialized intellectual instruction or study" has been interpreted to mean at least a bachelor's degree. This exemption is limited, moreover, to employees with degrees in science, engineering, or other advanced specialized fields. An employee with a bachelor's degree or higher in a field such as engineering or chemistry and who works in that respective field will qualify. An employee with a degree in English or business will not qualify.

Paralegals generally do not qualify for the learned professional exemption because there is no advanced course of study of law required to be a paralegal in California (though possession of a bachelor's degree, plus on-the-job experience, is one means of qualifying as a paralegal, the degree need not be in legal studies). A paralegal who has also completed an advanced course of study in another field that is the focus of the paralegal's work, however, such as a paralegal with an engineering degree who works for a patent law firm, would typically qualify for the exemption.

Artistic Professionals

The artistic professional exemption covers employees who meet the following criteria:

- Earn the applicable minimum required salary;
- Customarily and regularly exercise discretion and independent judgment;
- Spend more than half their working time performing work that is original and creative in character in a recognized field of artistic endeavor (as opposed to work that can be produced by a person with general manual or intellectual ability and training), and the result of which depends primarily on the invention, imagination, or talent of the employee (including work that is an essential part of or necessarily incident to such work); and
- Are engaged in work that is predominantly intellectual and varied in character (as opposed to routine mental, manual, mechanical, or physical work) and that is of such character that the output produced or the result accomplished cannot be standardized in relation to a given period of time.

The requirement of "invention, imagination, or talent" distinguishes the creative professions from work that primarily depends on intelligence, diligence, and accuracy. This exemption applies to most actors, musicians, composers, conductors, and soloists. Most painters and visual artists would qualify, but animators and others who merely apply technology to the creative process versus produce creative content would not qualify. Newspaper reporters typically do not qualify for the exemption but on-air reporters and correspondents, who research and investigate the stories they report and who provide editorial commentary, would likely qualify.

8.14 Computer Professionals

The computer professionals exemption applies to highly skilled and highly paid computer software professionals, although there is no educational prerequisite for this exemption. To qualify for this exemption in 2026, an employee must be paid at least $58.85 per hour, or a minimum salary of $10,214.44 monthly or $122,573.13 annually. The DIR's Labor Research and Statistics Office adjusts these amounts in October of every year to become effective on January 1 of the next year (the update can be found at https://www.dir.ca.gov/oprl/ComputerSoftware.htm). Unlike under the white-collar exemptions, there is no salary requirement for an exempt computer professional. Such an employee may be paid hourly and may be (but is not required to be) paid overtime at their usual hourly rate or at a premium rate.

In addition, to qualify for this exemption, an employee must exercise discretion and independent judgment and must spend more than half their working time engaged in work that is intellectual or creative and that involves one or more of the following:

- The application of systems analysis techniques and procedures, including consulting with users, to determine hardware, software, or system functional specifications.
- The design, development, documentation, analysis, creation, testing, or modification of computer systems or programs, including prototypes, based on and related to user or system design specifications.
- The documentation, testing, creation, or modification of computer programs related to the design of computer software or hardware for computer operating systems.
- The theoretical and practical application of highly specialized information to computer systems analysis, programming, and software engineering.

A job title will not be enough to qualify an employee for this exemption; a careful examination of the employee's actual duties is required. Employees who install and troubleshoot computer equipment will not qualify for this exemption even though the equipment may be complex. Likewise, "help desk" workers and other employees who fix equipment or systems by applying their skill and knowledge will not qualify. Also, per the wage orders, the following employees will not qualify for the exemption:

- Trainees or employees in an entry-level position who are learning to become proficient in the theoretical and practical application of highly specialized information to computer systems analysis, programming, and software engineering.
- Employees in a computer-related occupation who have not attained the level of skill and expertise necessary to work independently and without close supervision.
- Employees engaged in the operation of computers or in the manufacture, repair, or maintenance of computer hardware and related equipment.
- Engineers, drafters, machinists, or other professionals whose work is highly dependent on or facilitated by the use of computers and computer software programs and who are skilled in computer-aided design software, including computer-aided design (CAD) and computer-aided manufacturing (CAM), but who are not in a computer systems analysis or programming occupation.
- Writers engaged in writing material, including box labels, product descriptions, documentation, promotional material, setup and installation instructions, and other similar written information, either for print or for on-screen media, or who write or provide content material intended to be read by customers, subscribers, or visitors to web-based media.

- Employees engaged in any activities otherwise falling within this exemption for the purpose of creating imagery for effects used in the motion picture, television, or theatrical industry.

8.15 Outside Salespersons

Outside salespersons are not covered by any of the provisions of the wage orders, including minimum wage and overtime. An outside salesperson is an employee who customarily and regularly works more than half of their working time away from the employer's place of business selling tangible or intangible items or obtaining orders or contracts for products, services, or use of facilities.

This exemption is available only for employees whose jobs involve selling. Activities related to sales such as prospecting for customers, cold-calling, networking in trade and industry organizations for the purposes of developing new customers, and entertaining customers qualify as exempt duties. Activities such as delivering products, stocking merchandise, or performing services do not qualify even if the products or services involved were sold by the same employee. If the employee sells products or services that are provided by others, they are more likely to qualify for this exemption. If the employee personally delivers the products or provides the services they sell, the employee is not likely to qualify for the exemption. In determining whether an employee's duties qualify for the exemption, courts may analyze the nature of an employee's overall job duties, and in determining whether more than half the employee's time is spent on sales, will apportion various tasks as "sales" and "nonsales."

8.16 Inside Salespersons

Wage Orders 4 and 7 (the latter of which covers the mercantile industry) provide an overtime exemption for inside salespersons whose earnings exceed 1½ times the minimum wage, and when more than half the employee's compensation is in the form of commissions. A two-step process determines this exemption.

The first part of this test requires that in each workweek the employee must earn more than 1½ times the minimum wage for all hours worked. In 2026, this will be a minimum of $25.36. These earnings may be in the form of wages, salary, commissions, or guaranteed draw. This test must be met in every workweek for the exemption to apply. Although bona fide draws against a commission in a defined reconciliation period may be counted as a "commission," earnings from another workweek may not otherwise be imputed to a workweek for purposes of this calculation. For example, even though an employee receives a large commission payment at the end of the month, such payment may not be allocated over the other workweeks in the month to satisfy this test. Rather, you must make sure that the employee is timely paid more than $25.36 per hour worked in each of the pay periods during the month.

The second part of the test requires that more than half the employee's compensation be in the form of commissions. Commissions in California are defined as "compensation paid to any person for services rendered in the sale of such employer's property or services and based proportionately upon the amount or value thereof." A percentage of the sale price or of the profit on an item sold would constitute a commission. A flat amount paid for each item sold would also qualify as a commission. The essence of commission is that it is a reward for selling. Payment for services performed, such as a defined amount for each piece of equipment installed, is a piece rate and not a commission. Likewise, an incentive bonus amounting to a percentage of the profit of a retail store or division of a company is not a commission. Only commissions will potentially qualify an employee for the inside sales exemption. The second part of the test must also be satisfied for each workweek, but the test for compliance (that is, whether more than half the employee's compensation is in the form of commissions) may be deferred until commissions are calculated following month-end if commissions are calculated once monthly (as in most automobile dealerships). Also, for the test to be satisfied, the compensation arrangement must be a bona fide commission plan, which the Labor Commissioner defines as one in which commissions consistently exceed draws paid over a representative period of at least a month. If draws consistently equal or exceed commissions during a representative period, the draws will be viewed as fixed, noncommission compensation. Accordingly, the plan will not be deemed bona fide, and overtime will be due.

Note that the inside salesperson exemption does not appear in wage orders other than Wage Orders 4 and 7. A commissioned salesperson employed in a manufacturing company (Wage Order 1) or a hotel (Wage Order 5), for example, would not be eligible for this exemption. Moreover, the corresponding federal exemption, found in Section 7(i) of the Fair Labor Standards Act (FLSA), only applies to commissioned salespersons employed by retail or service establishments. Employees who sell products to other businesses for resale are not eligible for the federal exemption, and both the federal and state exemptions have to apply for an employee to be exempt from overtime.

Even if the inside salesperson exemption applies, it is only an overtime exemption. Unlike the white-collar exemptions, which also exempt the employee from mandatory meal and rest breaks, no such exemption applies to inside salespersons. Meal and rest breaks must be provided to them (see Sections 9.1 and 9.2). An accurate record of the hours worked by such employees must also be kept, to determine whether the first part of the test has been satisfied and to permit the calculation of overtime due if the test is not satisfied.

8.17 Truck Drivers

Truck drivers whose hours of service are regulated by the U.S. Department of Transportation (DOT) or the California Highway Patrol are exempt from federal and California overtime laws, respectively.

DOT regulations apply to vehicles weighing more than 10,000 pounds and that travel in interstate commerce. Both criteria must be met.

The DOT defines "interstate commerce" as "trade, traffic or transportation in the United States which is between a place in a State and a place outside of such State (including a place outside of the United States) or is between two places in a State through another State or a place outside of the United States." Goods may move in interstate commerce even though they are transported from only one point in a state to another point in the same state if they either originated in transit from a point outside the state or are ultimately bound for a destination beyond the state in a continuous movement. A truck driver who transports goods from a California seaport to a warehouse in California would be involved in interstate commerce even though they would never leave California. By contrast, a truck driver who delivers fresh produce grown in California from a distribution center in California to a retail store in California would not be involved in interstate commerce.

If the truck does not carry goods in interstate commerce, the driver would still be exempt from California overtime requirements if the truck is regulated by the California Highway Patrol. Its regulations cover trucks that meet one of the following criteria:

- Have three or more axles and gross vehicle weight of more than 10,000 pounds;
- Have a gross vehicle weight of at least 26,001 pounds;
- Have a gross vehicle weight of less than 26,001 pounds and transports hazardous materials or tow a trailer that transports hazardous materials;
- Tow a regulated trailer that, in combination with the truck, exceeds 40 feet in length;
- Tow a regulated trailer weighing more than 10,000 pounds;
- Are regulated by the California Public Utilities Commission; or
- Are farm labor vehicles.

California's overtime exemptions cover only employees whose duties actually involve driving. Helpers, loaders, fuelers, and mechanics are not covered by the state exemption. An employee who spends only part of their working time driving a truck covered by federal or state regulations may still be entitled to overtime compensation based on the time spent performing nondriving duties.

A driver may be exempt from California's overtime requirements but still be covered by federal overtime requirements if they do not qualify for the federal motor carrier exemption. For example, a driver who transports goods that originate in California to points within California and who drives a vehicle weighing more than 26,001 pounds would be exempt from state overtime requirements but not from federal overtime law.

8.18 Bus, Taxi, and Limo Drivers

Commercial buses designed to carry 16 or more passengers, including the driver, and school buses are regulated by the California Highway Patrol. Their drivers are exempt from California overtime laws. Commercial bus drivers are covered by federal overtime laws, however, unless they fall under the federal motor carrier exemption. Drivers of buses transporting passengers to and from seaports or airports may be covered by the federal exemption because the passengers they carry are traveling in interstate commerce. Drivers of buses that carry passengers to and from other locations within California are likely covered by federal overtime requirements.

Taxicab drivers are exempt from both federal and California overtime laws. Limousine or shuttle drivers generally are not exempt, however, and they must be paid overtime.

8.19 Paying Overtime to Exempt Employees

An employer may provide an exempt employee with additional compensation without losing the exemption or violating the salary basis requirement, so long as the employee is guaranteed at least the minimum weekly required amount paid on a salary basis. For example, an exempt employee may be paid an incentive bonus or commissions in addition to a set salary without disturbing the salary basis. An exempt employee also may be paid for overtime hours worked at an hourly rate based on their weekly salary divided by 40 for all or a certain number of hours worked over 40. An employee who is paid a guaranteed salary that is the same every week may be paid an unlimited amount of overtime pay in addition to their weekly salary. Such payments are not required but they may be offered as an incentive to exempt employees who are asked to work substantial amounts of overtime.

CHAPTER 9

Meals, Breaks, Pants, and Seats: Other Rights of Employees

California law generously vests employees with a multitude of rights not shared by employees in most other states.

9.1 Meal Periods

Nonexempt employees, exempt computer professionals, and exempt inside salespersons in California must be provided an unpaid, uninterrupted 30-minute meal period that begins before the end of their fifth hour of work. You need not ensure that employees take their meal breaks, but you must ensure that they have the *opportunity* to do so on a timely basis. This means that you must relieve employees of all duty, relinquish control over their activities (so that they are free to come and go as they please), and not impede or discourage them from taking their meal period.

If an employee's shift will last no more than 6 hours they may elect to waive the meal break if the employer consents. If an employee works more than 10 hours in a day, a second unpaid 30-minute meal period must be provided before the end of the tenth hour of work except that if the total hours worked in the day are no more than 12, the employee may waive the second meal period by mutual agreement of employer and employee if the first meal break was taken.

Waivers of a meal break when the employee does not work more than 6 hours, or of a second meal break when the employee works more than 10 but not more than 12 hours, should be in writing and signed by the employee and a supervisor. You can require a separate written waiver for each meal break waived, or you can utilize blanket waivers. If you use the former you must ensure that a waiver was timely executed every time the employee did not take a meal break; this should be monitored each pay period. If you use a blanket waiver it should provide that the employee may take a meal break in spite of the waiver at any time simply by notifying a supervisor.

Written waivers of the meal break where an employee works more than 6 hours (i.e., the employee elects to skip the meal break altogether) are not valid and should not be utilized.

When the nature of the employee's work prevents them from being relieved of all duty for the meal period, the employee may take a paid on-duty meal period, provided you have a written agreement with them for the on-duty meal period, and that agreement must state that it may be revoked by the employee at any time. The on-duty meal period is available only when it is impossible for the employee to be relieved for a meal period. More than mere inconvenience or added cost for the employer is required.

Employees who do not receive a timely and compliant off-duty meal period must be paid a premium of one hour's pay at the employee's "regular rate" for each day in which the meal period was not provided. This regular rate is the same rate used for purposes of calculating overtime (see Section 8.3). If an employee receives only an hourly wage, that wage will be the amount paid for a missed meal period premium. If the employee also receives bonus or incentive pay, or is paid a piece rate or commissions in addition to an hourly wage, those payments must also be taken into account in computing the missed meal period premium.

If you provide training to employees during the lunch hour or require them to be present for a lunch meeting, you must pay the cost of the meal and pay the employee for the time spent in the training or meeting. Such employees must be additionally provided a timely unpaid 30-minute meal period or an hour's pay as a missed meal period premium. If the meal period is to be provided, it generally must be provided before the lunch meeting so that it will be timely.

You should take three steps to prevent missed meal period claims. First, implement and publish a policy stating that employees will be entitled to take (1) a 30-minute, off-duty, unpaid meal period before the end of their fifth hour of work, and (2) another 30-minute, off-duty, unpaid meal period before the end of ten hours should they work more than 10 hours unless (a) the first meal period was taken, (b) they work less than 12 hours, and (c) they agree to waive the second meal period. The policy should instruct employees that if they are unable to take a timely duty-free meal period on any day to report it promptly to HR.

Second, ensure that every eligible employee is actually able to take the required meal periods. Even if you have a policy stating that meal periods will be provided, if employees' workloads are too heavy for them to leave their posts for 30 minutes, or if they are subject to supervisory pressure not to take a full 30-minute uninterrupted meal period, they will have a valid claim for missed meal period premiums. Such supervisory pressure could be as simple as calling, texting, or emailing an employee about work issues while they are on a meal break. Special care should be taken to ensure that tipped or commissioned employees are relieved of duty and provided an opportunity to take a meal period. These employees are often reluctant to take a full 30-minute break (or to take a break at all) yet later may claim that there were too many customers for them to be able to take their meal period.

Third, require employees to clock out at the beginning of their meal period and clock back in at the end of the meal period to provide a record that they took their breaks. You must review these time records every pay period to ensure compliance. If an employee has taken no meal period or less than a 30-minute break, or has started a meal period after the completion of five hours of work, the employee's supervisor should be alerted to the noncompliance and directed to counsel or discipline the employee. The supervisor should be held responsible for ensuring that employees get their meal breaks on a timely basis as well. Noncompliant meal breaks of fewer than 30 minutes may be prevented by programming your timekeeping system not to allow an employee to clock back in from a meal break less than 30 minutes from clocking out.

Rounding of meal period time punches is not allowed because it might result in employees receiving less than 30 minutes for their meal period, and it might reflect a timely meal break that was actually late (such as when an employee starts a meal break at 1:04 p.m. but the actual time is rounded to the nearest ten-minute increment, or 1:00 p.m.). Meal period time punches must reflect the actual number of minutes taken. Where a missed or noncompliant meal period occurs, you should consider paying the missed meal period premium on the employee's next paycheck to prevent them from filing a claim or lawsuit later that would likely result in your having to pay penalties, interest, attorneys' fees, and legal costs as well as the missed meal period premium.

9.2 Rest Breaks

Nonexempt employees, exempt computer professionals and inside salespersons must also be provided with a paid 10-minute rest break per 4 hours worked "or major fraction thereof." No rest break must be provided if the employee works less than 3½ hours. If the employee works more than 3½ hours but less than 6 hours, one rest break must be provided. An employee who works more than 6 hours and up to 10 hours is entitled to two 10-minute breaks. An employee who works more than 10 hours and up to 14 hours is entitled to three 10-minute breaks, and so on.

The rest break must be a *net* 10 minutes, such that if employees must travel some distance from their work area to a rest area, the 10 minutes begins to run when they arrive at the rest area. Employees may not be prohibited from leaving the premises during their rest breaks even though it might not be practical for them to do so. Employees may also use the restroom during their break time, but restroom breaks taken outside of the regular 10-minute break do not count toward their allotted break time.

Employees must be relieved of all duty during their rest breaks. They must not be "on call" or required to carry cell phones, radios, or pagers to use to respond to employer calls while on their rest breaks, even if they are rarely or never actually called. Employees who work in an office environment may wish to use their break time to make personal phone calls, send or return personal emails, or surf the internet at their desks. The problem with this is that if they answer the phone or respond to a work-related email while on break they can later claim that they did not receive a duty-free rest break. Employees therefore should be required to leave their work stations for their breaks or instructed that they must not respond to any phone calls, email, or coworker inquiries while on their rest breaks.

Employees must be relieved of all duty during their rest breaks. They must not be "on call" or required to carry cell phones or pagers to use to respond to employer calls while on their rest breaks, even if they are rarely or never actually called.

An employee who is not provided one or more required breaks in a workday is entitled to be paid a missed rest break premium of one hour of pay (one hour per workday, not one hour per missed break). As with a missed meal period premium, this premium must be calculated at the employee's "regular rate," which is the same rate used for purposes of calculating overtime (see Section 8.3). If an employee receives only an hourly wage, that wage will be the amount paid for a missed rest break premium. If the employee also receives bonus or incentive pay, or is paid a piece rate or commissions in addition to an hourly wage, those payments must also be taken into account in computing the missed rest break premium.

Because rest breaks are paid, employees typically do not clock out for them. As with meal periods, you are required to *provide* employees with rest breaks but not ensure that they are taken. You should have a written policy instructing employees to take their rest breaks. One means of limiting exposure to claims of missed rest breaks is to require employees to certify (usually on their time cards or time record) that they received all required rest breaks during the workweek or pay period except those specified by the employee. Should an employee state that they missed one or more rest breaks, the matter should be addressed with their supervisor, and the employee should be paid the missed rest break premium for all days in which a rest break was missed.

9.3 Pay for Rest Breaks

Employees who are paid hourly or on a salary simply receive their normal pay for their rest breaks. For employees who are paid on a commission or piece-rate basis, however, calculating rest break pay is more complicated.

Employees who are paid a draw against commissions must be paid separately for their rest breaks at an hourly rate that is at least the minimum wage. Thus, commission-paid employees must be paid for 1.67 hours per workweek (10 × 10 minutes) for their rest breaks (assuming they do not work more than 10 hours per day), and this pay must be separately reflected on their wage statements. Alternatively, commission-paid employees may be paid an hourly base (that will cover paid rest breaks) plus commission instead of a draw.

Calculation of rest break pay for employees paid on a piece-rate basis is more complex. Piece-rate employees generally include automotive technicians, spa therapists, massage therapists, and gym and sports instructors. They must be paid for their rest breaks at an average rate reflecting all nonovertime earnings during the workweek except for rest breaks. For example, assume an employee is paid an hourly base of $18.00 per hour plus a $25.00 piece rate for each job performed, completes 30 jobs, and works 40 hours in a workweek. Rest break compensation would be calculated as follows:

40 hours − 1.67 hours (rest breaks) = 38.33 hours
38.33 hours × $18.00 = $689.94
30 jobs × $25.00 piece rate = $750.00
$689.94 + $750.00 = $1,439.94 (total compensation for rest break pay purposes)
$1,439.94 ÷ 38.33 hours = $37.57 × 1.67 hours = $62.74

Such employee's rest break pay for this workweek therefore would be $62.74. This amount must be separately reflected on the employee's wage statement.

9.4 Cool-Down Breaks

Employees in all outdoor places of employment in California, and indoors where the temperature is 82 degrees Fahrenheit or greater, may take a paid cool-down break for a period of at least five minutes anytime when they feel the need to do so to protect themselves from overheating. No supervisor's permission is required, and there is no limit to the number of cool-down breaks that may be taken. These cool-down breaks are in addition to meal periods and regular ten-minute rest breaks required by law. Employees taking such cool-down breaks must be monitored for signs of heat illness.

Employers are responsible for providing shaded areas for cool-down breaks for employees working outdoors when the outdoor temperature in the work area exceeds

80 degrees. Such shaded areas must be either open-air or provided with ventilation or cooling. The amount of shade present must be at least enough to accommodate all of the employees taking a cool-down break at any given time, so that they can sit in a normal posture fully in the shade without having to be in physical contact with each other. Enough shade must also be provided to accommodate all employees taking a meal period at any given time. The employer may alternate groups of employees taking cool-down breaks or meal periods in the shade. When the outdoor temperature in the work area is less than 80 degrees, employers must still provide these shaded areas or else provide timely access to shade upon an employee's request. Drinking water must be available to employees taking cool-down breaks.

Employers must provide cool-down areas indoors where the temperature is maintained at lower than 82 degrees, blocked from direct sunlight and shielded from other high radiant heat sources, and is either open-air or where ventilation or cooling is provided. Drinking water must be provided as well.

On work sites in agriculture, construction, landscaping, oil and gas extraction, and transportation (other than by operation of an air-conditioned vehicle) of agricultural products, construction materials or other heavy objects (such as furniture or freight) where the temperature is 95 degrees or above, the employer must ensure that each employee takes a "preventative minimum net ten-minute cool-down rest period" every two hours. This cool-down rest period is in addition to cool-down breaks taken at the employee's initiative but it can be combined with employees' regular meal and rest breaks where practicable.

Pay for cool-down breaks for employees paid on a draw against commission or on a piece-rate basis is calculated the same as for paid rest breaks (see Section 9.4). Employees who are not provided with cool-down breaks as needed are entitled to be paid a premium of one hour of pay for each workday in which cool-down breaks were not provided.

9.5 The Right to Wear Pants to Work

Female employees in California have the statutory right to wear pants to work. Presumably, male employees have the same right, too. This law acknowledges an employer's right to require employees to wear uniforms but is unclear whether the uniform must provide the option of wearing pants.

9.6 Suitable Seats

Employers must provide employees with "suitable seats" when the nature of the work reasonably permits the use of seats. Whether the work "reasonably permits" the use of seats is an objective test. You should first look at the employee's job tasks, and whether those tasks can be performed while seated. In making this assessment, you should focus on the nature of the work itself, not on the characteristics of an individual employee. You then must look at whether providing a seat would unduly interfere with other standing tasks, whether the frequency of transition from sitting to standing would interfere with the work, whether activities performed while sitting would raise other ergonomic risks, and whether seated work would impact the quality and effectiveness of overall job performance. With respect to the last factor, an employer's mere preference that employees stand while working is not enough, but the analysis should consider the employer's right to determine job duties and its reasonable expectations regarding customer service. The physical layout of the work area is a relevant factor to consider too but you may not intentionally design a work area to preclude the use of a seat.

If the nature of employees' work requires standing, an adequate number of suitable seats must be placed in reasonable proximity to their work area for employees to use during lulls in operations when they are not on a formal rest break but are not actively engaged in any duties.

In the event of an employee challenge, the burden is on the employer to show that no suitable seating could be provided.

9.7 Day of Rest

California law provides that every employee is entitled to one day of rest in seven and that an employer may not "cause" its employees to work more than six days in seven. This rule does not apply when an employee's total hours of employment do not exceed 30 hours in a week or 6 hours in any one day of the week. Also, the law permits an accumulation of days of rest when the nature of the employment reasonably requires that the employee work seven or more consecutive days, if in each calendar month the employee receives days of rest equivalent to one day's rest in seven.

A California Supreme Court case has brought some clarity to these seemingly conflicting provisions. First, the court held that the one day of rest is required for each workweek, not for any rolling seven-day period. Periods of more than six consecutive days of work that stretch across more than one workweek are not prohibited. Second, the day of rest guarantee is not an absolute because California's overtime law anticipates that employees may work seven days in a workweek by requiring that they be paid one-and-a-half times their regular rate for the first 8 hours and double time for work in excess of 8 hours on the seventh day of work in a workweek. Third, an employer may require an employee to work all seven days in a workweek so long as the number of rest days received in a calendar month is at least the number of calendar days divided by seven.

Finally, the court defined how an employer can avoid "causing" its employees to work more than six days in a workweek. It maintained that the employer must apprise employees of their entitlement to a day of rest and thereafter maintain absolute neutrality as to the exercise of that right. An employer may not encourage its employees to forego rest or conceal their entitlement to rest, but it does not violate the law simply because an employee chooses to work a seventh day.

If employees must work seven days in a workweek, therefore, you must first ensure that (1) they are paid the overtime premium for the seventh day, and (2) that they receive enough days off in the month such that they receive the equivalent of one day per workweek. If the second requirement cannot be met then any further work must occur at the request of the employee and not as the result of any requirement or inducement by the employer.

9.8 Lactation Breaks

You must provide a reasonable amount of break time to accommodate an employee desiring to express breast milk for their infant child every time they need to do so. The break time should run concurrently with the employee's regular meal and rest breaks. If additional break time is required it may be unpaid.

You are additionally required to provide the employee with a room or place, other than a restroom, for them to express breast milk in private. The lactation room or location must be in close proximity to the employee's work area, shielded from view, and free from intrusion while the employee is expressing milk. In addition, the lactation room or location must be safe, clean, and free of hazardous materials. It must contain a surface on which to place a breast pump and personal items, as well as a place to sit. It must have access to electricity needed to operate an electric or battery-powered breast pump. You must also provide access to a sink with running water and a refrigerator suitable for storing milk in close proximity to the employee's workspace. If a refrigerator cannot be provided, you may provide another cooling device suitable for storing milk, such as a cooler. Where a multipurpose room is used for lactation, among other uses, the use of the room for lactation must take precedence over the other uses, but only for the time it is in use for lactation purposes.

If you are unable to provide a permanent space for lactation due to operational, financial, or space limitations, you may provide a temporary space so long as it is not a restroom and is in close proximity to the employee's work area, shielded from view, free from intrusion while the employee is expressing milk, and has the other elements required for a permanent lactation room.

Your employee handbook must contain a specific policy regarding lactation accommodations (see Section 4.11). If you cannot provide lactation break time or a location for expression of breast milk that complies with the requirements of the law you must provide a written response to any employee who requests lactation accommodations.

9.9 Illiterate Employees

Employers with 25 or more employees must reasonably accommodate and assist any illiterate employee unless to do so would impose an undue hardship. Employers must additionally make reasonable efforts to safeguard the privacy of illiterate employees. Reasonable accommodations do not include providing paid time off to attend an adult literacy education program. An employee who reveals their illiteracy to the employer but who otherwise satisfactorily performs their work may not be terminated on account of the disclosure of illiteracy.

9.10 Employees' Political Activities

Employers may not control or direct the political activities or affiliations of their employees, or forbid or prevent employees from participating in politics or becoming candidates for public office. Likewise, you may not coerce or influence employees by means of threat of discharge to adopt or follow any course of political activity or to refrain from doing so.

9.11 Secret Shoppers

You may not discipline or terminate an employee based on an outside "secret shopper's" report regarding the employee's performance, conduct, or honesty without first providing the employee a copy of the report. This law does not apply if you use your own employees to conduct secret shopper visits.

9.12 Smoke-Free Workplaces

Smoking is not allowed in enclosed spaces in the workplace, including lobbies, lounges, break rooms, waiting areas, stairwells, elevators, restrooms, and covered parking areas. A nonemployee who attempts to smoke in these areas must be directed not to do so. This ban on smoking in the workplace applies to e-cigarettes and vaporizer pens as well as cigars, cigarettes, and pipes.

9.13 Restrooms

Employers must provide restrooms for employees, and when there are five or more employees who are not of the same gender, a sufficient number of separate toilet facilities must be provided for each gender and must be clearly so marked.

9.14 Changing Rooms and Resting Facilities

When an employee's work requires a change of clothing, you must provide changing rooms or similar space apart from restrooms so employees may change their clothing in reasonable privacy and comfort. You must also provide a break room or resting area apart from restrooms for employees to use during rest breaks.

CHAPTER 10

Employee Privacy Rights

Employees in California have privacy rights from several sources, including the California Constitution, various statutes, and court decisions. Most of these rights are not absolute, however. In many instances employee privacy rights are balanced against other important interests, such as the public interest in finding the truth in court proceedings or the employer's interest in maintaining a safe and secure workplace. In some situations, the question is whether the employee has a reasonable expectation of privacy under the circumstances. This chapter will address the more important privacy rights that may be relevant in the workplace.

10.1 Sources of Privacy Rights

Pursuing and obtaining "privacy" is one of the inalienable rights set forth in Article I, Section 1 of the California Constitution. This right has been held to apply in private as well as in public workplaces.

Other privacy rights are provided via specific statutes. One prominent example is the California Consumer Privacy Act, discussed below, which applies in the employment context in at least some respects. Outside of specific statutory requirements, employee privacy rights are rarely absolute. A balancing test is usually applied. This balancing test provides employers with some latitude in most situations, but it also carries with it a measure of uncertainty as the law of privacy continues to evolve

10.2 California Consumer Privacy Act

The California Consumer Privacy Act (CCPA) provides extensive privacy rights for California residents. The law applies to three types of for-profit businesses that do business in California:

- Businesses that have annual gross revenues (worldwide) of over $25 million;
- Businesses that annually receive, sell, or share personal information of 100,000 or more California consumers or households; and
- Businesses that derive 50 percent or more of their annual revenue from selling or sharing personal information of consumers.

In addition to for-profit businesses that meet one of these thresholds, the CCPA applies to any other entity, including a nonprofit or subsidiary, that is "controlled by" and shares common branding with a covered business (for example, a nonprofit foundation formed by a large business that bears the same brand and is therefore known to be affiliated with that business).

The CCPA applies to these businesses if they collect "personal information," or if such information is collected on their behalf. Personal information is defined as information that identifies, relates to, describes, is capable of being associated with, or could reasonably be linked, directly or indirectly, with a particular consumer or household. Examples of covered personal information include:

- Personal identifiers, such as name, aliases, postal addresses, email addresses, account name, Social Security number, driver's license number, passport number, and online internet protocol address;
- Characteristics of protected classifications under California or federal law (race, sex, age, etc.);
- Commercial information such as records of personal property, products, or services purchased, obtained, or considered;
- Biometric information;
- Internet activity including browsing history, search history, and information regarding a consumer's interaction with an internet website, application, or advertisement;
- Geolocation data;
- Audio, electronic, visual, thermal, olfactory, or similar information;
- Professional or employment-related information;
- Education information that is not publicly available under the Family Educational Rights and Privacy Act (FERPA);
- Inferences drawn from any of the information listed above to create a profile about a consumer reflecting the consumer's preferences, characteristics, psychological trends, predispositions, behavior, attitudes, intelligence, abilities, and aptitudes; and
- Sensitive personal information.

Covered personal information does not include (a) publicly available information or lawfully obtained, truthful information that is a matter of public concern and (b) information that is deidentified or aggregated (meaning it is not capable of being linked back to a consumer or household). "Sensitive personal information" means:

- Social Security number, driver's license number, state ID card number, or passport number;

- A consumer's account log-in, financial account, debit card, or credit card number in combination with any required security or access code, password, or credentials allowing access to an account;
- A consumer's precise geolocation;
- A consumer's racial or ethnic origin, religious or philosophical beliefs, or union membership;
- The contents of a consumer's mail, email, and text messages unless the business is the intended recipient of the communication (i.e., contents of personal messages received or sent on company devices or company email);
- A consumer's genetic data;
- The processing of biometric information for the purpose of uniquely identifying a consumer;
- Personal information collected and analyzed concerning a consumer's health; and
- Personal information collected and analyzed concerning a consumer's sex life or sexual orientation.

Generally, consumers have the following key rights under the CCPA:

- The right to know what personal information is collected;
- The right to know what personal information is sold or shared and to whom;
- The right to correct inaccurate personal information;
- The right to delete personal information;
- The right to opt-out of the sale or sharing of personal information;
- The right to limit use and disclosure of sensitive personal information; and
- The right not to be discriminated or retaliated against for exercising these rights.

How Does the CCPA Apply to Employers?

The California Privacy Rights Act of 2020 (CPRA), enacted by California voters as Proposition 24, amended the CCPA and made it effective upon employers as of January 1, 2023. Under CCPA/CPRA, "consumers" include employees, job applicants, independent contractors, and family members and dependents and beneficiaries of employees who are California residents.

Employers subject to the CCPA/CPRA must conduct a data inventory to identify every piece of personal information and sensitive personal information collected from or about every consumer since January 1, 2022. Covered employers also must identify every piece of personal information and sensitive personal information that is shared with or accessed by any vendor or third party in the course of that vendor's or third party's business relationship with the employer. With respect to employees, job applicants, independent contractors, and family members, dependents, and beneficiaries of employees, you will need to know what personal information and sensitive personal information of theirs you collect and use or share with third parties such as health plans, background check vendors, and insurers (including workers' compensation).

Employers subject to the CCPA/CPRA may only collect data on employees, job applicants, independent contractors, and family members and dependents and beneficiaries of employees that is necessary to fulfill a business purpose and may only retain such data for as long as is needed to fulfill that business purpose. CCPA/CPRA requires that covered entities undergo a process of "data minimization," which includes development of a data retention policy, destruction of stale data, identification of data that does not need to be collected, and ceasing to collect that information. Before information is deleted, however, you should confirm that such information is not needed for any pending, reasonably anticipated, or threatened claims by the company or by any third party (including an employee) against the company.

Required Disclosures

CCPA/CPRA require covered entities to provide several disclosures to consumers, including employees, job applicants, independent contractors, and family members and dependents and beneficiaries of employees. The first is the organization's privacy policy. It should identify:

- All categories of personal information collected in any form, from any source in the last 12 months;
- All business purposes for which the information is used;
- All categories of sources from which the information was collected;
- All categories of third parties with which the information was shared in the last 12 months;
- The retention period for each category of information or the criteria to be used in deciding how long to keep the data;
- What sensitive personal information is collected; and
- Whether you "sell" any of the data, which includes any sharing of data with a third party that is not a service provider in exchange for valuable consideration, not necessarily money.

The second required disclosure is the Notice at Collection. At or before the point of collection of information from a job applicant, employee, or other consumer, you must disclose which categories of personal information are collected, the business purpose for collecting this information, and whether the information is sold or shared. For example, the notice to job applicants and employees might list the following information:

- Personal identifiers;
- Financial information;
- Protected classification information;
- Professional and employment-related information;
- Medical and health information;
- Education information;
- Internet and network activity; and
- Mobile device security information.

The reasons listed for your use of this information might include:

- To comply with state and federal law and regulations requiring employers to maintain certain records (such as immigration compliance records, personnel files, wage and hour records, payroll records, accident or safety records, and tax records);
- To process payroll;
- To maintain workers' compensation and other liability insurance;
- To manage workers' compensation claims;
- To administer and maintain group health insurance benefits, 401(k), and/or retirement plans;
- To evaluate job applicants and candidates for employment or promotions;
- To obtain and verify background checks on job applicants and employees;
- To evaluate, make, and communicate decisions regarding an employee's employment, including decisions to hire, terminate, promote, demote, transfer, suspend, or discipline;
- To communicate with employees regarding employment-related matters such as upcoming benefits enrollment deadlines, action items, availability of W2s, and other alerts and notifications;
- To grant employees access to secure company facilities and maintain information on who accessed the facility;
- To implement, monitor, and manage electronic security measures on employee devices that are used to access company networks and systems;
- To administer medical and other types of leaves of absence; and
- To evaluate whether an employee's disability or work restrictions are subject to a reasonable accommodation.

These examples are not exhaustive. You should list the types of information you actually collect and the actual reasons you collect it. The disclosure to job applicants should be given to the applicant at or before the time they submit an application for employment or résumé.

The third required disclosure is the Notice of Right to Limit Use and Disclosure. It informs consumers of their rights to limit the use and disclosure of their sensitive personal information and how to exercise those rights. Consumers may make the following requests:

- **Request to Know:** Consumers are entitled to make up to two requests in a 12-month period regarding what personal information of theirs you have collected, from which sources you collected it, with whom you have shared it, and what was the business purpose of your collecting such information. This requires an individualized response looking back to January 1, 2022. Your response must be provided within 45 calendar days, but the deadline may be extended another 45 days.
- **Request to Access:** Consumers may make up to two requests per 12-month period for access to or disclosure of the specific pieces of personal information collected on them since January 1, 2022.
- **Request to Delete:** Consumers may request twice in a 12-month period that their personal information collected by your organization be deleted. The information to be deleted may have been collected at any time, before or after January 1, 2022. The information must be deleted within 45 calendar days, but the deadline may be extended another 45 days.
- **Request to Opt-Out of Sale/Sharing of Personal Information:** This request must be granted within 15 business days. A consumer may opt-in again after opting out.
- **Request to Correct:** Consumer may request that an organization correct inaccurate information that it maintains on them. The request must be acted upon within 45 calendar days to respond, which can be extended by another 45 calendar days. The information maintained on a consumer need not be corrected if it is more likely than not that the information is accurate.
- **Request to Limit Use or Disclosure of Sensitive Personal Information:** Upon a consumer's request, use of their sensitive personal information must be limited to that which is necessary to perform the services or provide the requested good. In the employment context, use would be limited to that which is necessary to conduct any required background checks, compensate the employee, withhold required taxes, and provide employee benefits. This limitation extends to any service provider (such as a health plan) upon your notification that the job applicant or employee has requested such limitation.

Limits on Exercise of CCPA/CPRA Rights

Consumers, including employees, job applicants, independent contractors, and family members, dependents, and beneficiaries of employees, cannot exercise their CCPA/CPRA rights in a manner that would restrict an organization's ability to do any of the following:

- Comply with federal, state, or local laws;
- Comply with a civil, criminal, or regulatory inquiry, investigation, subpoena, or summons by federal, state, or local authorities;
- Cooperate with law enforcement agencies concerning conduct or activity that the business, service provider, or a third party reasonably and in good faith believes may violate federal, state, or local law;
- Exercise or defend legal claims;
- Collect, use, retain, sell, or disclose consumer information that is deidentified or aggregated; or
- Collect or sell a consumer's personal information if every aspect of that commercial conduct takes place wholly outside of California.

Data Security

Employers must comply with the data security requirements of CCPA/CPRA, including the requirement of an annual independent security audit. If a data breach of an employee's sensitive personal information occurs as the result of an employer's failure to implement reasonable security measures as required by CCPA/CPRA, regardless of whether any employee suffered any actual harm, the employee can sue for penalties of between $100 and $750 per employee per data breach incident or their actual damages, whichever is greater. Employers therefore must ensure that the information collected on their employees is subject to adequate data security and that third parties who are provided access to employee information have also implemented adequate security measures.

Training Requirements

Employers must ensure that any employee involved in implementing, managing, or overseeing compliance with the CCPA and CPRA receives training. Such employees may include executives, general managers, human resources professionals, directors of marketing, social media managers, and information technology employees. Additionally, any employee who is involved with receiving and responding to requests from consumers must receive the training. Finally, employees who regularly interface with consumers— such as sales representatives—should receive training on the basic requirements of the CCPA and CPRA and know where to direct consumer questions and requests regarding data privacy.

10.3 Personnel Records

California employees have a recognized privacy interest in their personnel records. Personnel files should therefore be maintained in a secure location. Access to personnel files should be limited to those persons with a legitimate need to work with them, such as HR personnel. Specific rules apply to employees' right to access their own personnel files, and to third-party access to personnel files.

Employee Access to Personnel Files

You must allow employees to inspect or copy their personnel files within 30 days of a written request to do so. You must provide a form for employees to use if they wish to request their personnel files, but any written request from the employee will suffice.

You must produce the personnel file of a current employee at the location where the employee works, and the employee need not be paid for the time spent reviewing the file. If the file cannot be produced at the employee's worksite, the employee must be paid for the time spent traveling to the location where the file is kept.

You must produce the personnel file of a former employee where the file is kept, or you may mail a copy of it to the former employee. You may charge an employee or former employee the actual cost of copying and mailing the personnel file. If a former employee was terminated for harassment or workplace violence, you may produce the personnel file at a location other than the workplace that is within a reasonable driving distance of the former employee's home, or you may mail a copy of the file to the former employee. You need not comply with more than one request per year from a former employee to inspect or copy their personnel file. Finally, if an employee or former employee files a lawsuit over an employment issue, the right to inspect or copy the personnel file is suspended during the pendency of the lawsuit.

Personnel files should include the employment application, résumé (if any), all onboarding documents, arbitration agreement, confidentiality agreement (if any), performance evaluations, written disciplinary action, and termination documents or resignation letter. It may also include other employment-related notices and documents, but it should not include:

- Medical information (see Section 10.4);
- Internal correspondence regarding the employee;
- Correspondence with legal counsel regarding the employee;
- Investigation documents such as complaints of harassment and witness statements; or
- Information (including disciplinary action) regarding other employees.

All contents of the personnel file must be produced for inspection or copying except:

- Letters of reference for the employee;
- Documents relating to the investigation of a criminal offense; and
- Names of nonsupervisory employees (these may be redacted).

Confusion sometimes arises because another California statute provides that employees are entitled to receive copies of all documents in their files that they have signed. Although that statute is still on the books, the law described above is broader in that it gives employees and former employees the right to obtain copies of all documents in their files except for those documents listed above. Employees covered by a collective bargaining agreement are not covered by this law if the agreement sets forth a procedure for inspection and copying of personnel records.

Employees also have the right under California law to obtain copies of their payroll records (that is, the itemized wage statement that accompanies each paycheck) required to be maintained by Labor Code Section 226 (see Section 7.26). A request for these records may be made orally or in writing, and you must produce the records within 21 days of the request. Often an employee or an attorney representing the employee will request copies of both the employee's personnel file and payroll records. When such a combined request is made, the payroll records must be provided within 21 days even though the personnel file need not be produced until 30 days from the request. These deadlines are important because a $750 penalty may be assessed by the Labor Commissioner or a court for an employer's failure to timely provide a personnel file, and a separate $750 penalty may be assessed for failure to timely produce payroll records. An employee or former employee may also sue for an injunction to compel compliance with these laws and, if successful, recover litigation costs and attorneys' fees.

Third-Party Access to Personnel Files

Given that personnel files contain private information, they may not be released to persons outside the employer's organization without proper authorization. There are two kinds of acceptable authorization.

The first is simply a written authorization signed by the employee authorizing release of the file to a designated person or entity.

The second is a subpoena. Personnel records are considered "consumer records" under the California Code of Civil Procedure, which specifies that when consumer records are subpoenaed by a third party, a "Notice to Consumer or Employee" must be provided to the employee stating that the requested records will be provided unless the employee serves an objection to production of the records on the person who subpoenaed the records and the custodian of those records on or before the date specified in the subpoena for production of the records. If the employee is a party to the lawsuit in which the records are sought, to block production of the records the employee must file a motion to quash or modify the subpoena and give notice to the custodian of records and the deposition officer (which is usually the copy service that will copy the records) at least five days before the date specified for production of the records. Subpoenas from government agencies or for the claimant's personnel records in a workers' compensation case need not comply with this notice requirement.

10.4 Medical Information

Employers sometimes receive medical information on employees, such as results of preemployment physical examinations, reports of fitness-for-duty examinations, or workers' compensation information. California law requires employers that receive such medical information to establish appropriate procedures to ensure the confidentiality and protection from unauthorized use and disclosure of that information. These procedures include training of employees who have access to employee medical information and implementation of security systems that restrict access to files containing employee medical information.

Federal and state regulations require that employee medical information be kept in a file separate from the personnel file and that such file be accessible only by employees with a specific need to know, such as HR or benefits personnel.

An employer may not use or disclose employee medical information without the employee's written authorization. Exceptions to this authorization requirement are that employee medical information may be used or disclosed in the following situations:

- In administering employee benefit plans;
- In administering medical leaves;
- In administering workers' compensation claims; and
- If compelled by a subpoena or order of a court or administrative agency.

In addition, if the employee has filed a lawsuit or grievance against the employer and placed into issue their medical history, mental or physical condition, or treatment, medical information relevant to those issues may be disclosed.

Employers must guard not only against disclosure of written medical records or information but also against an employee's verbally disclosing confidential medical information about another employee, such as that the employee has a particular disease or disorder. Access to employee medical information should therefore be limited only to those employees who have a specific need to know that information. For example, an employee's supervisor would ordinarily have no need to know the employee's medical information. To the extent an employee requires a medical leave or job restrictions, the need for leave (and its duration) or the nature and duration of the restrictions may be communicated to the supervisor but not the underlying medical reason for the need.

Workers' compensation insurers or third-party administrators are prohibited from disclosing to employers medical information concerning a workers' compensation claimant except information relating to the following:

- The diagnosis of the mental or physical condition for which workers' compensation is claimed and the treatment provided for the condition; and
- Restrictions regarding work or job duties.

This law does not prohibit an insurer from discussing claim information with an employer that affects the employer's premium so long as medical information relating to specific employees not falling within the above-noted exceptions is not disclosed.

10.5 Biometric Information

An increasing number of employers use biometric data such as fingerprints, iris scans, or facial recognition software for timekeeping purposes. There is presently no California law regulating this practice but California Labor Code Section 1051 prohibits an employer from obtaining photographs or fingerprints of applicants or employees and sharing the data with a third party where the data could be used to the detriment of the applicant or employee. While this law, when enacted, was directed primarily at blacklisting, it can be read potentially to apply to the timekeeping context as well. Therefore, biometric data obtained for purposes of timekeeping should not be accessible by the vendor of the timekeeping program or any other outside party. It must be used only for timekeeping purposes, moreover.

Employers that use biometric data must include it in disclosures to applicants and employees under the CCPA (see Section 10.2).

10.6 Immigration Enforcement

California's new "Workplace Know Your Rights Act" places two requirements on employers. First, employers must provide an annual written notice to all employees that explains certain workers' rights, including their rights during an immigration enforcement operation. The rights that must be stated in the notice are:

- The right to workers' compensation benefits, including disability pay and medical care for work-related injury or illness;

- The right to notice of inspection by immigration agencies;
- Protection against unfair immigration-related practices;
- The right to organize a union or engage in concerted activity in the workplace; and
- Constitutional rights when interacting with law enforcement at the workplace, including the rights to be free from unreasonable searches and seizures, to due process, and against self-incrimination.

The first notice must be provided on or before February 1, 2026. The Division of Labor Standards Enforcement will provide a template notice.

Second, employers must, if requested by an employee, notify the employee's designated emergency contact in the event the employee is arrested or detained at work, and employers must give employees an opportunity to designate this emergency contact no later than March 30, 2026 (or at the time of hire for employees hired after that date).

Additionally, when an employer receives a Notice of Inspection of I-9 forms or other employment records, within 72 hours of receipt of the notice it must post a notice to employees containing the following information:

- The name of the immigration agency conducting the inspections of I-9 Employment Eligibility Verification forms or other employment records;
- The date that the employer received notice of the inspection;
- The nature of the inspection to the extent known; and
- A copy of the Notice of Inspection of I-9 Employment Eligibility Verification forms for the inspection to be conducted.

The Labor Commissioner has developed a template for such a notice; it may be found at https://www.dir.ca.gov/DLSE/LC_90.2_EE_Notice.pdf. This notice must also be given to any union(s) representing the affected employees.

Upon receipt of the written immigration agency notice providing the results of the inspection of the I-9 forms and other employment documents, within 72 hours the employer must provide a copy of such notice to each employee found during the inspection to lack work authorization, or whose work authorization documents were found to have deficiencies. Such notice shall state the obligations of the employer and the affected employee arising from the inspection of I-9 forms and other employment records. This notice must be given by hand, or by mail and email if the employee's email address is known, and it shall contain the following information:

- A description of any and all deficiencies or other items identified in the written immigration inspection results notice related to the affected employee;

- The time period for correcting any potential deficiencies identified by the immigration agency;
- The time and date of any meeting with the employer to correct any identified deficiencies; and
- Notice that the employee has the right to representation during any meeting scheduled with the employer.

A copy of such notice must also be given to the affected employee's union, if any.

10.7 Social Security Numbers

Employers are prohibited by California law from showing more than the last four digits of an employee's Social Security number (SSN) on itemized wage statements. Employers are additionally prohibited from printing an employee's SSN on any documents that are mailed to the employee, unless state or federal law requires the SSN to appear on the document (such as a Form W-2).

Employers that store employee names and SSNs electronically are required to promptly notify affected employees in the event of a data security breach if (1) the data was unencrypted, or (2) the data was encrypted and the encryption key or security credential that could render the information readable or usable was also compromised. Such notice must be given no later than 30 days after the security breach. If the employer is the source of the breach, it must offer to provide appropriate identity theft prevention and mitigation services to affected persons for at least one year if the breach exposed or may have exposed SSNs or other specified personal information such as driver's license numbers or health insurance information.

10.8 Searches of Employees and Their Possessions

No California law specifically addresses searches of employees or their possessions while on company property. To negate any expectation of privacy, you should provide notice to employees that they and their possessions, such as bags, briefcases, toolboxes, backpacks, and vehicles, are subject to search at the discretion of the employer and that employees are expected to cooperate. Such notice may be provided in the employee handbook or in a stand-alone policy. If employees are provided with lockers, you should provide locks and notify employees that a master key or combination may be used to open the lock when necessary.

An employee should be asked to consent to any search of their person or possessions. An employee who refuses to consent to the search should be reminded of the employer's policy on searches and, if the refusal continues, may be terminated.

10.9 Monitoring Telephone Conversations

California law prohibits monitoring or recording telephone conversations without the consent of all parties to the conversation. Such consent may be implied if employees are notified in writing that their telephone calls may be monitored. The other party to such conversations would need to be notified as well, such as via a warning to incoming callers or to the recipient of a call that the call may be monitored.

Employer monitoring of voice mail messages on the company telephone system is permissible provided employees are notified in advance that such monitoring might occur.

10.10 Video and Audio Recording of Employees

California law prohibits employers from causing an audio or video recording to be made of an employee in a restroom, locker room, or other room designated for changing clothes, unless authorized by a court order.

Secret video recording of employees in private offices or cubicles should not be conducted as courts have found that employees have a reasonable expectation of privacy in such areas. Such an expectation may be overcome by prior written notice to employees that they may be subject to surveillance. The right to privacy of employees in larger open work areas such as manufacturing plants and warehouses is less settled under California law. Employees in those areas should therefore be notified in writing that they are subject to video surveillance should the employer wish to monitor those areas.

California law prohibits trespassing to capture a visual image or sound recording of a person "engaged in a personal or familial activity." It similarly prohibits use of a visual or auditory enhancing device to capture a visual image or sound recording of a person "engaged in a personal or familial activity under circumstances in which the [person] had a reasonable expectation of privacy" that would not have been accessible without trespassing. "Personal and familial activity" is defined to include:

- Intimate details of the person's personal life;
- Interactions with the person's family or significant others; and
- Other aspects of the person's private affairs or concerns.

This law was enacted to address paparazzi activity, but it would likely apply as well to employer investigations outside the workplace of employee misconduct such as violation of a nonfraternization policy or workers' compensation fraud. Surveillance of employees in open public areas would not violate this law because there would be no reasonable expectation of privacy there, but the law would likely be construed to bar surveillance of employees in private homes, hotels, or other areas where an expectation of privacy might exist.

10.11 Use of Employee Photograph or Likeness

It is unlawful in California to use another person's name, photograph, or likeness on any product or goods or in the advertisement of any goods or services without that person's consent. Therefore, if employee photographs are to be included in any company advertisement or written materials, the written consent of the employee(s) involved should be obtained in advance.

10.12 GPS Tracking

GPS tracking devices may be used on vehicles owned or leased by the company. Otherwise, it is unlawful in California to use an electronic tracking device (such as a smartphone app, even on a company-owned phone) to track the movements of employees.

10.13 Monitoring of Email, Internet Use, and Social Media

Employers that notify their employees in advance that company-owned computers and other communications devices are subject to monitoring may monitor employees' internet use, emails sent over the company's email system, and text messages sent or received on a company-issued device. A comprehensive electronic communications policy (see Section 4.22) will make it clear to employees that they should have no expectation of privacy in communications sent using company-owned devices or networks.

Employees who are issued laptop computers or smartphones for business use should be informed that such devices are covered by the employer's electronic communications policy and may be monitored at any time. Employees should further be advised that any personal information they might store on such devices will be subject to the employer's inspection or monitoring.

California's Labor Code Section 980 prohibits employers from requiring or requesting an employee or applicant for employment to:

- Disclose a username or password for the purpose of accessing personal social media;
- Access personal social media in the presence of the employer; or
- Divulge any personal social media unless relevant to an investigation of employee misconduct or violation of law.

This law defines "social media" as including emails, text messages, internet profiles, and online accounts. An exception to the prohibition applies to requests for usernames or passwords to access an employer-owned device. Otherwise, you should refrain from asking employees to provide access to their social media, usernames, or passwords. You should additionally refrain from monitoring employees' use of personal email accounts via company computers unless done in connection with an investigation of specific misconduct such as harassment, misappropriation of trade secrets, or violation of the company's electronic communications policy.

10.14 Drug and Alcohol Testing

California employers have the right to expect that their employees come to work free of drugs and alcohol. Although you may not conduct testing of most applicants and employees for non-psychoactive tetrahydrocannabinol (THC) metabolites and you may not inquire about a job applicant's prior use of marijuana, you need not allow or accommodate the use or possession of, or impairment by, marijuana or medical marijuana while an employee is at work.

There are four instances in which drug or alcohol testing might occur—pre-employment, reasonable suspicion, post-accident, and random—and the lawfulness of such testing varies according to the type of testing involved. An employer wishing to subject applicants and employees to drug or alcohol testing must have a policy in place that describes when testing will occur as well as the consequences of failing a test or failing to cooperate in the testing process.

Pre-Employment Testing

Pre-employment drug testing is lawful in California. Because drug testing is not deemed a "medical examination" under the federal Americans with Disabilities Act or the California Fair Employment and Housing Act, an applicant need not be given a conditional offer of hire to be drug tested. As a practical matter, however, most employers wait until they have made a conditional offer of employment before sending the candidate for a drug test. The employer must pay the cost of the drug test, but applicants need not be paid for the time they spend being tested as they are not yet considered employees.

To avoid claims of discrimination, all applicants, or all applicants for certain classes of positions, should undergo pre-employment drug testing.

Should a candidate fail a pre-employment drug test, the conditional offer of employment may be withdrawn. Candidates who fail a pre-employment drug test should not be hired, no matter how stellar their credentials. In spite of their protestations that they do not regularly use drugs, they are likely to have a drug problem that will cause other problems in the workplace such as poor attendance, a greater risk of accidents and workers' compensation claims, and even theft. Moreover, by excusing one candidate or employee from the consequences of failing a drug test, you risk a discrimination claim every time you subsequently terminate or decline to hire someone who fails the test.

Drug testing of current employees who are candidates for promotion is not permitted in California.

Reasonable Suspicion

To send a current employee for drug or alcohol testing in most instances, you must have a reasonable suspicion that the employee is currently impaired. Such suspicion may be found, for example, in the employee's erratic behavior, physical manifestations such as a glassy-eyed stare or slurred speech, reliable reports of observed recent drug use, or the smell of alcohol on the person. The manager who has the suspicion should document the grounds for that suspicion in writing.

When reasonable suspicion of employee drug or alcohol use exists, it is important to promptly send the employee for a drug or alcohol test, as alcohol and most drugs do not remain in the body for long. If days are allowed to elapse from the time the suspicion arose until the time testing occurs, the suspicion will have grown stale, and the employee may have grounds to attack the lawfulness of the test.

For obvious reasons, if there is current suspicion to justify a drug or alcohol test, the employee should not drive alone to the testing facility. The employee should be driven there by a manager or another employee.

Post-Accident Testing

Many industrial medicine clinics automatically subject employees with workplace injuries to drug testing. Testing every injured employee without regard to how the injury occurred is overbroad, however, and it risks a legal challenge. Some injuries occur under circumstances in which the injured employee plainly is not at fault. An employee rear-ended while stopped at a traffic light in a company vehicle is one example. Therefore, before an injured employee is drug tested, there should be some reason to believe that drugs or alcohol might have contributed to the incident that caused the injury.

Random Testing

Random drug and alcohol testing of employees is not generally lawful in California. The only exceptions are employees covered by the U.S. Department of Transportation's (DOT's) drug testing regulations, which includes intrastate drivers regulated by the California Highway Patrol (see Sections 8.17 and 8.18). Random testing is required for these employees. Employees who are engaged in work that creates a direct threat to the safety of the employee or others in the workplace may also be required to undergo random testing. The threat must be real and immediate, not merely speculative. Employees operating dangerous equipment or working with dangerous chemicals would likely qualify for random testing. Employees working on computers typically would not.

If random testing is implemented, a truly random method of selecting employees for testing, such as is described in the DOT regulations, should be used.

10.15 Lawful Off-Duty Conduct

California Labor Code Section 96(k) authorizes the Labor Commissioner to take assignments of claims for "loss of wages as the result of demotion, suspension, or discharge from employment for lawful conduct occurring during nonworking hours away from the employer's premises." Though written broadly, this provision to date has been construed narrowly by the courts to apply only to claims for violation of civil rights guaranteed by Article I of the California constitution. In one case interpreting this law, the court held that a manager did not have a constitutional right to engage in a romantic relationship with a subordinate in violation of their employer's nonfraternization policy. In another case the court rejected a claim that an employee was terminated for exercising their constitutional right to free speech, noting that the guarantee of free speech applies only to government action, not action by private employers. Both courts maintained that this statute does not create a basis for public policy wrongful termination claims based on an allegation that an employee was terminated simply for engaging in lawful conduct in off-duty hours.

This statute does not apply to hiring decisions, moreover. You may lawfully decide not to hire a job applicant because of lawful conduct you deem undesirable, such as having a nonmarital relationship with a current employee or acting in pornography.

10.16 Defamation in the Employment Context

Former employees sometimes claim the employer's representatives defamed them, particularly when reasons for termination of employment are communicated to other employees or to persons outside the organization.

California law includes an anti-blacklisting statute that prohibits an employer from making a misrepresentation designed to prevent a former employee from obtaining a new job. Employers are expressly permitted, however, upon a request for a reference on a former employee, to provide a truthful statement concerning the circumstances of the employee's termination or resignation.

Truth is an absolute defense to claims for defamation, but the burden of proof is on the employer. Therefore, it is important, when providing a reason for terminating an employee, to provide no more than what you can objectively prove.

Current or former employees may also invoke California's common law actions for slander and libel. Slander is a false and unprivileged oral statement that, among other things, tends directly to injure a person in their trade or business or which causes actual damages. Libel is a false and unprivileged written statement that tends to injure a person in their occupation. For both slander and libel the statements must be of fact, not of opinion.

Truth is an absolute defense to claims for defamation, but the burden of proof is on the employer. Therefore, it is important, when providing a reason for terminating an employee, to provide no more than what you can objectively prove. For example, when money is missing for which an employee was responsible, the employee should be terminated for loss of funds while in their custody, not for stealing. An employee terminated for an altercation with another employee should be terminated for engaging in a fight with a coworker, not for assault and battery.

California law additionally recognizes a privilege against claims for slander and libel for communications made without malice to another person who was also interested in the subject or who requested the information. This is known as the "common interest" privilege. California courts have found employers' statements to other employees regarding the reasons for a coworker's termination for a breach of integrity to be covered by this qualified privilege. For this privilege to apply, however, communications should be limited to those with a "need to know" (such as a terminated employee's peer group) and should be limited only to the reasons for termination and should not include other negative information about the terminated employee.

Note that an employer may be liable in California for providing a falsely positive reference that omits information that a former employee poses a risk of harm to others. Sometimes a former employee terminated for misconduct or poor performance will request a letter of reference as part of an agreement not to sue. You should not provide a letter that misrepresents a poor employee as a good employee, especially when the employee engaged in misconduct that harmed another. Letters of reference, if given, should be limited to dates of employment and position(s) held.

CHAPTER 11

Protecting Trade Secrets

Protecting trade secrets and other confidential information can pose a challenge in California. This is because California courts, unlike the courts of many states, will not enforce noncompete covenants regardless of their reasonableness. California law provides maximum protection for employee mobility. Business and Professions Code Section 16600 states: "Except as provided in this chapter, every contract by which anyone is restrained from engaging in a lawful profession, trade, or business of any kind is to that extent void." The rationale for this rule is that employees' interest in their own mobility and betterment is paramount to employers' competitive interests.

11.1 Sale of Business Exception

The statutes that follow Section 16600 set forth a few exceptions to the rule against enforcing restrictive covenants:

- An owner of a business who sells all of their ownership interest in the company, or who sells all the assets of the business as well as its goodwill, may lawfully agree with the buyer to refrain from carrying on a similar business within a specified geographical area in which the business sold had been carried on.
- A partner in a partnership may agree that, upon leaving the partnership or the partnership dissolving, they will not carry on a similar business within a specified geographical area where the partnership business has been transacted, so long as any other partner continues to do business there.
- A member of a limited liability company (LLC) may lawfully agree that, upon leaving the LLC or the LLC dissolving, they will not carry on a similar business within a specified geographical area where the LLC's business has been transacted, so long as any other member of the LLC continues to do business there.

For these exceptions to apply, the sale price of the ownership interest sold must reflect the sale of the respective portion of the goodwill of the business. Merely selling a few token shares of a business to employees will not support enforcement of a noncompete agreement against them when they leave and sell back their shares for a price that does not include the fractional value of the goodwill of the business attributable to those shares. To reflect the value of goodwill, the shares must be sold at their market value, not at their book value.

11.2 It Is Unlawful to Require Employees to Sign Noncompete Agreements

In the past, sometimes employers would require new hires or existing employees to sign noncompete agreements even though they were not enforceable, in the hope that such an agreement might nonetheless deter an employee from attempting to compete after leaving the employer. However, it is now unlawful for an employer to require new or existing employees in California to sign a noncompete agreement. An employee who is terminated or an applicant who is denied employment for refusing to sign such an agreement may sue for an injunction, damages, and attorneys' fees. Unfortunately, the law making it illegal to require an employee to sign a noncompete agreement does not define what is meant by such an agreement. It is safe to assume that it would include any agreement prohibiting an employee from going to work for a competitor after employment with your company terminates, and it likely includes a nonsolicitation of customers provision not tied to the use of trade secrets or confidential information. Whether it also includes a nonsolicitation of employees provision or other provisions is presently unclear.

11.3 Noncompete Agreements Are Unlawful and Unenforceable in California

Apart from the sale-of-business exceptions noted in Section 11.1, it is unlawful in California for an employer to attempt to enforce an agreement restricting a former employee's ability to accept employment with a competitor. It does not matter that a noncompete agreement may have been signed in another state where such provisions are lawful, or that it contains a choice-of-law provision stating that it is to be governed by another state's law. California law makes it unlawful for an employer to enforce noncompete agreements regardless of where the agreement was signed or where the employee worked when the agreement was signed. For example, if an employee had signed a noncompete agreement in a state that allows them and then moves to California, that agreement would not be enforceable in California, either by an employer in California or an employer outside of California.

Moreover, California law specifically prohibits an employer from requiring an employee to sign an employment contract that contains a provision (1) requiring the employee to adjudicate a claim arising in California in a forum outside of California, or (2) depriving the employee of the protection of California law with respect to a claim arising in California.

11.4 Obligation to Notify Current and Former Employees Regarding Invalid Noncompete Agreements

California law requires that employers notify employees and former employees who were employed after January 1, 2022, and who signed contracts containing invalid noncompete provisions, that such provisions are void. Such notice must have been provided on or before February 14, 2024, and it must be delivered to the last known mailing address and email address of the employee or former employee. Failure to provide such notice is deemed an act of unfair competition.

11.5 Lawful Means of Protecting Trade Secrets

Although an employer generally cannot prohibit a former employee from going to work for a competitor in California, there are lawful means available for an employer in California to protect its trade secrets. The Uniform Trade Secrets Act has been adopted in California (it is found at Section 3426 of the California Civil Code). It prohibits the misappropriation, use, or disclosure of the trade secrets of another. It provides that a court may enjoin the actual or threatened misappropriation, use, or disclosure of a trade secret as well as award damages for loss of the trade secret or for unjust enrichment. If willful and malicious misappropriation is shown, the court may award punitive damages, costs, and attorneys' fees to the injured party.

California courts, however, have rejected the notion of "inevitable disclosure," which assumes that a former employee with access to trade secrets will necessarily disclose those trade secrets to a new employer because they are known to the former employee, even when no physical manifestations of the trade secrets were taken. California courts will refuse to enjoin a former employee from working for a competitor based merely on the possibility that trade secrets might be divulged. Rather, an employer seeking such an injunction must show that actual or threatened misappropriation of trade secrets has occurred, and misappropriation involves both taking and using trade secrets.

In 2016 Congress enacted the Defend Trade Secrets Act (DTSA), which also provides a remedy in federal court for misappropriation of trade secrets. The DTSA authorizes federal courts to enjoin actual or threatened misappropriation of trade secrets. Such an injunction cannot prevent a person from entering into an employment relationship, however, and any conditions placed on a person's employment must be based on evidence of actual or threatened misappropriation and not merely on information the person knows.

fyi **What Is a Trade Secret?**

A "trade secret" is information, including a formula, pattern, compilation, program, device, method, technique, or process, that:

- Derives independent economic value, actual or potential, from not being generally known to the public or to other persons who can obtain economic value from its disclosure or use; and
- Is the subject of efforts that are reasonable under the circumstances to maintain its secrecy.

The DTSA also bars federal courts from issuing injunctions that conflict with state law prohibiting restraints on the practice of any lawful trade, profession, or business. Thus, while the DTSA provides a federal court remedy for trade secret misappropriation, California employers should not expect to obtain any broader restrictions on competition by a former employee in federal court than in state court. The DTSA authorizes a federal court to award compensatory damages, plus punitive damages and attorneys' fees where willful or malicious conduct is shown, provided certain employee notice requirements are met (see Section 11.5). The DTSA also authorizes a court to order the seizure of property, under certain extraordinary circumstances, to prevent dissemination of a trade secret.

The DTSA provides protection for whistleblowers who divulge a trade secret in the course of reporting a violation of law to a federal, state, or local government official or to an attorney. The DTSA also requires an employer to provide notice to an employee in any contract or agreement governing the use of a trade secret or other confidential information that the employee will be immune from criminal and civil liability for the disclosure of a trade secret that either:

- Is made in confidence to a law enforcement or government official, or an attorney, solely for the purpose of reporting or investigating a suspected violation of any law; or
- Is made in a complaint or other document filed under seal in a lawsuit or other legal proceeding.

This notice must be included in any agreement executed after the date the DTSA was enacted (May 11, 2016), and failure to include it will prevent an employer from obtaining punitive damages and attorneys' fees in a successful lawsuit for misappropriation of trade secrets under the DTSA. This notice must be provided in the agreement itself or via a cross-reference to a policy document provided to the employee that sets forth the employer's reporting policy for a suspected violation of law.

11.6 Confidentiality Agreements

Confidentiality agreements provide an important measure of protection against former employees competing illegally. Employees may be required to sign a confidentiality agreement as a condition of employment or continued employment, and no additional consideration is required for such an agreement to be enforceable. All employees who have access to trade secrets or other confidential information should be required to sign such an agreement covering the following areas.

Agreement to Keep Trade Secrets Confidential

Employees may be required to agree contractually that during their employment they will not without authorization disclose the employer's trade secrets and confidential business information to any person or entity outside the organization, and that they will not personally use such information in competition with the employer or to the employer's detriment. Employees may also be required to protect the confidentiality of the employer's trade secrets and not reveal them to competitors or other outside parties after they are no longer employed. The confidentiality agreement should include a list of the types of information the employer deems to be trade secrets or confidential business information so that it is clear to the employee what is protected. Just designating information as a trade secret does not make it so, however. It must still meet the legal definition, which requires that it not be generally known and that it be subject to reasonable efforts to maintain its secrecy. A database containing the contact information of customer representatives and those customers' purchasing history might qualify as a trade secret, for example. Mere knowledge, acquired through experience in the industry, of which customers might be interested in purchasing a particular product would not likely qualify.

Agreement Not to Compete While Employed

California law is not clear to the extent which employees who are not officers of a company owe it a duty of loyalty. Historically, California courts have held that such a duty exists on the part of all employees. One federal court in California held, however, that there is no duty of loyalty on the part of employees who are not fiduciaries of a company. That court recognized that employers may contractually prohibit employees from competing or from aiding a competitor while still employed. All confidentiality agreements should include such a provision, therefore.

Agreement to Return All Employer Property upon Termination of Employment

Employees may be contractually required to return all company property and data, without retaining copies or duplicates, upon termination of employment. The confidentiality agreement should specify the types of property and information the employee is likely to have and that will need to be returned, such as notebook computers, personal data assistants or smartphones, hard drives, flash drives, blueprints, designs, formulas, specifications, price lists, customer lists, financial records, marketing materials, client files, and access cards. If employees are allowed to store company information on their personal computers or devices, they should be required to agree to submit these devices to the company for inspection and removal of any company information when their employment terminates.

Agreement Not to Solicit Customers

Employees may not generally be prohibited from soliciting customers of their former employers. California courts are not uniform on the issue, but most are willing to enforce a nonsolicitation of customers provision to protect an employer's trade secrets. In other words, an ex-employee may be prohibited from using the employer's trade secrets to solicit the employer's customers but may not be prohibited from soliciting those customers without the aid of the employer's trade secrets. This is an area that often leads to dispute, as it is not always clear that an employee has used a former employer's trade secrets in obtaining new business from a customer. Merely contacting a customer of the former employer with whom the former employee regularly dealt would not typically involve use of trade secrets. Quoting that customer a lower price though use of a former employer's confidential product cost and pricing information, by contrast, would be much more vulnerable to attack. Similarly, contacting all customers on a former employer's confidential customer list to ask them for a chance to do business with them would likely be found to violate an anti-solicitation provision.

Agreement Not to Recruit Employees

The lawfulness and enforceability of a contractual provision prohibiting a former employee from soliciting employees of the former employer to leave their employment is presently in question. For many years, these provisions were considered lawful, so long as they were for a reasonable period of time (no more than two years) and were designed to protect a legitimate business interest of the former employer such as the time and cost spent assembling and training employees. In *AMN Healthcare, Inc. v. AYA Healthcare Services, Inc.* (2018), however, the court held that such a provision in a contract covering recruiters of travel nurses was unlawful under Section 16600 of the Business & Professions Code because it amounted to a restraint of the nurse recruiters to practice their occupation. Because of the unique context of the *AMN Healthcare* case it is unclear whether a court would reach the same conclusion where the former employee's job was not recruiting employees. Until this issue is clarified, therefore, there is some risk that an employee forced to sign a confidentiality agreement containing a nonsolicitation of employees provision, or an employee who refuses to sign such an agreement and is met with adverse consequences as the result, might pursue a claim against the employer for unfair business practices.

Note also that an agreement among competing firms not to hire one another's employees might be subject to criminal prosecution for violation of federal antitrust laws.

Assignment of Interest in Inventions

An employee may be required to assign to their employer all interest in any inventions (a) that are made with the employer's equipment, supplies, facilities, trade secrets, or time; (b) that relate, at the time of conception or of reduction to practice, to the business of the employer or the employer's research and development activity; (c) that result from any work performed by the employee for the employer; or (d) that were made by the employee using the employer's trade secrets after termination of employment with the employer. The employee should additionally be required to disclose to the employer all inventions that the employee makes during their employment with the employer, as well as all patent applications filed by the employee during employment or within a reasonable period of time after termination. The assignment of inventions provision must reference Labor Code Section 2870, a copy of which should be attached to the agreement. The Section 2870 reference should state that the employee is not required to assign to the employer any invention for which no equipment, supplies, facilities, or trade secrets of the employer were used; that was developed entirely on the employee's own time; that does not relate to the business of the employer or the employer's actual or demonstrably anticipated research or development; and that does not result from any work performed by the employee for the employer.

No Prior Agreements or Restrictions

An employee may be required to disclose any existing agreements or restrictions with any prior employers that might prevent the employee from performing their duties as an employee of the current employer. Though a noncompete agreement with a prior employer would not be enforceable in California, it is important to know whether a new employee is bound by a nondisclosure or nonsolicitation agreement with a prior employer that might be violated by the employee in the current job. The confidentiality agreement should require disclosure of all such agreements and restrictions. It should also state that the employee has returned all property, trade secrets, and confidential information belonging to others and is not in possession of any such items, as well as an acknowledgment by the employee that they are not permitted to use trade secrets or confidential information of any prior employer in the current job. The agreement may further contain indemnification language under which the employee agrees to indemnify and defend the employer against all claims by third parties as a result of the employee's failure to disclose prior agreements or restrictions or the employee's use of a prior employer's trade secrets or confidential information in the current employment.

11.7 Hiring Employees of a Competitor

There are no legal restrictions against hiring at-will employees of a competitor, unless such hiring is done via unlawful methods such as the use of fraudulent or deceptive means, or use of the competitor's trade secrets or confidential information. An example of the latter would be the use of a confidential list of a competitor's employee salaries to lure away the competitor's employees by offering them more money. In addition, an employer that hires employees from a competitor with knowledge that those employees are presently under an unexpired contract for a specific term may be liable for tortious interference with contract. In industries in which such contracts are common, employers should therefore inquire of prospective hires whether they presently are under contract with their current employers.

CHAPTER 12

Employment Discrimination

California law prohibits employers of five or more employees from discriminating against applicants or employees on the basis of:

- Race or color;
- National origin or ancestry;
- Age;
- Sex;
- Sexual orientation;
- Gender, gender identity, or gender expression;
- Religion;
- Physical or mental disability;
- Medical condition;
- Genetic information;
- Marital status;
- Reproductive health decision-making;
- Military or veteran status; or
- Cannabis use.

Discrimination based on any combination of these protected classifications is also prohibited. The bar on discrimination applies to hiring, selection for training leading to employment, termination of employment, compensation, benefits, and other terms and conditions of employment. More than just "ultimate acts" such as demotion or termination are subject to the discrimination laws, but there must be a substantial adverse change to the employee's working conditions. Minor acts or events that merely anger or upset an employee are generally not unlawful, but the U.S. Supreme Court has ruled that a forced lateral job transfer – with no change in pay or benefits – may be unlawful if it is based on discriminatory reasons and produces some harm to the employee. Note that California's prohibition against discrimination applies to unpaid interns and volunteers too.

The California Constitution also prohibits discrimination based on sex, race, creed, color, or national or ethnic origin. Employers may be sued for constitutional violations as well, and there is no minimum number of employees required for the California Constitution to apply.

There are three types of employment discrimination. The first is when there is *direct evidence* of discrimination. An example is when an employer terminates a pregnant employee, telling them, "This job is too dangerous for a pregnant woman." Direct evidence cases are rare.

The second type of discrimination case involves *disparate treatment.* This occurs when an employee is treated differently on account of a protected classification. It does not require intentional bias on the part of the employer; a showing of inconsistent treatment of similarly situated employees is usually enough. The employer may defend such a claim by showing either that the employee was not in fact treated differently or that there was a legitimate and nondiscriminatory reason for the inconsistent treatment. The employee may still succeed in proving discrimination if they can show that the employer's explanation was pretextual, that is, that the employer's explanation was not true. For this reason, it is essential that you give the true reason for taking adverse action against an employee or applicant. Often employers will give another reason to avoid a confrontation or to protect the person's feelings. An example is calling a termination for poor performance a "layoff." It is not a layoff if you hire someone to replace the terminated employee, and if the employee learns that they have been replaced following a layoff, they are likely to be able to establish pretext. Examples of disparate treatment may include:

- Giving one employee who fails a drug test a "last chance" while firing another employee of a different race for failing a drug test;
- Firing an employee for failing to meet their sales quota when other employees of different ethnicities have missed their quotas and not been fired; or
- Suspending a female employee for an insubordinate outburst toward a supervisor when a male employee received only a warning for similar conduct.

To prevail in a disparate treatment lawsuit the plaintiff must prove that their protected status was a *substantial motivating factor* in the employer's decision to terminate the employee or take other adverse action against them.

The third type of discrimination is *disparate impact.* This occurs when a seemingly neutral practice has a harsher impact on a protected classification of employees. Once such a harsher impact is shown (usually via statistics), the employer may defend the practice by showing that it is related to the job and consistent with business necessity. The employee may still succeed in proving discrimination, however, if they can show that a less discriminatory alternative exists. Examples of disparate impact may include:

- A blanket policy of not hiring job applicants with criminal convictions regardless of the relevance of the conviction to the job; or
- A requirement that applicants have a high school diploma or a college degree for a job when a diploma or degree is not necessary for the employee to perform the job.

Aside from these general considerations, specific rules apply to discrimination based on certain protected classifications. These are addressed in the remainder of this chapter.

12.1 Age

Federal and state age discrimination laws cover persons who are age 40 and older. It is not illegal to favor older workers over younger workers, and a requirement that employees be at least 18 years of age is lawful.

Employers must be careful in hiring not to express a preference only for younger applicants. You should not state a preference for a "recent graduate," for example, and applicants should not be asked their date of high school graduation. You may, however, state that a job is "entry level" or that "no experience is required."

Age discrimination claims often arise in reductions in force. California law provides that use of salary as a criterion for selecting employees for layoff may amount to age discrimination if older workers are adversely affected as a group. When selecting employees to be laid off, therefore, do not use compensation as a selection criterion. Nor should you use an employee's proximity to likely retirement as a criterion for layoff because this is an age-related factor.

A mandatory retirement age is not permitted for most jobs. The exceptions are the following:

- Firefighters and police officers over the age of 55 may be required to retire at such age as is established by a bona fide state or local government retirement policy.
- Employees who have worked in an executive capacity for at least two years before retirement and who will receive an annual retirement benefit of at least $44,000 may be required to retire at age 65.

An employer may lawfully offer voluntary retirement incentives to employees or groups of employees so long as there are no adverse consequences for employees who choose not to retire. Employees who elect such an incentive should be required to sign a release of claims that is compliant with the Older Workers Benefit Protection Act (see Section 18.2).

12.2 Cannabis Use

California employers may not discriminate against an applicant or employee for that person's use of cannabis off the job and away from the workplace. Employers also may not inquire of job applicants about their prior use of cannabis. The law does not permit an employee to possess, be impaired by, or use cannabis on the job, and it does not affect an employer's rights and obligations to maintain a drug-free workplace.

The law also prohibits an employer from discriminating against an applicant or employee for testing positive for non-psychoactive cannabis metabolites in their hair, blood, urine, or other bodily fluids. Testing that detects tetrahydrocannabinol (THC), the chemical compound in cannabis that causes psychoactive effects and potential impairment, is still allowed, although such tests are not yet widely available.

The non-discrimination mandates and testing prohibition in this law do not apply to employees in the building and construction trades, to persons required by federal, state, or local laws to be tested for controlled substances (including those covered by the Department of Transportation's drug testing requirements), or to persons hired for positions requiring a federal government background investigation or security clearance.

12.3 Disability and Medical Condition

California law prohibits discrimination based on physical or mental disability. This topic is covered separately in Chapter 14.

California law also prohibits discrimination based on "medical condition," but not all medical conditions are covered. Rather, only cancer and genetic characteristics are covered by this prohibition.

12.4 Gender

Gender, as defined in California's anti-discrimination law, includes a person's gender identity and gender expression. Gender identity means a person's identification as male, female, a gender different than the person's sex at birth, or transgender. Gender expression means a person's gender-related appearance and behavior whether or not stereotypically associated with the person's sex assigned at birth. Transgender refers to a person whose gender identity differs from the person's sex at birth. A transgender person may or may not identify as transsexual, and no surgery or hormone treatments are required in California for an employee to qualify as transgender.

California law protects transgender applicants and employees from discrimination in employment. Transgender employees are also protected from harassment based on their gender identity or gender expression. Exclusion or segregation of transgender persons cannot be justified by "customer preference" or other employees' religious objections.

A transgender employee should be addressed by their chosen name and pronoun (that is, "he," "she," or "they"). You can require evidence of a legal name change before changing an employee's official employment record, however. California courts offer a streamlined name-change procedure where the change is the result of a gender transition. Where a transgender employee has changed names, you can also require proof of a name change with the Social Security Administration before changing payroll records.

California law protects transgender applicants and employees from discrimination in employment. Transgender employees are also protected from harassment based on their gender identity or gender expression.

Which Restroom?

Although previously there was some confusion over which restroom a transgender employee should use, federal and state law is now clear that employees must be allowed to use restrooms, locker rooms, and changing rooms that correspond to their gender identity. Objections by other employees to a transgender employee's use of their restroom or locker room are not a valid basis for prohibiting such use. Of course, you may discipline any employee, transgender or not, for misconduct in restrooms or locker rooms.

All single-occupancy restrooms must be identified as "all gender" and be universally accessible. Single-occupancy restrooms are those with no more than one toilet and one urinal, and with a locking mechanism controlled by the user. While you may make a unisex restroom available for transgender employees, you may not require its use.

Dress Codes

You may enforce dress codes, but you must allow transgender employees to follow the dress code that aligns with their gender identity. You may prohibit wearing of certain items for safety reasons (dangling earrings or high heels, for example) so long as the prohibition applies to all employees.

Training

Managers must be trained regarding the prevention of harassment and discrimination against transgender employees and applicants. A portion of the required Assembly Bill 1825 (AB 1825) training must be devoted to transgender issues so that managers do not unwittingly discriminate, and so they will be alert for incidents of coworker harassment. Sensitivity training for employees might be considered as well if transgender employees are a part of your workforce.

Poster

Employers must post a "Transgender Rights in the Workplace" poster. It may be accessed at https://calcivilrights.ca.gov/Posters.

12.5 Genetic Information

Both federal (the Genetic Information Nondiscrimination Act, or GINA) and California law prohibit discrimination based on genetic information. The definition of genetic information includes any of the following:

- The individual's genetic tests;
- The genetic tests of family members of the individual;
- The manifestation of a disease or disorder in family members of the individual; and
- Any request for, or receipt of, genetic services, or participation in clinical research that includes genetic services, by an individual or any family member of the individual.

Genetic information does not include a person's age or sex.

12.6 Marital Status

Marital status means a person's status as married, unmarried, separated, divorced, or widowed, and this includes marriage to a same-sex spouse.

It is unlawful to consider the marital status or the employment status of the spouse of an employee or applicant in making employment decisions. You may ask whether an applicant is the spouse of a current employee, but you may not use that fact in determining whether to hire the person. For business reasons of supervision, safety, security, or morale you may:

- Refuse to place one spouse under the direct supervision of the other spouse; and
- Refuse to place both spouses in the same department, division, or facility if the work involves potential conflicts of interest or other hazards greater for married couples than for other persons.

You may ask an applicant to disclose all other names used so that you can obtain a complete background check, even though the applicant's maiden name or prior married name(s) might be disclosed. You may not require a female employee to use their husband's name.

12.7 Military or Veteran Status

"Military or veteran status" is defined as a member or veteran of the U.S. armed forces, the reserves, or the National Guard. The addition of this protected status under California law was intended to address discrimination against veterans primarily in hiring in light of potential employer concerns that veterans may be too old, not willing to take orders from younger employees, or suffering from posttraumatic stress disorder or other service-related conditions.

The federal Uniformed Services Employment and Reemployment Rights Act (USERRA) provides detailed requirements for the re-employment of a member of the military who took a leave of absence to perform military service (see Section 15.7).

12.8 National Origin or Ancestry

"National origin" refers to the nation of an employee or applicant's birth; "ancestry" refers to the nation in which an employee's parents, grandparents, or other ancestors were born. In addition, national origin may additionally refer to:

- Physical, cultural, or linguistic characteristics associated with a national origin group;
- Marriage to or association with persons of a national origin group;
- Tribal affiliation;
- Membership in or association with an organization identified with or seeking to promote the interests of a national origin group;
- Attendance or participation in schools, churches, temples, mosques, or other religious institutions generally used by persons of a national origin group; or
- A name that is associated with a national origin group.

A "national origin group" includes ethnic groups, geographic places of origin, and countries that are not presently in existence.

Language Restrictions

Among the national origin discrimination issues that arise today are those that involve rules on language use. California law provides that an employer may not limit or prohibit use of any language in the workplace unless:

- The language restriction is justified by business necessity;
- The language restriction is narrowly tailored; and

- Employees are notified of the time and circumstances when the language restriction applies and the consequences for violating that language restriction.

"Business necessity" for purposes of this law means that the language restriction is necessary for the safe and efficient operation of the business, the language restriction effectively fulfills the business purpose it is supposed to serve, and there is no alternative that would serve the business purpose equally well and have a lesser discriminatory impact. It is not sufficient that a language restriction merely promotes business convenience or is due to customer or coworker preference. An English-only requirement, moreover, is not lawfully applicable during nonworking time such as meal and rest breaks.

You may not discriminate against an applicant or employee whose accent makes them difficult to understand unless the ability to speak clearly in English is necessary for the job. For example, a front desk clerk at a hotel may be required to speak and understand English clearly because their failure to do so could lead to guest service problems and potential safety issues. A housekeeper at the same hotel, by contrast, would not have to speak and understand English clearly to do their job, particularly if the employee and their supervisor are fluent in the same language. You may ask a job applicant about their ability to speak, read, and write any language, including English, if justified by business necessity.

Height and Weight Requirements

Where height or weight requirements create an adverse impact on the basis of national origin they are unlawful, unless the employer can demonstrate that they are job related and justified by business necessity. Where such a requirement is job related and justified by business necessity, it is still unlawful if the applicant or employee can prove that the purpose of the requirement can be achieved as effectively through less discriminatory means. Any minimum or maximum height or weight restrictions therefore should be carefully tailored to the requirements of the job.

Immigration-Related Practices

California has several laws protecting undocumented immigrants. These include a prohibition against requiring an applicant or employee to present a driver's license, unless possession of a driver's license is required by law or required by the employer for a lawful reason. For example, applicants for a position involving driving of vehicles may be required to show a valid driver's license. New hires may also be required to produce a driver's license (or other acceptable forms of identification) in the course of completing the Form I-9. An employer may not, however, discriminate against an applicant or employee based on that person having the type of California driver's license issued to undocumented immigrants.

Employers also are prohibited from including a statement in a job advertisement, posting, application, or other material that an applicant must have a driver's license unless (1) the employer reasonably expects driving to be one of the job functions for the position, and (2) the employer reasonably believes that using an alternative form of transportation, such as a ride hailing service, a taxi, carpooling, bicycling or walking, would not be comparable in travel time or cost.

California law also prohibits an employer from taking adverse action against an employee who updates their personal information based on a lawful change of name, Social Security number, or federal employment authorization document. It is not clear whether this law would protect an employee who initially submitted a fake Social Security card or work permit but then later submitted a genuine document, but this seems to be its intent.

California law cannot and does not force employers to employ persons lacking the proper documents, however. New hires who cannot produce the required documents for completion of the I-9 form should not be allowed to start working. Employees who present a work authorization document that later expires should be suspended until they can produce a renewed and valid work authorization document. Note that permanent resident status, once granted, does not expire even though permanent resident cards ("green cards") show an expiration date. An employee whose permanent resident card has expired should not be suspended or required to present a renewed card.

Employees whose work authorization documents expire and are not renewed, or whose documents are found to be forged or fraudulent, should be terminated. The discovery, after an employee has filed an employment lawsuit, that the employee had false immigration documents will not serve as a basis for having the lawsuit dismissed, however.

12.9 Race or Color

Race discrimination includes discrimination based on skin color and characteristics associated with race such as facial hair or hair styles. Hair texture and hairstyles such as braids, locs, and twists are specifically protected. You nonetheless may regulate hair styles and beards when a legitimate health or safety concern exists.

Unlawful race discrimination includes discrimination against an applicant or employee for associating with (or being married to) a person of a different race.

Reverse race discrimination is unlawful as well. Although you should strive to have a diverse workforce, hiring (or considering for hire) persons only of a particular race in the interest of improving diversity is illegal.

12.10 Religion

You may not discriminate against applicants or employees based on their religion or lack of religion. The law protects not only those who are members of organized religions but also those who have sincerely held ethical or moral beliefs. Most religious discrimination issues involve accommodation of religious dress and grooming practices or time off for religious holidays. Your obligation to accommodate religious beliefs and practices is the same in California as your obligation to accommodate a disability. That is, you must engage in an interactive process with the employee, and you must provide a reasonable accommodation unless an undue hardship would result. A typical request for accommodation involves time off for the Sabbath or for a religious holiday. Generally these accommodations should be provided if possible. If the essence of a job requires work on weekends, however (such as a retail sales position), you would not be required to give weekends off to an employee who affiliates with a religion that prohibits working on the Sabbath, particularly if to do so would disrupt operations or produce a substantial inequity for other employees.

Modification of a dress code or grooming standards might be required to accommodate religious beliefs or practices such as the wearing of head scarves or beards. Head scarves or religious jewelry may be prohibited if they pose a direct safety threat and if the employee's duties cannot be modified to eliminate such threat without imposing an undue hardship. For example, if an employee must wear a respirator to safely perform their duties, it might be impossible to accommodate their growing a beard that would interfere with the creation of a seal between their face and the respirator. On the other hand, it would be difficult to argue that accommodation of an employee wearing a head scarf or a cross on a chain in an office environment would be unreasonable. You are not permitted to segregate an employee from other employees or the public as part of an accommodation of a religious dress or grooming practice unless expressly requested by the employee.

Employees do not have a right to impose their religious beliefs on other employees or customers. This includes quoting scripture in emails and instigating discussions of religion or church attendance, especially by managers or supervisors. Employees may also be prohibited from criticizing other employees for their different religious beliefs or their lack of religious belief as well as from condemning coworkers for their moral and lifestyle choices such as living together outside of marriage, marrying someone of the same sex, having an abortion, or using contraception.

Nonprofit religious corporations and associations are not generally covered by California's anti-discrimination laws. They are still covered by federal law, however, except with respect to the employment of individuals of a particular religion to perform work connected with the religious organization's activities. A religious nonprofit corporation that operates an educational institution may restrict employment to members of that religion, but the institution is subject to the laws prohibiting other forms of discrimination. A Catholic school may require that all of its teachers be Catholic and that they adhere to the teachings of the Catholic Church. Such a school would not be free to discriminate based on race, however. Hospitals that are operated by religious organizations but that provide services to persons of other faiths are subject to the laws against discrimination, with the exception of employment of executives and of pastoral-care personnel or others who perform religious duties at the hospital.

12.11 Reproductive Health Decision-making

This includes, but is not limited to, a decision by an applicant or employee to use or access a particular drug, device, product, or medical service for reproductive health.

12.12 Sex

The law against sex discrimination in California covers several topics.

Dress and Grooming Standards

Male and female employees may be required to meet different dress and grooming standards, so long as neither sex is unequally burdened compared with the other sex. For example, men may be required to keep their hair short and may be prohibited from wearing makeup. Women may be required to wear makeup, nail polish, and stockings or pantyhose with skirts (but note that women have the statutory right to wear pants to work in California; see Section 9.5). Visible tattoos and piercings may be regulated or prohibited with respect to both sexes.

Height, Weight, and Attractiveness Standards

Male and female employees or applicants may be required to meet different height and weight standards so long as the standards are proportionally equal and are related to the job. Discrimination based on appearance or attractiveness is not prohibited in California as long as no other protected classification such as age or disability is involved. You may lawfully prefer a more attractive candidate over a less attractive candidate.

Pregnancy

California law prohibits an employer from discriminating against an employee on account of pregnancy or perceived pregnancy. Pregnant employees are entitled to up to four months of job-protected leave for pregnancy, childbirth, or related medical conditions (see Section 15.4). This entitlement to up to four months of leave is per pregnancy.

A pregnant employee who is not on leave is entitled to reasonable accommodations if their health care provider determines that such accommodations are advisable, or if the need for an accommodation is obvious. Such accommodations might include a change of work duties or job restructuring, a reduced work schedule, intermittent leave, a transfer to a less strenuous job, more frequent or longer break periods and restroom breaks, relocation of work areas, closer or reserved parking spaces, seating accommodations, and allowing the employee to drink water while working. Note that while you need not eliminate an essential function of a job for a disabled employee, in accommodating a pregnant employee you might have to eliminate an essential function temporarily if such amounts to a reasonable accommodation.

You may not require a pregnant employee to take a leave of absence if they have not requested one. Nor may you transfer a pregnant employee to another position (such as a less strenuous job) against their will unless they are on a reduced work schedule or taking intermittent leave. Such an alternative position must have the same rate of pay and benefits as the employee's regular job, but it need not have the same duties.

You must provide a reasonable accommodation, if needed, for pregnancy-related conditions such as fertility and infertility treatments and the termination of a pregnancy. A California court has held that procedures to retrieve eggs for freezing or donation are not covered by the law prohibiting pregnancy discrimination, however.

You must post in a conspicuous place a notice titled "Your Rights and Obligations as a Pregnant Employee." A copy of the notice may be found at https://calcivilrights.ca.gov/wp-content/uploads/sites/32/2023/01/Your-Rights-and-Obligations-as-a-Pregnant-Employee_ENG.pdf.

Breastfeeding

California law prohibits discrimination against breastfeeding employees. Employers must also provide a reasonable amount of break time (which may coincide with the employee's statutorily required rest breaks) for an employee to express breast milk for an infant child as well as provide a room, other than a toilet stall, near the employee's work area for the purpose of expressing breast milk in private.

12.13 Sexual Orientation

California law prohibits discrimination based on sexual orientation, which is defined as heterosexuality, homosexuality, and bisexuality.

12.14 Bona Fide Occupational Qualifications

California law recognizes the bona fide occupational qualification (BFOQ) defense in certain narrow circumstances. When an employer seeks to exclude an entire group of individuals based on a protected classification (sex or religion, for example), it must prove that such exclusion is reasonably necessary to the operation of the business, that all or substantially all of the excluded individuals are unable to safely and efficiently perform the job in question, and that it is impossible or highly impractical (a) to consider whether each person excluded is able to safely and efficiently perform the job and (b) to rearrange job responsibilities to avoid excluding all individuals in the protected classification.

Customer preference for employees of a particular race, sex, or other classification will not qualify as a BFOQ. Nor will the fact that members of one sex traditionally have been hired to perform the job, or the necessity of having to provide separate restroom or locker room facilities for both sexes. Personal privacy considerations may justify a BFOQ when:

- The job involves observing others in the nude or conducting body searches;
- It would be offensive to prevailing social standards to have an individual of the opposite sex present; and
- It is detrimental to the mental or physical welfare of persons being observed or searched to have someone of the opposite sex present.

Given the difficulty of establishing a BFOQ, you should seek guidance of legal counsel before implementing a BFOQ.

CHAPTER 13

Harassment

The laws prohibiting workplace harassment grew out of the laws prohibiting discrimination, as harassment is deemed a form of unlawful discrimination. Today the laws prohibiting harassment are distinct in many ways from the laws against discrimination, with one exception: Both are tied to the same protected classifications. The term "harassment" has a much broader meaning in popular usage than in employment law. The same goes for the term "hostile working environment." Many employees think they have a hostile working environment, and the basis for a lawsuit, because they have a demanding boss or unfriendly coworkers, but under the law the term has a much narrower meaning.

fyi ▸ What Is the Legal Definition of a "Hostile Working Environment"?

The term "hostile working environment" was coined by the Equal Employment Opportunity Commission in 1980 to describe the form of unlawful sexual harassment that does not involve submission to sexual conduct as a condition of employment. In other words, sexual language, jokes, insults, gestures, and touching can amount to a "hostile working environment," and thus unlawful sexual harassment, if they are sufficiently severe or pervasive as to alter an employee's working conditions and create an abusive working environment. The U.S. Supreme Court adopted this definition of a hostile working environment in *Meritor Savings Bank v. Vinson* (1986).

Today, employees often consider demanding or unpleasant bosses, rude or gossipy coworkers, difficult customers, the pressure of meeting deadlines or production quotas, harsh criticism, or "unfair" discipline or performance reviews to amount to "harassment" or a "hostile working environment," and the potential basis for a lawsuit. This is not correct. Only if harassment is tied to a protected classification such as race, sex, or national origin will it be potentially unlawful. As one California appellate court in *Doe v. Department of Corrections* (2019) put it, "workplaces can be stressful and relationships between supervisors and their subordinates can often be contentious," but the law against harassment was "not designed to make workplaces more collegial; its purpose is to eliminate more insidious behavior like discrimination and harassment based on protected characteristics."

In addition, claims of unlawful harassment cannot be based on ordinary management decisions such as work assignments, office assignments, performance evaluations, deciding who will and who will not attend meetings, enforcing workplace rules, and the like. Even if a manager performs these tasks in a manner that is perceived as insensitive, arbitrary, or unfair, it does not make the manager's conduct unlawful harassment.

Sometimes an employee will complain of being "harassed" based on a protected classification because she received disciplinary action, a negative evaluation, or some other unfavorable treatment when other employees outside the protected classification did not. Such might be the basis for a claim of unlawful *discrimination*, if similarly-situated employees were treated differently without justification, but not of unlawful *harassment*.

13.1 The Legal Standards

Harassment is potentially unlawful in California only if it is based on one or more of the protected classifications under the anti-discrimination laws:

- Race or color;
- National origin or ancestry;
- Age;
- Sex;
- Sexual orientation;
- Gender, gender identity, or gender expression;
- Religion;
- Physical or mental disability;
- Medical condition;
- Genetic information;
- Marital status;
- Reproductive health decision-making;
- Military or veteran status; and
- Cannabis use.

Harassment based on one of these protected classifications is unlawful if it is ***severe*** or ***pervasive***. This means that one serious incident, such as a sexual assault or a racial slur involving use of the "N" word, will be sufficient to establish a violation of law, but for less serious misconduct, such as off-color jokes or most racial or ethnic insults, more than one incident will likely be required. As the misconduct increases in seriousness, fewer incidents are required to establish a violation.

Harassment must be ***unwelcome*** to be unlawful. For harassment to have been "welcomed" means more than just that the target of the harassment went along with it or failed to complain; the target must have instigated the conduct.

Finally, to be unlawful, harassing conduct must be offensive as viewed from the perspective of a *reasonable person* in the same protected classification as the person complaining. Conduct that would be offensive only to a hypersensitive person is not illegal. For example, an employee telling a coworker "I like your new hair style" would not ordinarily be deemed offensive by a reasonable person and would therefore not qualify as unlawful harassment. On the other hand, an employee's use of a racial slur to refer to a coworker would likely be found offensive by reasonable persons of the coworker's race. The laws against harassment in California apply to all employers with one or more employees (unlike California's laws against discrimination and retaliation, which apply to employers of five or more employees). Also unlike under California's discrimination and retaliation laws, employees may be held personally liable for unlawful harassment.

Independent contractors, vendors, customers, unpaid interns, and volunteers, in addition to employees and applicants, are covered by California's laws against harassment. Likewise, employees are protected from unlawful harassment by customers, vendors, and independent contractors.

The employer will be held strictly liable for harassment committed by managers and supervisors. The employer will be held liable for harassment committed by coworkers or nonemployees if it knew or should have known of the harassment and failed to take immediate and appropriate corrective action.

There is no constitutional right to free speech in private workplaces that protects the right of employees to use language or make statements that violate the laws against unlawful harassment.

13.2 Sexual Harassment

The U.S. Equal Employment Opportunity Commission defines sexual harassment as "unwelcome sexual advances, requests for sexual favors, and other verbal or physical conduct of a sexual nature." There are two types of sexual harassment.

Hostile environment harassment involves conduct that interferes with the target's ability to do their job. It may consist of jokes, comments, propositions, emails, text messages, cartoons, displaying or viewing of sexually related pictures or websites, unwanted touching, multiple requests for dates, derogatory comments, and sex or gender-based insults. Harassing conduct need not be based on sexual desire, and same-sex as well as opposite-sex harassment may be illegal.

Quid pro quo harassment involves an express or implied promise of a job benefit in exchange for sexual favors, or an express or implied threat of some job detriment if sexual favors are not granted. Quid pro quo harassment typically occurs in the context of a supervisor-subordinate dating relationship. Decades ago, quid pro quo cases often involved managers imposing themselves sexually on or making blatant sexual demands of their subordinates. Today, quid pro quo claims typically arise after a manager and a subordinate have commenced—and ended—a dating relationship. Such claims may also arise if a manager or supervisor invites a subordinate out on a date even if sexual conduct neither occurs nor is even suggested. Managers and supervisors, therefore, should be cautioned against inviting subordinates on dates or social encounters after hours because, should the invitation be declined and the subordinate later experience some negative job action, a quid pro quo harassment claim is likely to arise.

The laws against sexual harassment apply after hours as well as during working time. A manager's sexual advances or comments made while socializing with subordinates after work, or during business travel, can just as easily be the basis for a sexual harassment claim as if the conduct occurred in the workplace. California's harassment laws apply to harassment occurring on business travel out of state because it affects the employee's working conditions in California. Managers must understand that they are on duty 24/7 and that they can create liability for themselves and their employer by the use of poor judgment in relating to their subordinates during business travel or nonworking time.

Contrary to the advertising slogan, what happens in Vegas can still find its way back to a California courtroom.

13.3 Coworker Dating and "Love Contracts"

Dating or sexual relationships between coworkers can lead to sexual harassment claims. A relationship between peer employees may be distracting to the employees and disruptive to the workplace. Relationships between a manager and a subordinate may in addition create potential liability for quid pro quo harassment claims as well as complaints by employees not involved with the boss that the boss's paramour is receiving favored treatment.

Employers should therefore have a policy addressing dating and sexual relationships between employees. Employees who are involved in relationships with coworkers should be instructed that their relationships must not become a source of disruption of the workplace due to conduct such as public displays of affection, bringing arguments and relationship conflicts into the workplace, or wasting working time discussing personal issues.

Managers should be prohibited from becoming involved in dating or sexual relationships with nonmanagement employees due to the potential for such relationships to lead to disruption, sexual harassment claims, and complaints of favoritism. Employees should be required to report such relationships to management and should be informed that they may be terminated or disciplined for violating the policy. In spite of such a policy, however, some employees are still likely to pursue romantic relationships with one another.

A common scenario is when a valued manager and an excellent employee become involved in a relationship, and it does not make good business sense to fire them. One means of protecting the company in the event of such a supervisor-subordinate dating relationship is to have both parties sign a "love contract." This is a document in which both employees acknowledge that:

- Their relationship is wholly consensual and not the result of any pressure or coercion;
- The employer has a policy against harassment (which should be attached to the agreement);
- They understand to whom they should bring complaints of harassment should it occur;
- They must keep their relationship discreet while at work; and
- They agree to avoid conflicts of interest such as the manager evaluating the subordinate for promotion or pay increases.

Such an agreement, once signed, will be useful in defending against claims that the relationship was coerced or involuntary should it end and the jilted party sue.

13.4 Other Forms of Unlawful Harassment

Hostile working environment harassment based on other protected classifications (for example, race, religion, national origin) may also be unlawful. The same legal standards apply that apply to sexual harassment claims; that is, the conduct must be severe or pervasive, must be unwelcome, and must be offensive to a reasonable person in the same protected classification as the complaining employee. Such unlawful harassment may include:

- Racial slurs (including use of the "N" word);
- Ethnic slurs;
- Religious slurs;
- Criticism of lifestyle choices as, for example, not being "moral" or "Christian";
- Proselytization;
- Jokes or insults about religious beliefs, practices or attire;
- Jokes or insults about Latinos or Hispanics;
- Jokes or insults about Arabs or Muslims;
- Jokes or insults about or directed at gay persons (including negative comments about same-sex marriage);

- Jokes or insults about people with disabilities; and
- Pranks involving nooses, "KKK" symbols, or vandalism involving swastikas or racist graffiti.

Such unlawful harassment might also include physical altercations or assaults, threats, emails, text messages, cartoons, pictures, and the like if relating to one or more protected classifications.

If management hears or sees such harassment occurring, the employer will be deemed under law to have known about it, leading to liability for the harassment. It is important, therefore, that managers and supervisors understand that they must be vigilant for incidents of harassment and take prompt corrective action when it occurs. Such action might include verbal coaching for minor violations ("We don't talk that way about each other here") to written reprimands, suspension, and even termination for more serious violations.

"We were just joking around" is not a valid defense to a harassment claim. It does not matter that comments were made in jest and that no harm was intended.

13.5 Failure to Prevent Discrimination and Harassment

California employers must take all reasonable steps to prevent and promptly correct discriminatory and harassing conduct from occurring. It is a separate violation of California law for an employer to fail to do so, but such a violation can be established only if a claim of unlawful discrimination or harassment is also proven. You fulfill your obligation under this law by:

- Distributing a policy against discrimination and harassment to all employees;
- Distributing the California Civil Rights Department's (CRD) CRD-185 brochure or an equivalent document to all employees that, among other things, describes how employees may contact the CRD to file a complaint;
- Posting the required CRD poster in the workplace;
- Promptly and objectively investigating all complaints of discrimination or harassment;
- Taking prompt and effective corrective action if unlawful discrimination or harassment occurs; and
- For employers of 5 or more employees, providing the training to managers, supervisors, and nonsupervisory employees that is required under California law.

Under federal law, an employer sued for hostile working environment harassment may avoid liability by showing (a) that it exercised reasonable care to prevent and promptly correct any sexually harassing behavior, and (b) that the employee unreasonably failed to take advantage of any preventive or corrective opportunities or to avoid harm otherwise. This is known as the *Faragher/Ellerth* defense, named after the two U.S. Supreme Court cases in which the defense was recognized.

The *Faragher/Ellerth* defense does not apply under California law. A different variation of it is available that does not permit an employer to avoid liability for harassment but which might limit a plaintiff's damages. If an employer shows (a) that it took reasonable steps to prevent and correct workplace harassment, (b) that the employee unreasonably failed to use the preventive and corrective measures provided, and (c) that reasonable use of the preventive and corrective measures provided would have prevented at least some of the harm that the employee suffered, then the amount of damages the employee may recover is reduced accordingly.

Therefore, not only are you required by California law to take steps to prevent and correct unlawful harassment, but your doing so could provide an important means of limiting a plaintiff's damages in some harassment lawsuits. When you have taken all the steps outlined above, yet the employee failed to complain about harassment before quitting, a good argument may be made that the plaintiff should not recover lost wages because they should have remained on the job and complained under the company's policy.

13.6 Drafting an Effective Policy Against Harassment

All California employers must distribute to all employees a policy against harassment. This may be included in the employee handbook or distributed as a separate document. A detailed description of what such a policy should include may be found in Section 4.5. One important feature of such a policy is that it must provide employees with an effective means of complaining about harassment, particularly when a company has multiple locations or when the harasser is the employee's supervisor. Instructions should be included regarding how to contact HR to lodge a complaint, or if the company does not have an HR person or department, the policy should direct employees to complain to some other official outside the chain of command, such as the controller or chief financial officer. Alternatively, a small employer without an onsite HR department should consider contracting with an outside HR consulting firm for an employee hotline service to which complaints of harassment may be directed. Each manager or supervisor must be given a copy of your policy against harassment and must sign a receipt for the policy indicating that the manager or supervisor has read the policy. A statement of your policy that is separate from your employee handbook therefore should be provided to managers and supervisors.

13.7 Harassment Training

Employers of five or more employees (not all of whom must be in California) must conduct training of their supervisors and managers on sexual harassment and other forms of harassment every two years. Newly hired or newly promoted supervisors and managers must receive training within six months of hire or promotion. The California Civil Rights Department (CRD) has developed an interactive video course for supervisors and managers (it may be found at https://calcivilrights.ca.gov/shpt/). You are not required to utilize the CRD training, however.

The training must be at least two hours in duration and may be presented in person in a classroom setting or online in an interactive webinar or e-learning format. Trainers must meet one of the following criteria:

- Attorneys admitted to practice for at least two years and whose practice includes discrimination and harassment law.
- HR professionals with at least two years of experience in training employees regarding harassment, responding to or investigating harassment complaints, or advising employers or employees on prevention of harassment, discrimination, and retaliation.
- Professors or instructors in law schools, colleges, or universities who have either an advanced degree or California teaching credential and at least two years of experience teaching about discrimination and harassment law.

The content of the training must include:

- Definitions of sexual and other forms of harassment under federal and California law;
- That harassment, discrimination, and retaliation are prohibited by federal and California law;
- Types of conduct that constitute unlawful harassment;
- Remedies available for harassment victims who prevail in lawsuits;
- The potential for employees to be held personally liable for harassment;
- Strategies to prevent harassment in the workplace;
- Supervisors' obligation to report harassment, discrimination, and retaliation when they become aware of it;
- Practical examples, such as role plays or case studies, involving examples of harassment, discrimination, and retaliation;
- The limited confidentiality of the complaint process;
- To whom victims of harassment should report such harassment;
- The employer's obligation to conduct a prompt investigation of all harassment complaints and to take effective remedial action when harassment has been found to have occurred;

- What to do if the supervisor is accused of harassment; and
- The essential elements of an effective policy against harassment.

"Abusive Conduct"

In addition, the training must include a review of the definition of "abusive conduct" under California law, which is essentially bullying conduct "with malice" that a reasonable person would find hostile or offensive and that is not related to an employer's legitimate business interests (including performance standards). Examples of abusive conduct may include repeated infliction of verbal abuse, such as the use of derogatory remarks, insults, or epithets; verbal or physical conduct that a reasonable person would find threatening, intimidating, or humiliating; or the gratuitous sabotage or undermining of a person's work performance. The training should include an explanation of the negative effects that abusive conduct has on the victim of the conduct as well as on others in the workplace. The discussion should also include information about the detrimental consequences of abusive conduct on employers—including a reduction in productivity and morale. Finally, the training should emphasize that a single act does not constitute abusive conduct unless the act is especially severe or egregious. Notably, bullying or abusive conduct is not unlawful in California even though the topic must be covered in mandatory harassment training.

Gender and Sexual Orientation

The training must include a component on discrimination and harassment based on gender identity, gender expression, and sexual orientation. The training should address what it means to be transgender as well as issues involving transgender employees such as restroom use, dress codes, and use of an employee's preferred name and pronouns.

Practical Examples

For training of supervisors and managers to be most effective, it should not only cover those topics specifically required by law but in addition it should address the types of practical situations that may lead to complaints of harassment. For example, supervisors and managers should be reminded of the substantial risks involved in:

- Dating or becoming sexually involved with subordinates or other nonmanagement employees;
- Socializing with subordinates outside of work, especially where alcohol is involved;
- Texting subordinates after hours or on weekends, especially about nonwork matters;

- Inviting subordinates into managers' homes, or managers visiting subordinates in their homes;
- Lending money to subordinates;
- Becoming involved in subordinates' personal lives;
- Commenting on political or lifestyle issues that others may perceive as indicating bias against persons in protected classifications (such as making comments about same-sex marriage or enforcement of the immigration laws); and
- Inviting subordinates to join in prayer or attend religious services.

Managers also should be reminded that, as managers they are always "on duty" and can create liability for themselves and their employer for harassment committed outside of regular business hours.

Employee Training

Nonsupervisory employees of employers with five or more employees must receive one hour of sexual harassment training. Such training must be provided to new employees within six months of hire and the training must be repeated every two years thereafter. Training may be conducted for employees individually or in groups, and it may be completed in shorter segments so long as a total of one hour of training is provided. Like the training program for managers and supervisors it must also cover abusive conduct, gender identity, gender expression, and sexual orientation. The CRD has developed an optional interactive video course for nonsupervisory employees similar to the one that is available for supervisors and managers (it may be found at https://calcivilrights.ca.gov/shpt/).

"Bystander Intervention" Training

An employer may, but is not required to, provide "bystander intervention" training that includes information and practical guidance on how to enable bystanders to recognize potentially problematic behaviors and to motivate bystanders to take action when they observe problematic behaviors. The training and education may include exercises to provide bystanders with the skills and confidence to intervene as appropriate and to provide bystanders with resources they can call upon that support their intervention.

Training Records

You must keep for at least two years records of harassment training provided, including sign-in sheets or electronic documentation that training has been completed, copies of certificates of completion of the training provided to participants, and a copy of the training materials used.

CHAPTER 14

Accommodating Employees with Disabilities

Many employers find the law regarding disability discrimination and the duty to accommodate employees and applicants with disabilities to be confounding. Employees with almost any health condition may qualify as disabled, and the "interactive process" of accommodating a disabled employee or applicant can seem endless.

When the federal Americans with Disabilities Act (ADA) was enacted in 1990, it was designed to apply to persons with significant disabilities such as deafness, blindness, and mobility impairments. California's version of the law provided broader coverage, and then Congress broadened the ADA in the ADA Amendments Act in 2008 because of its concern that too many plaintiffs were losing their ADA lawsuits. In so doing, Congress decreed that the focus of ADA lawsuits should no longer be on whether the plaintiff is disabled but rather on whether the employer discriminated against or reasonably accommodated the plaintiff. Thereafter, California law became broader still as its regulations governing disability discrimination were amended.

14.1 Who Is Disabled?

Initially, to qualify for protection under the anti-discrimination laws, an employee or applicant must have a physical or mental disability.

Physical Disability

A physical disability means any physiological disease, disorder, condition, cosmetic disfigurement, or anatomical loss that affects one or more of the following body systems:

- Neurological;
- Immunological;
- Musculoskeletal;
- Special sense organs;

- Respiratory, including speech organs;
- Cardiovascular;
- Reproductive;
- Digestive;
- Genitourinary;
- Hemic and lymphatic;
- Skin; or
- Endocrine.

Such a disease, disorder, condition, cosmetic disfigurement, or anatomical loss must also *limit a major life activity* (this is addressed further below). Physical disabilities specifically include deafness, blindness, partially or completely missing limbs, mobility impairments requiring the use of a wheelchair, cerebral palsy, and chronic or episodic conditions such as HIV/AIDS, hepatitis, epilepsy, seizure disorder, diabetes, multiple sclerosis, and heart disease.

Mental Disability

A mental disability is any psychological disorder or condition, such as intellectual disability, organic brain syndrome, emotional or mental illness, or specific learning disability that limits a major life activity. Mental disabilities include autism spectrum disorders, schizophrenia, and chronic or episodic conditions such as clinical depression, bipolar disorder, posttraumatic stress disorder (PTSD), and obsessive-compulsive disorder.

"Limits"

Unlike under the ADA, which requires that a physical or mental impairment *substantially limit* a major life activity, California law requires only that a physical or mental disorder or condition "limit" a major life activity. A physical or mental disorder or condition limits a major life activity if it makes the achievement of the major life activity "difficult." This requires an individualized assessment that may consider what most people can perform with little or no difficulty or what the individual would be able to perform with little or no difficulty in the absence of a disability.

Whether the achievement of a major life activity is difficult must be determined without regard to mitigating measures such as medications, assistive devices, or reasonable accommodations, unless the mitigating measure itself limits a major life activity. For example, antidepressant medication may be a mitigating measure that relieves the symptoms of depression such that a person with depression might not meet the definition of disabled. Yet the person would still likely qualify as having a disability because symptoms of depression would be present in an unmedicated state. Moreover, the mitigating measure (antidepressant medication) might also limit a major life activity if, for example, it interferes with the person's sleep patterns, making sleep or waking difficult.

As a practical matter just about every medical or psychological condition can be said to make at least one major life activity difficult, especially when the breadth of qualifying major life activities is considered. This therefore amounts to a low threshold that is likely to screen out hardly any claimed disabilities.

Major Life Activities

Major life activities are construed broadly and include caring for oneself, performing manual tasks, seeing, hearing, eating, sleeping, walking, standing, sitting, reaching, lifting, bending, speaking, breathing, learning, reading, concentrating, thinking, communicating, interacting with others, and working. Major life activities also include the operation of major bodily functions, including functions of the immune system, special sense organs and skin, normal cell growth, digestive, genitourinary, bowel, bladder, neurological, brain, respiratory, circulatory, cardiovascular, endocrine, hemic, lymphatic, musculoskeletal, and reproductive functions. Major bodily functions additionally include the operation of an individual organ within a body system. Again, given the breadth of qualifying activities and that virtually every bodily function is included, almost every physical or mental disorder is likely to limit some major life activity and qualify as a covered disability.

Although interacting with others is a major life activity, an employee's inability to get along with a supervisor or coworkers does not mean that they are limited in the major life activity of interacting with others. Rather, a profound limitation on a person's ability to function socially is required. One who is able to communicate with others, but whose communications are at times offensive or inappropriate or create a hostile environment for colleagues is not substantially limited in their ability to interact with others.

Working is a major life activity, regardless of whether an individual is limited in performing a particular job or a class or broad range of jobs. An employee who can show that they have a physical or mental disability that makes performance of their job difficult will likely qualify as disabled.

Other Ways to Qualify as Disabled

There are other ways in which a person may qualify as "disabled" under the law:

- A person has a special education disability that does not fit the definition of a physical or mental disability but that requires or in the past has required special education. This includes learning disabilities resulting from brain injury or brain dysfunction or conditions such as dyslexia or developmental aphasia.

- A person has a record or history of disability. This includes having a prior disability of which the employer is aware, such as substance use disorder, cancer, or mental illness.
- A person is perceived or regarded as disabled. This could happen if the employer believes that a person has a disabling physical or mental condition when in fact they do not, or if the person in fact has a physical or mental condition that the employer considers to be disabling when in fact it is not. Examples would include refusing to hire a military combat veteran for fear that they might have PTSD or refusing to hire an overweight person out of fear that the individual might have diabetes or other health conditions.
- A person is associated with another person who has, or is perceived to have, a disability. An example of associational disability would be an employee who has a spouse, child, or parent with a disability. In *Castro-Ramirez v. Dependable Highway Express, Inc.* (2016), the court held that the employer's refusal to provide an earlier work schedule for an employee who needed to be home to assist their son with dialysis and then terminating the employee after they refused to work a later schedule was a form of disability discrimination based on association. The court stopped short of deciding that an employer must reasonably accommodate an employee who associates with a disabled person, but the practical effect is largely the same. You should use caution in terminating employees because they require special consideration to allow them to care for a disabled relative or other close associate.

Excluded Conditions

Certain conditions are excluded from the definition of disability as a matter of law:

- Compulsive gambling;
- Kleptomania;
- Pyromania;
- Psychoactive substance use disorders resulting from current unlawful use of controlled substances or other drugs;
- Pedophilia;
- Exhibitionism; and
- Voyeurism.

In addition, mild and short-term conditions such as colds, the flu, minor cuts and sprains, muscle aches and soreness, nonmigraine headaches, and minor and nonchronic gastrointestinal disorders typically will not qualify as disabilities.

Substance Use Disorder

Current users of illegal drugs are not protected by the anti-discrimination laws. This includes users of medical marijuana. Current individuals suffering from alcohol use disorder are covered, provided they can perform the essential functions of the job and do not pose a direct threat to themselves or others. Persons who have completed treatment for addiction and no longer use drugs or alcohol are also covered.

A "one-strike" rule, under which an applicant or employee who fails a drug test is forever ineligible for hire by the employer, is lawful. It is not deemed to be discrimination against one with a record of a disability.

14.2 "Qualified"

An employee with a disability will not come under the protection of the antidiscrimination laws unless they are *qualified* for the job in question. This means that they meet the following criteria:

- Has the required skill, experience, education, licensure, and other job-related qualifications for the job they hold or desire; and
- Can perform the *essential functions* of the job, with or without *reasonable accommodation.*

14.3 Essential Job Functions

Essential job functions are the fundamental duties of the job. In other words, they are the reason why the job exists. Some indications of whether a job function is essential include:

- Whether it is identified as essential in the written job description;
- The amount of working time spent performing the function;
- The consequences if the function were not performed; and
- Whether other employees are available and able to perform the function.

Essential functions do not include marginal job functions, which are not the essence of the job or can readily be performed by other employees. An example is a receptionist who also opens and distributes the mail. Answering the phone and greeting visitors are essential functions of the job. Opening and distributing the mail are marginal functions because they can be readily performed by other employees.

14.4 Reasonable Accommodation

A reasonable accommodation is a change in how or when the job is performed such that an individual with a disability is able to perform the essential functions of the job. A reasonable accommodation, such as an adjustment in the application or interview process, might also be necessary to give an applicant with a disability an equal opportunity to be considered for a desired job. A reasonable accommodation likewise might be necessary to allow a disabled employee to enjoy equivalent benefits and privileges of employment as employees without disabilities. An example of this might be to provide a disabled employee an alternative means to qualify for a benefit resulting from participation in a wellness program.

There is no clear definition of what constitutes a ***reasonable*** accommodation, except that it does not amount to an "undue hardship." Unfortunately, undue hardship is defined more in terms of financial cost than disruption of the employer's operation. Nonetheless, the law has developed to the point that some boundaries have been drawn regarding what is and is not a reasonable accommodation. The purpose of a reasonable accommodation is to enable a disabled employee to perform their job or an alternate job. If the accommodation sought will not advance that purpose or is merely a matter of personal convenience, it is not a reasonable accommodation that you must provide. Examples would include transferring an employee away from annoying coworkers or allowing a later start time to avoid traffic.

Making the Workplace Accessible

Making the workplace accessible may be a reasonable accommodation depending on the extent and cost involved. Providing accessible restrooms, break rooms, and training facilities; providing reserved parking spaces (where parking is available); and acquiring or modifying furniture, equipment, or devices are typically considered reasonable accommodations. Examples of furniture and equipment that may constitute a reasonable accommodation include ergonomic chairs and keyboards, telephone amplifiers, and dictation software. Transferring an employee to a more accessible worksite might also be a reasonable accommodation. An employer is not required to make major structural changes to the workplace, however, such as installing an elevator in a building that lacks one.

Providing Assistive Aids or Services

Providing readers or interpreters for applicants or employees may be a reasonable accommodation depending on the cost and the resources of the employer. By contrast, an employer is not required to furnish personal assistive devices such as eyeglasses or hearing aids. Moreover, whereas providing a job coach might be a reasonable accommodation under certain circumstances, hiring or assigning an employee to perform the essential job duties of an employee with a disability is not required.

Modifying Examinations, Training Materials, or Policies

Modifying examinations may be a reasonable accommodation if the purpose is to make the examination more accessible to a disabled applicant or employee. However, an employer need not reduce its standards as a reasonable accommodation. Modifying training materials to make them more accessible may also be a reasonable accommodation. Likewise, providing additional training as may be required by an employee with a learning disability might also be a reasonable accommodation. Modification of some policies may be required. An example is the policy that employees may take only one break every four hours. Such a policy might have to be modified for a disabled employee who needs more frequent work breaks. Policies need not be modified to accommodate erratic attendance or disruptive, threatening, or dangerous conduct, however.

Modifying Supervisory Methods

Modifying supervisory methods such as providing one-on-one instruction or providing directions in writing as well as orally may be reasonable accommodations. Yet an employee who does not care for their boss is not entitled to a new boss as a reasonable accommodation.

Job Restructuring

Elimination or reassignment of nonessential job functions may be a reasonable accommodation. Essential job functions need not be eliminated or reassigned, however. In the example given above of a receptionist who also opens and distributes mail, the mail distribution functions are likely nonessential and could be reassigned. The functions of answering the telephone and greeting visitors are essential to the job of receptionist and need not be eliminated or reassigned.

Lowered performance standards or a reduced quota are not required accommodations. Nor is an employer required to reduce or eliminate the stress inherent in a job as a reasonable accommodation.

> The stress of a job need not be reduced or eliminated as a reasonable accommodation. A job without stress is called a "hobby."

Reassignment to a Vacant Position

If an employee can no longer perform the essential functions of the position they hold, reassignment to a vacant position for which the employee is qualified may be a reasonable accommodation. However, an employer is not required to *create* a new position for a disabled employee who no longer can perform their present job. Likewise, a disabled employee who cannot perform their current job is not entitled to a promotion to a higher-rated position. If no comparable positions are available, the employee may be reassigned to a lower-rated position. In such an event the employee would be paid the wage rate applicable to the lower-rated job.

A disabled employee who is qualified for a vacant position is entitled to priority for that position over a more qualified outside applicant. When a seniority system is in place, a disabled employee is not entitled to override seniority to transfer to a vacant position that a more senior employee desires. The only exception is when the employer has disregarded or allowed variations to seniority in the past.

Reassignment to an available vacant position is available as an accommodation only for existing employees. An applicant who cannot perform the essential functions of the posted job they seek is not entitled to be considered for other, non-posted, vacancies.

Modified Work Schedule

A modified or reduced work schedule might be a reasonable accommodation depending on whether the employee's presence on the job at particular times is essential. Such an accommodation might not be reasonable when, for example, the employee is required to open the business at the start of the workday and no other employees are available to perform that function. In jobs in which the employee's presence for the entire workday is not essential, a modified or reduced schedule will likely be a reasonable accommodation when the reduced schedule is necessary for the employee to obtain therapy or treatment, or to ease back into the job after an absence due to disability.

Leave of Absence

A leave of absence to obtain treatment or to recover from an illness or injury may be a reasonable accommodation, provided that the leave is likely to enable the employee to return to work at the end of the leave. This includes additional leave for an employee who has exhausted their leave provided under the federal Family and Medical Leave Act (FMLA) or the California Family Rights Act (CFRA; see Section 15.1). Indefinite leave is not required to be provided, however. An employer is not required to allow an employee to continue on leave who is unlikely ever to be able to return to work in their current job or in an alternate vacant position.

fyi **When Does Leave Become "Indefinite"?**

The law is clear that an employer need not accommodate an indefinite leave of absence. In many cases, an employee never requests an indefinite leave, but the leave seems to have become indefinite after a series of extensions from the initial leave. How should you deal with a situation in which an employee continues, month after month, to submit 30-day leave extensions?

First, look at whether the position the employee holds is a high-turnover position. If you are always hiring for the position held by the employee on leave, there is little hardship attendant to maintaining the employee on unpaid leave for an extended period because you will likely have a need if and when the employee is able to return to work. If you cannot hold the position open indefinitely, after receiving a few 30-day leave extensions, contact the employee and ask them if they are likely to be able to return to work at the end of the current extension. If the employee says no, ask the employee when they expect to return. If they do not know, you are relatively safe in concluding that the leave is an indefinite one, but for an added layer of safety you might ask the employee to have their doctor send a letter estimating the employee's likely return-to-work date. If the doctor is equivocal or fails to respond, such would be further evidence that the employee is on an indefinite leave.

Working from Home

Working from home might be a reasonable accommodation if the job can be performed independently. Jobs requiring the physical presence of the employee or personal interaction with customers or coworkers are not well suited to working from home.

Employers should use caution in allowing employees without disabilities to work from home as a matter of convenience, as doing so will make it difficult to argue that allowing a disabled employee performing the same or a similar job to work from home would create an undue hardship.

Use of Assistive Animals

Allowing an applicant or employee to use an assistive animal in the workplace might be a reasonable accommodation if two conditions are met:

- The animal is housebroken and free from offensive odors; and
- The animal does not present a danger to the health or safety of the disabled employee or applicant or others in the workplace.

Assistive animals include guide dogs trained to guide an employee who is blind or visually impaired, signal dogs or other animals trained to alert an employee who is deaf or hearing impaired to sounds, service dogs or other animals trained to assist a person with a disability, or support dogs or other animals that provide emotional, cognitive, or similar support to a person with a disability. Whether an assistive animal constitutes a reasonable accommodation requires an individualized analysis reached through the interactive process (see Section 14.6).

You may require an employee who seeks to bring an assistive animal to work to provide a letter from their health care provider stating that the employee has a disability and explaining why the employee needs the animal as an accommodation to enable the employee to perform the essential functions of the job. You may require annual certification of the employee's continued need for the animal. You may also require certification from the employee or another source that the animal meets the two conditions stated above.

14.5 "My Disability Made Me Do It!"—Accommodation of Misconduct

Whether misconduct caused by a disability must be accommodated is not always clear. Federal courts in California and other western states have held that disability-related misconduct must be accommodated unless it involves substance or alcohol use disorder or serious criminal conduct, or poses a direct threat to the health or safety of the employee or others. California courts have been somewhat more conservative, but given the position of the federal courts, employers should use caution when considering termination for misconduct of an employee with a disability. In the absence of substance use disorder, criminal conduct, or a direct threat, termination for disability-related misconduct might still be warranted when accommodation of the misconduct would constitute an undue hardship. Some examples might include profanity or emotional outbursts in the presence of clients or customers, or inappropriate behavior that affects the integrity or reputation of the employer such as a bank employee committing theft, a teacher or coach engaging in inappropriate sexual behavior, or a police officer brandishing a weapon without justification.

14.6 The Interactive Process

The interactive process is the process by which the employer and an employee or applicant with a disability communicate with each other about the need for an accommodation and the reasonable accommodations that are available. Both employer and employee or applicant must conduct the interactive process in good faith. Frequently, however, the interactive process breaks down, and a lawsuit results. It is essential, therefore, that you engage in the interactive process in a timely and thorough manner and that you document the process in detail. You must document each step you took, and when, and you must document all points at which the employee or applicant failed to cooperate.

You must initiate the interactive process when:

- The employee or applicant requests a reasonable accommodation;
- You become aware of the need for an accommodation by your own observation or from a third party such as a relative or physician; and

- An employee has exhausted the medical leave available under the FMLA, the CFRA, or both, yet the employee or the employee's doctor has indicated that additional leave is necessary for the employee to be able to return to work.

When the need for accommodation is not obvious, you may require the employee to provide medical documentation regarding the existence of a disability and the need for an accommodation. Disclosure of the nature or the cause of the disability is not required, but the medical documentation must describe the employee's or applicant's functional limitations in performing the essential functions of the job. For example, an employee requesting accommodation for a back injury need not provide detailed medical information about the injury but must provide information regarding any weight or other restrictions they may have with respect to lifting, carrying, bending, stooping, sitting, standing, and the like. If the information provided is insufficient, you must explain why the information is insufficient and give the employee or applicant time to provide additional information. If the employee still fails to provide sufficient medical documentation, you may require them to be examined by a doctor of your choice to determine the extent of their limitations.

Once the employee's or applicant's limitations are clear, you should meet with them in a face-to-face discussion, if possible, to explore potential accommodations. If a face-to-face meeting is not possible, you should use whatever other form of communication that is available to ensure that the interactive process is timely pursued.

Ask the employee what accommodation they seek. If such an accommodation appears reasonable and effective, implement it and document it, and the interactive process will be completed. Often this is no more complicated than an employee saying, "I need six weeks off to have surgery, and here's my doctor's certification," and you arrange for the employee to take the leave.

In more complex cases you do not have to grant the employee's preferred form of accommodation, but if you do not grant the employee's requested accommodation, you must discuss with the employee what alternative forms of accommodation are available. An analysis of the essential functions of the job may be part of the interactive process. The communications between employer and employee must involve give-and-take. Neither side may take a "my way or the highway" approach. The employee, for example, might request to be relieved of the heavy lifting requirements of their job as a reasonable accommodation. You might counter that heavy lifting is an essential function of the job and that the lifting requirements cannot be modified without changing the nature of the job. You would then have to explore other accommodations, such as a possible transfer to another vacant position that does not require heavy lifting but that has a wage rate lower than that applicable to their current job. Should the employee reject that alternative, you would have to explore whether any other accommodations are available, such as a leave of absence for the employee to obtain treatment for their condition so that the employee could safely perform the heavy lifting required for the position.

Each time a potential accommodation is offered, it should be documented by a memo to file or in a letter or email to the employee or applicant. The responses from the employee or applicant must be similarly documented. The back-and-forth discussion of possible accommodations must continue until a reasonable accommodation is implemented, or until all possible reasonable accommodations have been identified and rejected by the employee or applicant. If a reasonable accommodation is agreed upon and implemented but proves ineffective, the interactive process must start again to attempt to identify an alternative reasonable accommodation. This process must continue until all possible reasonable accommodations have been exhausted.

You may require medical recertification on an annual basis of an employee's continuing need for a reasonable accommodation.

All documents received or created during the interactive process must be kept in a file separate from the employee's personnel file and must be kept confidential except that the employee's supervisors may be informed of the employee's work restrictions, and first aid and safety personnel may be informed if the employee's condition may require emergency treatment.

14.7 Direct Threat

An applicant with a disability need not be hired, and an employee need not be permitted to work, if after engaging in the interactive process, no reasonable accommodation can be identified that would allow the person to perform the job without posing a direct threat to the health or safety of the employee or others.

Assessment of the risk of harm must be based on reasonable medical judgment that takes into account current medical knowledge and the best available objective evidence. A mere subjective fear that harm might result is not enough. Factors that must be considered in evaluating the risk of harm are:

- The duration of the risk;
- The nature and severity of the potential harm;
- The likelihood that potential harm will occur;
- The imminence of the potential harm; and
- The employee's work history.

The risk of harm, moreover, must be current. The mere fact that an employee has a condition that might in the future create a risk of harm is not sufficient to exclude the employee from the workplace. This point is particularly relevant when mental illness is concerned. The simple fact that an employee has a psychiatric illness does not necessarily mean that they will pose a danger to self or others. This can only be determined by a qualified physician after a fitness for duty examination.

14.8 Disability Discrimination and Workers' Compensation

Employers sometimes mistakenly believe that the disability discrimination laws do not apply to employees who are injured on the job. In fact, the disability discrimination laws affect employees on workers' compensation leaves in several ways.

First, terminating or otherwise discriminating against an employee who has filed a workers' compensation claim may not merely subject an employer to exposure for a retaliation claim before the Workers' Compensation Appeals Board. It may also result in a lawsuit for disability discrimination. Extreme caution is necessary, therefore, if you are considering not returning an employee from a workers' compensation leave. A mere subjective fear that, if reinstated, an employee might be reinjured and file another workers' compensation claim is not a valid reason for refusing to reinstate the employee.

Second, the interactive process applies to employees who are disabled on account of an injury at work just as it applies to employees with other types of disabilities. Should an injured employee's doctor allow the employee to return with certain restrictions, you must pursue the interactive process with the employee to determine whether the restrictions can be accommodated in the employee's current job or, if not, in another vacant position for which they are qualified. If the first accommodation selected does not work, you must continue the interactive process to determine if another reasonable accommodation is available.

Third, a "permanent disability" rating in the workers' compensation system does not necessarily mean that the employee is unable to perform any work. Many employers have made the mistake of terminating an employee as soon as they are declared permanently disabled by a workers' compensation doctor. This almost always leads to a lawsuit. Instead, upon an employee's receiving a permanent disability rating, you must begin the interactive process to determine the extent of the employee's ability to work and whether any vacant positions exist for which they are qualified. A warehouse worker who is declared permanently disabled as a result of a back injury might still be able to perform a quality inspector job, for example, if such a job were available.

Finally, you may not have a "100 percent healed" requirement before reinstating an employee from workers' compensation leave. Rather, if an employee is able to return to work with restrictions, you must initiate the interactive process to determine whether those restrictions may be accommodated.

14.9 Medical Exams and Inquiries

You may not conduct a medical or psychological examination or inquiries of a job applicant before you make an offer of employment. This restriction does not apply to pre-employment testing for illegal drug use. It also does not apply to personality or aptitude testing designed to determine whether the applicant is a good fit for the job (such as aptitude for sales or customer service) versus whether the applicant has a medical or mental health condition. Nor does the restriction prohibit physical agility testing to determine whether the applicant is physically able to perform the job.

After you make an offer of employment, you may conduct medical or psychological examinations or inquiries before the candidate's starting work to determine their fitness for the job, provided that:

- All new hires in similar positions are subject to the same examinations and inquiries;
- If the results of such examinations or inquiries would disqualify the candidate, the candidate must be allowed to submit other medical opinions before a final determination of disqualification is made; and
- The results of such examinations and inquiries are maintained in confidential medical files separate from the employee's personnel file.

You may withdraw an offer of employment based on the results of medical or psychological examinations or inquiries only if one of the two following conditions is met:

- The examinations or inquiries reveal that the candidate is unable to perform the essential duties of the job with or without a reasonable accommodation.
- The candidate would endanger their own health or safety, or the health or safety of others if permitted to work, and there is no reasonable accommodation that would eliminate such danger.

You may require an employee to undergo a fitness-for-duty examination if the examination is both related to the job and consistent with business necessity. An examination is related to the job if it is tailored to assess the employee's ability to perform the essential functions of the job or to determine whether the employee poses a danger to their own health or safety or the health or safety of others. Business necessity will justify a fitness-for-duty examination if, absent the examination, the employee might create a safety hazard or disrupt the employer's operations in a substantial way. An employee may be disciplined or terminated for refusing to undergo a validly requested fitness-for-duty examination.

CHAPTER 15

Leaves of Absence

California law provides many types of leaves for employees. Managing these leaves can be a daunting challenge for California employers. This chapter will examine each of these types of leave and how some of them may intersect.

15.1 Family and Medical Leave Act/California Family Rights Act Leave

Both the federal Family and Medical Leave Act (FMLA) and the California Family Rights Act (CFRA) provide California employees with job protected leave rights. The coverage of the CFRA is significantly broader than that of the FMLA, however. In some respects, the CFRA still mirrors the FMLA, but in other respects it does not. As with other laws, whichever provision (state or federal) is most favorable to the employee is the one that will apply.

Coverage of Employers

The FMLA covers employers of 50 or more employees. The 50-employee threshold is met if an employer has 50 or more employees for 20 or more workweeks (that need not be consecutive) in the current or prior calendar year. Part-time as well as full-time employees are counted, and employees on leaves of absence are counted as well if there is a reasonable expectation that they will return to work at the end of the leave. All public employers in California are covered by the FMLA and CFRA regardless of their size. The FMLA but not the CFRA applies to private elementary and secondary schools regardless of their size.

The CFRA covers employers that regularly employ five or more employees. Those five employees need not be within a 75-mile radius, or even be in California at all. A company with only one employee in California would be covered by the CFRA as to that employee if it has at least four more employees out of state. The five employees may be full-time or part-time, and employees who are on leaves of absence are counted as well.

> The CFRA now covers smaller employers as well as large ones. In fact, an employer having just one employee in California must apply the CFRA to that employee if it has at least four more employees elsewhere.

Coverage of Employees

In order to be eligible to take FMLA leave an employee must meet the following criteria:

- Work at a location where the employer employs at least 50 employees within a 75-mile radius on the date the employee gives notice of the need for leave;
- Have been employed by the employer for at least 12 months, but this period of employment need not be consecutive; and
- Have worked at least 1,250 hours in the 12 months before taking leave.

In order to be eligible to take CFRA leave an employee must meet the following criteria:

- Have been employed by the employer for at least 12 months, but this period of employment need not be consecutive; and
- Have worked at least 1,250 hours in the 12 months before taking leave.

Part-time employees may be eligible for FMLA/CFRA leave if they meet the above qualifications. Time worked for the employer before a break in service of at least 7 years need not be counted toward the 12-month threshold unless the break was due to military leave.

Maximum Amount of Leave Available

A covered employee may take a maximum of 12 weeks of FMLA/CFRA leave in a 12-month period. For a full-time employee, the 12 weeks of leave amount to 60 eight-hour working days. For employees who work other than 5 eight-hour days per week, the 12 weeks of leave amount to 12 workweeks of the employee's usual work schedule.

The employer may designate the method in which the 12-month measuring period is determined. The options are:

- Calendar year;
- Employee's anniversary year;

- 12-month period measured forward from the first day of leave ("rolling forward" method); or
- 12-month period measured backward from the first day of leave ("rolling backward" method).

For leave taken under the FMLA for care of an injured or ill military service member, the 12-month period must begin on the first day of leave.

You must provide notice to employees, typically in the employee handbook, of which method you will use to designate the 12-month period, and you must apply that method consistently to all employees. If you change your method of measuring the 12-month period, you must provide employees with at least 60 days' notice of such change. If you do not designate any method, the method that is most favorable to the employee is the one that will apply.

Under the calendar year method, an employee could take a 12-week FMLA/CFRA leave in October through December of one year and another 12-week leave in January through March of the next year. Similarly, under the anniversary date method, an employee could take 12-week leaves on either side of their anniversary date. These methods are not recommended. Under the rolling forward method, an employee who took an eight-week leave beginning June 1, 2026, would be eligible to take only four additional weeks of leave before June 1, 2027, but on that date would be eligible to take another 12 weeks of leave.

The rolling backward method is most favorable to the employer. Under this method, you look backward to see how much leave the employee has taken during the prior 12 months. Should the employee who took an 8-week leave beginning June 1, 2025 seek to take a leave beginning June 1, 2026, they would be limited to taking four weeks because the employee already took 8 weeks of leave during the prior year. Compare this amount of leave entitlement to the 12-week entitlement that would result from use of the rolling forward method. Where a holiday falls during a whole week of FMLA/CFRA leave, the holiday is counted as a day of leave taken. Where only a partial week of leave is taken and a holiday falls during that week, the holiday is not counted as a day of leave taken.

Reasons Leave May Be Taken

An eligible employee may take FMLA leave for the following reasons:

- The employee's own serious health condition;
- To care for a parent, child, or spouse with a serious health condition;
- Pregnancy and childbirth;
- Care for and bonding with a newborn or newly adopted child;

- Up to 12 weeks for a qualifying exigency relating to a close family member being deployed in military service to a foreign country; and
- Up to 26 weeks to care for a spouse, child, parent, or next-of-kin who is an ill or injured current or former military service member.

A "serious health condition" is defined under the FMLA as an injury, illness, or condition that involves either inpatient care or continuing treatment by a health care provider. "Inpatient care" means an overnight stay in a hospital or other residential care facility and any subsequent treatment in connection with such inpatient care. "Continuing treatment by a health care provider" means any one or more of the following:

- Incapacity (defined as missing work or school) for more than 3 consecutive days plus treatment by a health care provider that involves a regimen of continuing treatment, meaning either (a) two or more treatments by a health care provider within 30 days of the first day of incapacity or (b) one treatment by a health care provider and a subsequent regimen of treatment;
- Pregnancy and childbirth;
- A chronic condition (such as asthma, diabetes, or migraines) that continues over an extended period of time and requires periodic visits (at least two per year) to a health care provider;
- Permanent or long-term conditions (such as Alzheimer's, a severe stroke, or a terminal illness) requiring supervision but not active treatment by a health care provider; and
- Any period of absence to receive treatments ordered by a health care provider, such as surgery, chemotherapy, radiation therapy, or dialysis.

An eligible employee may take CFRA leave for the following reasons:

- The employee's own serious health condition;
- To care for a parent, parent-in-law, child (regardless of age), spouse, sibling, grandparent, grandchild, or registered domestic partner with a serious health condition;
- To care for a "designated person" with a serious health condition. A "designated person" is an individual related by blood or whose association with the employee is equivalent to a family relationship. An employee may be limited to identifying one "designated person" per 12-month period;
- To care for and bond with a newborn or newly adopted child; and

- Because of a qualifying exigency related to the covered active duty or call to covered active duty of an employee's spouse, domestic partner, child, or parent in the Armed Forces of the United States.

Under the CFRA, the definition of "serious health condition" differs from the FMLA definition in the following ways:

- An overnight stay in a hospital or residential care facility is not required for inpatient care if the person is admitted with the expectation that they will remain overnight but it later develops that the person can be discharged or transferred to another facility;
- Pregnancy and childbirth are not covered by the CFRA; and
- There is no express requirement that at least two visits to a health care provider occur with respect to a chronic condition.

Both the FMLA and the CFRA define serious health conditions to include treatment of substance use disorder. Cosmetic surgery and minor conditions such as colds, flu, stomachaches, routine dental problems, and the like do not qualify as serious health conditions under either law.

To be eligible for leave to care for an ill or injured relative, an employee must actually participate in the ongoing treatment of the relative's medical condition, such as driving the relative to medical appointments, helping administer medications, or providing emotional support. Merely spending time with aged parents or assisting them in their move to a new residence will not qualify.

Under the FMLA, if both parents work for the same employer, they are only entitled to a total of 12 weeks of leave combined for bonding with a new child. This is not so under the CFRA. Under the latter law each parent is entitled to take up to 12 weeks apiece for baby-bonding leave.

Obligations of an Employee Taking Leave

Under both the FMLA and the CFRA, an employee is required to provide at least 30 days' notice of the need for leave when the need for leave is foreseeable. When the need for leave is not foreseeable, no amount of advance notice is required.

The employee must request leave, orally or in writing, and indicate that the leave is for a covered reason, but there is no requirement that the employee refer specifically to the FMLA or the CFRA. For an eligible employee to say simply "I need some time off for drug rehab" or "I am going to be out for back surgery" is sufficient notice of the employee's need for leave. On the other hand, the employee must indicate that a medical leave is necessary for a serious health condition. An employee stating only that they are going to take a sick day, or that they will miss work for some doctors' appointments, is not sufficient. If the employee is unable to provide notice because they are hospitalized or otherwise incapacitated, a relative, a friend, or the employee's physician may communicate the employee's need for leave.

You may request the employee to complete a written application for FMLA/CFRA leave, but if the employee fails to do so or is unable to do so on account of illness or injury, you are not relieved of your obligation to designate the leave as FMLA/CFRA leave if you have sufficient information to warrant such a designation.

You may require an employee to submit a medical certification of the need for leave within 15 days of the employee's request for leave. This certification must be completed and signed by the employee's health care provider. You should not use the U.S. Department of Labor medical certification form, Form WH-380, because it asks the health care provider to list medical facts justifying the employee's need for leave, and medical facts may not be disclosed under California law without the employee's written consent. Instead, use the form provided by the California Civil Rights Department, available on that agency's website, https://calcivilrights.ca.gov.

If you doubt the validity of the medical certification or of the employee's need for leave, you may require the employee to obtain a second and even a third opinion at the company's expense. You may not, however, challenge the validity of the certification of a family member's health care provider submitted in support of an employee's request for leave to care for a family member. If the employee fails to submit the required medical certification, you may deny designation of the leave as FMLA/CFRA-protected leave and terminate the employee for being absent without leave. As a practical matter, though, it is best to make several attempts to obtain the medical certification form from the employee or their physician, and to document those attempts, before denying designation of FMLA/CFRA leave, given the likelihood that an employee fired for failing to provide medical certification will sue for denial of leave or retaliation.

Should an employee take a subsequent FMLA/CFRA leave for the same reason as a prior leave when medical certification was provided and the maximum amount of available leave was not taken, the employee does not need to provide a new medical certification of the need for leave. If an employee takes another FMLA/CFRA leave for a different reason, a new medical certification would need to be submitted.

Obligations of an Employer When an Employee Requests Leave

Within five days of your receipt of all required information, you need to determine whether a leave is covered by the FMLA, the CFRA, or both, and you must provide written notice to the employee designating the leave as FMLA/CFRA-covered leave or not. The leave may be designated retroactively to the first day of the employee's absence for the FMLA/CFRA-qualifying condition. You must also provide an explanation of the employee's rights and responsibilities while on leave, and you must provide a guarantee (in writing if the employee requests it) that the employee will be reinstated in the same or an equivalent position at the conclusion of the leave.

If you deny the employee's request for FMLA/CFRA leave, you must provide at least one reason for such denial.

You do not have to pay an employee while on FMLA/CFRA leave. An employee may elect to use, or you may require an employee to use, accrued vacation or paid time off (PTO), other than accrued sick leave, during the unpaid portion of an FMLA/CFRA leave. An employee may also elect to use, or you may require an employee to use, any accrued sick leave during the unpaid portion of an FMLA/CFRA leave if the leave is for the employee's own serious health condition. If an employee is receiving a partial wage replacement benefit during the FMLA/CFRA leave (such as state disability benefits, see Section 15.2), you and the employee may agree to have vacation, PTO, or paid sick leave supplement the partial wage replacement benefit. An employee receiving paid family leave (see Section 15.3) to care for the serious health condition of a family member or to bond with a new child is not on "unpaid leave," and so you may not require the employee to use paid accrued vacation or PTO.

You must continue the employee's group health insurance benefits during FMLA/CFRA leave on the same terms as if the employee continued working. If the employee pays a portion of their insurance premium, they may be required to pay the same portion while on leave. If the employee fails to pay the premium within 30 days of the due date, you may cancel their coverage after providing 15 days' notice and issue a Consolidated Omnibus Budget Reconciliation Act (COBRA) notice. If such an employee wishes to reinstate coverage upon returning from leave, however, coverage must be reinstated without any waiting period or conditions.

You may recover from an employee the premiums paid for maintaining the employee's group health care coverage during any period of unpaid FMLA/CFRA leave provided the following conditions are met:

- The employee fails to return from leave at its expiration (an employee is deemed to have failed to return from leave if they work less than 30 days after returning from leave, but an employee who retires during leave or during the first 30 days after returning is deemed to have returned from leave); and
- The employee's failure to return from leave is for a reason other than the continuation, recurrence, or onset of a serious health condition that entitled the employee to FMLA/CFRA leave, or other circumstances beyond the control of the employee.

Upon completion of an FMLA/CFRA leave, an employee must be returned to the same position they left or to a comparable position with the same duties, compensation, and working conditions. You may require a medical release from the employee's physician that confirms the employee is able to return to work with or without restrictions. You may also require the employee to undergo a fitness-for-duty examination if, after the employee returns from leave, you have a good faith doubt, based on objective evidence, regarding the employee's ability to perform their essential job functions without posing a direct threat to their own health or safety, or the health or safety of others.

You may refuse reinstatement to the employee if they would have otherwise been terminated had the employee not been on leave. For example, if a layoff occurred while the employee was on leave that would have included the employee, you need not reinstate them. Likewise, if while the employee was on leave, you discover that they committed serious misconduct, such as theft or embezzlement, you may terminate the employee.

fyi **Three Good Ways to Get Sued by an Employee Who Took Leave**

The following are *not* lawful reasons for failing to reinstate an employee returning from leave:

- You discovered during the employee's absence that you no longer needed them;
- You hired a temp to cover for the employee on leave, and you like the temp better; or
- You did not think the employee would be returning from leave, so you replaced them.

Failing to return an employee from leave for one of these reasons will almost certainly result in a lawsuit.

What If an Employee Fails to Return from Leave?

Should an employee notify you that they will not be able to return to work upon the expiration of FMLA/CFRA leave, you must determine whether to grant additional leave as a reasonable accommodation of the employee's disability (see Section 14.4).

Should an employee simply fail to show up for work upon the expiration of FMLA/CFRA leave, you should not immediately terminate the employee for job abandonment. Rather, you should contact the employee and inquire whether they need additional leave and, if so, how much leave. You may require a medical certification of the employee's need for additional leave. If the employee has not exhausted their 12 weeks of FMLA/CFRA leave, you must give the employee 15 days to respond. Otherwise, you must give the employee a reasonable amount of time to respond, but you should set a specific deadline. Only if the employee fails to respond to such a communication regarding need for additional leave would termination for job abandonment be warranted.

The "Key Employee" Exception

A "key employee" is defined as a salaried employee who is among the highest paid ten percent of all the employees employed by the employer within 75 miles of the employee's worksite. An employer may decline to reinstate a key employee following FMLA leave if reinstating such an employee would cause "substantial and grievous economic injury" to the operations of the employer. It is the employee's reinstatement, not the employee's absence, that must cause such injury. If permanent replacement of a key employee on leave is unavoidable, the cost of reinstating that employee can be considered in evaluating whether substantial and grievous economic injury will occur from such reinstatement, that is, the effect on the operations of the company of reinstating the employee in an equivalent position after they have been permanently replaced. Note that the "key employee" exception does not apply under the CFRA. Thus, the "key employee" exception will not apply in California unless an employee has exhausted their CFRA leave but still has FMLA leave available.

The "substantial and grievous economic injury" standard under the FMLA is more stringent than the "undue hardship" standard relating to reasonable accommodation under the disability discrimination laws. No precise test has been set for the level of hardship or injury to the employer that must be sustained. If the reinstatement of a key employee threatens the economic viability of the firm, such would constitute substantial and grievous economic injury. An example of this might be where the company must hire a highly paid executive to replace a key employee and would face a costly lawsuit should it fire the replacement to reinstate the key employee. A lesser injury that causes substantial, long-term economic injury would also be sufficient according to federal regulations. However, minor inconveniences and costs that the employer would experience in the normal course of doing business would not constitute substantial and grievous economic injury.

A key employee must be provided FMLA leave. The issue is whether such a key employee may be denied reinstatement following such leave. An employer anticipating that reinstatement may be denied to a key employee must give written notice to the employee at the time the employee gives notice of the need for FMLA/CFRA leave (or when leave commences, if earlier) that they qualify as a key employee. The employee must also be informed of the potential consequences with respect to reinstatement and maintenance of health benefits if the employer should determine that substantial and grievous economic injury to its operations will result if the employee is reinstated from leave.

As soon as the employer makes a good faith determination that substantial and grievous economic injury to its operations will result if a key employee is reinstated from FMLA leave, it must notify the employee in writing of its determination and that it intends to deny reinstatement upon completion of leave. You must serve this notice either in person or by certified mail. This notice must explain the basis for your finding that substantial and grievous economic injury will result, and, if leave has commenced, must provide the employee a reasonable time in which to return to work, taking into account the circumstances, such as the length of the leave and the urgency of the need for the employee to return.

If a key employee does not return to work in response to your notification of your intent to deny restoration, you must continue the employee's health benefits for the duration of the leave or until the employee notifies you of their intent not to return. You may not recover the cost of health insurance premiums paid for a key employee while on leave. Even after you have notified a key employee of your intent not to reinstate them, the employee is still entitled to request reinstatement at the end of the leave period. You must then again determine whether there will be substantial and grievous economic injury from reinstatement, based on the facts at that time. If you again determine that substantial and grievous economic injury will result, you must notify the employee in writing (in person or by certified mail) that reinstatement will be denied.

Given the complexity of these requirements and the heavy burden the employer must satisfy to deny reinstatement to a key employee, employment counsel should be consulted in the event you contemplate that a key employee might not be reinstated following FMLA leave.

Intermittent Leave

An employee may use FMLA/CFRA leave on an intermittent basis up to the total amount of leave available, which is 480 hours per year for a full-time employee. Intermittent leave may be taken in daily increments, or in increments as small as the smallest increments you allow employees to take vacation or PTO. Common examples of the use of intermittent leave include whole or part-day absences for therapy or treatment. Unfortunately, however, employees who qualify for intermittent leave due to chronic conditions that may flare up, such as migraine headaches or bipolar disorder, may take intermittent leave with little or no prior notice.

You may require an employee who is taking intermittent leave to transfer to an alternate position at the same pay and benefits during the period of such leave. If an employee needs leave intermittently or on a reduced leave schedule for planned medical treatment, the employee must make a reasonable effort to schedule the treatment so as not to disrupt unduly the employer's operations.

"Stacking" of FMLA and CFRA Leave

Because the FMLA and CFRA are not entirely congruent, employees in California might qualify for more than 12 weeks of leave per year in various situations.

For example, pregnancy and childbirth qualify as a "serious health condition" under the FMLA but not under the CFRA. As a result, a California employee eligible for FMLA/CFRA leave may take up to 4 months of pregnancy disability leave (PDL; see Section 15.4) and then take another 12 weeks of CFRA leave for care and bonding with their new child. Note that fathers who qualify for CFRA leave may take up to 12 weeks for care and bonding with a newborn or newly adopted child, too. Therefore, employees who take California PDL should also be put on FMLA leave, so they exhaust some or all of their 12 weeks of FMLA entitlement while on PDL. Otherwise, an employee could take 12 weeks of PDL for pregnancy and childbirth, plus another 6 weeks of CFRA baby-bonding leave, and soon after returning to work, go on another 12-week leave for a qualifying reason under the FMLA.

The FMLA but not the CFRA provides for leave to care for an injured or ill current or former military service member. Thus, an employee could take up to 26 weeks under the FMLA to care for a family member who became injured or ill in military service, and then upon returning take up to 12 weeks of leave under the CFRA for another qualifying reason. Should an employee take up to 26 weeks of leave under the FMLA to care for an ill or injured current or former service member who is a spouse, child, parent, sibling, grandparent, grandchild, or registered domestic partner, the first 12 weeks of such leave should be designated as CFRA leave as well.

The CFRA but not the FMLA provides for leave for the care of a sibling, grandparent, grandchild, registered domestic partner, or "designated person" with a serious health condition. Thus, an employee could take 12 weeks of CFRA leave to care for a seriously ill grandparent, then take up to 12 weeks of additional leave for a qualifying reason under the FMLA.

When administering FMLA and CFRA leaves, therefore, it is important to consider whether the leave is qualifying under both the FMLA and CFRA, or under only one of the laws. If it qualifies under both, the leave designation document given to the employee should say so. If it only qualifies under one of the laws it should not be taken into account in using the "rolling backward" method of determining how much leave is still available.

The FMLA/CFRA and Workers' Compensation

Employees injured on the job are entitled to take a leave of absence for the duration of the period in which they are temporarily disabled from working. Employers have the right under the workers' compensation laws to replace employees on workers' compensation leave when business necessity dictates, but the law in this area has largely been superseded by the courts' application of the disability discrimination laws to employees injured on the job, so extreme caution must be used in replacing or terminating employees on workers' compensation leaves (this subject is addressed in more detail in Section 14.8).

Moreover, if an employee is off work receiving treatment under workers' compensation for a workplace injury, they would easily qualify as having a "serious health condition" under the FMLA/CFRA in most instances. If the employee is otherwise eligible for FMLA/CFRA leave, the employee will be entitled to job-protected leave for the first 12 weeks of leave (or whatever amount of unused FMLA/CFRA leave the employee has available). Many employers do not designate leaves taken for industrial injuries as FMLA/CFRA leave. This is a mistake. If the employee is otherwise qualified for FMLA/CFRA leave, you should designate their workers' compensation leave time also as FMLA/CFRA time, for three reasons:

- You must determine how much job-protected leave the employee has under FMLA/CFRA before you can consider terminating or replacing the employee, in those situations when such termination or replacement is allowed under the workers' compensation and disability discrimination laws.
- Even though an employee may be off work for medical reasons, the time off does not count toward FMLA/CFRA leave unless you designate it as such. An employee could be out for a year or more on workers' compensation leave and then return only to take more time off under the FMLA/CFRA. This can be prevented by ensuring that an employee uses their FMLA/CFRA leave allotment while on workers' compensation leave.
- If your health insurance plan provides for coverage of employees only while on job-protected leaves such as FMLA/CFRA leave, you need not continue providing coverage to an employee who has exhausted their 12 weeks of FMLA/CFRA leave. Assuming you have an insured health plan and the language of your plan allows it, you may issue a COBRA notice to employees on workers' compensation after they have exhausted their available FMLA/CFRA leave.

15.2 State Disability Insurance Benefits

California's Employment Development Department (EDD) operates a state disability insurance (SDI) program that provides employees short-term disability benefits that are funded through employee payroll deductions. The weekly benefit amount for employees whose wages are less than ⅓ of the state average quarterly wage is 70 percent of the employee's wages paid during the quarter of the employee's individual base period in which those wages were highest, divided by 13. The weekly benefit amount for employees whose wages are more than ⅓ of the state average quarterly wage is 60 percent of the employee's wages paid during the quarter of the employee's individual base period in which those wages were highest, divided by 13. The maximum weekly benefit payable in any event cannot exceed the maximum workers' compensation temporary disability weekly event, which is currently $1,764.11. SDI benefits are available for the duration of the employee's disability or for a maximum of 52 weeks, whichever is less. SDI benefits, like unemployment benefits in California, are paid via a debit card.

There is an initial seven-day waiting period before SDI benefits are paid. You may require or allow an employee to use accrued sick leave, vacation, or PTO during this time. After the initial waiting period, you may require or allow employees to take enough accrued sick leave to equal their regular pay until their accrued sick leave is exhausted.

For pregnancy and childbirth, four weeks of SDI benefits are generally available before delivery, and six weeks are available afterward, although the EDD may extend the period in which benefits are paid upon a physician's certification that additional time off work is needed.

Receipt of SDI benefits does not itself provide job-protected leave, even though many employees who receive SDI benefits may be on a job-protected leave. The right to job protection must be found in some other law such as the FMLA/CFRA, pregnancy disability leave, or federal or state disability discrimination laws.

SDI benefits generally are not available for time off work due to industrial injuries, as such injuries are covered by workers' compensation insurance, which includes temporary disability benefits.

15.3 Paid Family Leave

California's paid family leave (PFL) law causes much confusion. The law does *not* provide a right to job-protected leave. It merely provides for payment of benefits similar to SDI benefits that are funded via employee payroll deductions and paid by the EDD. Up to eight weeks per year of PFL benefits are available for employees who take time off work to care for a seriously ill child, parent, spouse, registered domestic partner, parent-in-law, grandparent, grandchild, sibling, or "designated person," or for bonding with a new child. Baby-bonding leave must be taken within the first year of the child's life.

Benefits are paid according to the same formula as SDI benefits.

An employee receiving PFL benefits is not automatically entitled to job-protected leave. The right to such leave must be found in the FMLA or the CFRA, as there is no right to leave to care for a disabled relative under the Americans with Disabilities Act or similar state law. There may be numerous situations in which an employee may be eligible for PFL benefits but not for job-protected leave under the FMLA/CFRA, such as:

- The employee works for an employer with fewer than five employees;
- The employee has not been employed by the employer for a year or has not worked 1,250 hours before the start of leave; or

- The employee has exhausted their 12 weeks of leave for the year.

Although an employer may provide job-protected leave to employees receiving PFL benefits who are ineligible for FMLA/CFRA leave, it is not required to do so. If it does so, it must do so consistently to avoid claims of discrimination.

15.4 Pregnancy Disability Leave

Pregnant employees in California who work for employers with five or more employees are entitled to up to four months of job-protected pregnancy disability leave (PDL) for pregnancy, childbirth, or related medical conditions. There is no minimum period that an employee must work to be eligible for PDL.

The period of leave available is the actual period of disability as certified by the employee's physician up to the four-month maximum. For a full-time employee, up to 17⅓ weeks or 693 hours of leave are available. For employees who work more or less than 40 hours per week, the total leave available is the amount of time the employee would normally work in a four-month period. The limit on leave time is per pregnancy, not per year.

Leave is available not only for disability for pregnancy and childbirth but also for related medical conditions occurring before or after delivery, such as pregnancy-induced hypertension, preeclampsia, gestational diabetes, loss of pregnancy, postpartum depression, and lactation-related medical conditions such as mastitis. Leave may be taken intermittently, in increments no greater than the shortest period of time the employer uses to account for other forms of leave but not greater than one hour. You may transfer an employee on intermittent leave to another position with equivalent pay and benefits for the duration of the intermittent leave.

The employee has a right to be reinstated to their same position upon return from leave, unless they would have been terminated from that position (for example, due to plant closure or layoff) had they not been on leave. An employee who cannot return to work after four months of PDL as a result of a continuing disability may be entitled to additional leave as a reasonable accommodation.

PDL is unpaid leave, although the employee may be eligible for SDI benefits while on leave. You may require an employee to use, or they may elect to use, any accrued sick leave during the unpaid portion of PDL before SDI benefits begin. The employee may elect, but you cannot require them, to use any accrued vacation or PTO time while on PDL. You must continue the employee's group health coverage while they are on PDL on the same terms and conditions as if the employee was not on leave. Unlike under the FMLA/CFRA, the PDL statute and the regulations interpreting it contain no provision authorizing an employer to terminate group health coverage should the employee fail to pay their share of the premium or for dependent coverage.

The period during which an employer continues health coverage for an employee on PDL is not applicable to reduce the period (of up to 12 weeks) that an employer must continue health coverage for the employee should they take FMLA/CFRA leave, even if PDL leave is also designated as FMLA leave. Should an employee not return to work at the end of their PDL, you may recover the amount of premiums paid for continuation of their health coverage while on leave provided their failure to return from leave is for a reason other than one of the following:

- Taking CFRA leave, unless the employee chooses not to return to work following the CFRA leave;
- The continuation, recurrence, or onset of a health condition that entitles the employee to further PDL, unless the employee chooses not to return to work following the leave;
- Non-pregnancy-related medical conditions requiring further leave, unless the employee chooses not to return to work following the leave; or
- Any other circumstance beyond the control of the employee, including circumstances in which the employer is responsible for the employee's failure to return (for example, the employer does not return the employee to their same position or reinstate the employee to a comparable position), or circumstances in which the employee must care for a family member (for example, the employee gives birth to a child with a serious health condition).

Because pregnancy and childbirth are not "serious health conditions" under the CFRA, an employee may take up to four months of PDL, and then take up to 12 weeks of CFRA leave for bonding with the child if they are otherwise eligible for CFRA leave. Such bonding leave must be taken immediately following the conclusion of PDL, or at some other time within a year of childbirth.

15.5 Paid Sick Leave

Employers are required to provide paid sick leave to their employees in California. This law covers all employers; there is no exception for small employers. It also covers almost all employees who work 30 or more days for the same employer in California—full-time, part-time, exempt and nonexempt, regular and temporary. The only exceptions are certain employees in the construction industry covered by a collective bargaining agreement, and airline flight crews who accrue at least as much paid sick leave as is required by law.

Under this law, employees accrue paid sick leave at the rate of one hour per 30 hours worked. Employees may begin using their accrued paid sick leave on their 90th day of employment. You may limit employees to using no more than 40 hours or 5 days of paid sick leave per year. Unused sick leave will carry forward to the next year, but you may limit an employee's total sick leave accrual to 80 hours or 10 days, whichever is more. These limitations on the use and accrual of paid sick leave must be stated in your policy; they are not automatic.

Your policy may specify a different accrual method (other than providing 1 hour of leave for every 30 hours worked), so long as an employee can accrue at least 24 hours of paid sick leave or paid time off (PTO) by the 120th day of employment or in each calendar year, and can accrue no less than 40 hours of accrued sick leave or PTO by the 200th calendar day of employment, or in each calendar year or year of employment.

For sick leave or PTO policies that existed before January 1, 2015, and that comply with the accrual, carry-over, and use requirements of current law, you need not provide additional paid sick days so long as employees are able to earn at least five days or 40 hours of sick leave or PTO within six months of employment. If such a grandfathered plan does not meet this standard it must be modified so as to provide accruals consistent with the paid sick leave law.

As an alternative to the accrual method, you may simply credit employees with five days or 40 hours of paid leave at the beginning of each year, which may be a calendar year, anniversary year, or other twelve-month period. Those credited days will not carry over to the next year if they are not used, and they need not be cashed out upon termination.

Employees may take paid sick leave for their own illnesses or preventive care (such as medical checkups) or to provide care for an ill spouse, registered domestic partner, child (regardless of age), parent (including stepparents and parents-in-law), grandparent, grandchild, sibling, or a "designated person." Employees may identify such a "designated person" when they request to use paid sick leave, and the employer may limit an employee to one "designated person" per twelve month period. Employees who are victims of domestic violence, sexual assault, or stalking may also take paid sick leave (see Section 4.14), and employees may use their paid sick leave while on jury duty or while appearing in court as a witness.

Unused accrued sick leave need not be paid out upon termination of employment, but any unused time must be reinstated if the employee is rehired within a year unless it was paid out when the employee was terminated.

Employers may not deny employees the use of paid sick leave, nor may an employer discharge or otherwise retaliate against an employee who uses paid sick leave. There is no meaningful advance notice requirement and no requirement for medical certification in this law, so there will not be much you can do to prevent employees from calling in sick without prior notice or to ensure that they are actually sick or caring for a sick relative, so long as they have paid sick leave available. You will not be able to take paid sick days into account in disciplining employees for poor attendance.

The record-keeping requirements of this law are onerous. On each payday you will need to provide each employee with a written notice of the amount of paid sick leave available. This must be provided on the itemized wage statement provided with the employee's paycheck, or on a separate document. You must also keep for at least three years records documenting the hours worked and paid sick days accrued and used by each employee. Employees have the right to inspect and copy their accrued sick leave records in the same manner as they may inspect and copy their itemized wage statements (See Section 10.3).

Calculation of the Amount of Sick Pay Due

Employees who are covered by the executive, administrative, and professional exemptions from overtime are simply paid their regular salary for sick days taken, with the amount of sick time taken being deducted from their leave balance. Exempt outside salespersons should be paid their regular salary, not including commissions, for sick days taken.

For nonexempt employees it is more complicated. Sick leave for nonexempt employees may be paid either:

- At the employee's "regular rate" for calculation of overtime in the workweek in which leave was taken (that is, divide total earnings during the workweek, including commissions, bonuses and piece-rate pay, by total hours worked during the workweek); or
- At the rate derived by dividing the employee's total wages, not including overtime premium pay, by the employee's total hours worked in the full pay periods of the prior 90 days of employment.

Ordinarily the first method will be the easiest to use, but the second method should be used where the employee has unusually high earnings in the workweek when the employee takes a sick day, such as when a substantial bonus or commission is paid.

Local Paid Sick Leave Ordinances in California

Several local jurisdictions in California have enacted their own paid sick leave ordinances that provide a greater amount of paid leave to employees in those jurisdictions than under state law. Where the state and local laws conflict, whichever law is more favorable to employees is the one that applies. For example, some local ordinances permit employers to request medical documentation of the need for leave, but California law does not permit employers to require a medical excuse. No such documentation may be required for use of the minimum paid sick leave provided under California law, but such documentation could be required for use of such paid leave required by applicable municipal ordinance that exceeds the state law requirement.

Requirements of local sick leave ordinances in California's larger cities are as follows:

Los Angeles: Employees who have worked at least 30 days in a year and at least 2 hours in the city "in a particular week" must accrue 1 hour of leave for every 30 hours worked in the city or be given 48 hours of leave at the beginning of a year. Employees who work outside the city and travel through the city without stopping are not covered by the law; however, time spent traveling through the city counts toward the employee's eligibility for paid sick leave if the employee makes any work-required stop in the city. Accrued leave may be capped at 72 hours per year and employees may be limited to using 48 hours of leave per year. Unused leave need not be paid upon termination of employment, but the unused balance must be reinstated if the employee is rehired within a year. Leave may be used for the employee's own illness or to care for sick family members as under California law, and in addition for care of "individuals related by blood or affinity whose close association with the employee is the equivalent of a family relationship." Employers may require reasonable documentation of the reason for the employee's use of sick leave for absences of more than three consecutive workdays so long as it does not deter employees from taking legitimate paid sick leave. There is no exemption for employees covered by a collective bargaining agreement.

Hotel employers in Los Angeles with 60 or more guest rooms must provide employees with 96 hours of compensated time off per year for sick leave, vacation, and other personal purposes. Hotel employees accrue this paid time off at the rate of 96/52 hours per week worked. Employees may use the paid time off after six months of employment. Unused accrued time off carries over to the next year and once the accrual reaches 192 hours, the employer must provide a cash payment once every 30 days for the amount of accrued compensated time off over the maximum. Hotel employers must additionally provide 80 hours of unpaid time off per year to be used for the employee's own illness or the illness of an immediate family member where paid time off has been exhausted. This unpaid time off accrues at the rate of 80/52 hours per week worked, and employees may use the unpaid time off after six months of employment. This law does not apply to managerial, supervisory, or confidential employees.

Oakland: Employees who work at least 2 hours in the city "in a particular week" must accrue 1 hour of leave for every 30 hours worked in the city. There is no provision for vesting employees with a lump sum of leave at the beginning of a year. Employers with ten or more employees may cap accrual at 72 hours; employers of fewer than ten employees may cap accrual at 48 hours. Leave may be used to care for the employee's own illness and to care for sick family members as under California law, plus an employee without a spouse or registered domestic partner may designate a person for whom leave may be taken to provide care. Employers may take reasonable measures to verify that an employee's use of sick leave is lawful and cannot require an employee to incur expenses in excess of $5.00 to show their eligibility for paid sick leave. Employees may not be required to use paid sick leave in increments larger than one hour. Unused leave need not be paid upon termination of employment, but the unused balance must be reinstated if the employee is rehired within a year. Employees covered by a collective bargaining agreement are exempt if the agreement contains a clear and unambiguous written waiver of the right to leave under the ordinance.

San Diego: Employees who perform at least 2 hours of work in the city in one or more calendar weeks in a year must accrue 1 hour of leave for every 30 hours worked in the city. Accrued leave may be capped at 80 hours and employees may be limited to using 40 hours of leave per year. Unused leave will roll over to the next year subject to the 80-hour cap on total accrued leave. Alternatively, employees may be given a lump sum of 40 hours of available leave at the beginning of a year, which need not be carried over. Leave may be used to care for the employee's own illness and to care for sick family members as under California law, plus leave also may be used when the employee's place of business is closed due to a public health emergency or the school or child-care provider of a child in the employee's care is closed due to a public health emergency. Employers may require reasonable documentation of the reason for the employee's use of sick leave for absences of more than three consecutive workdays. Employees may not be required to use paid sick leave in increments larger than 2 hours. Unused leave need not be paid upon termination of employment, but the unused balance must be reinstated if the employee is rehired within six months of termination. There is no exemption for employees covered by a collective bargaining agreement.

San Francisco: Employees who perform any work in the city must accrue 1 hour of leave for every 30 hours worked in the city. Employees who only work occasionally in the city or who attend conferences or meetings there are not covered unless they work 56 or more hours in the city. Employers of fewer than ten employees may cap accrual at 40 hours. Employers of ten or more employees may cap accrual at 72 hours. Employees may be given a lump sum of leave in any amount at the beginning of the year, but they will begin accruing leave again after working the number of hours required to accrue the lump sum amount granted. Unused leave will roll over to the next year subject to the applicable accrual cap. Leave may be used to care for the employee's own illness and to care for sick family members as under California law and for organ or bone marrow donation by the employee or a family member. An employee without a spouse or registered domestic partner may designate a person for whom leave may be taken to provide care. Unused leave need not be paid upon termination of employment, but the unused balance must be reinstated if the employee is rehired within a year. Employees may not be required to use paid sick leave in increments larger than one hour. Employees covered by a collective bargaining agreement are exempt if the agreement contains a clear and unambiguous written waiver of the right to leave under the ordinance.

Other Cities: Other California jurisdictions, including Berkeley, Emeryville, and Santa Monica, have enacted their own paid sick leave ordinances. You should check with your legal counsel or the websites of the jurisdictions in California where you have employees to determine if a local paid sick leave ordinance applies to them.

fyi **Paid Sick Leave Required of Certain Federal Contractors**

Employees who work on certain federal contracts and subcontracts awarded, renewed, or extended after January 1, 2017, are entitled to up to seven days of paid sick leave per year. The contracts covered by this requirement are construction contracts under the Davis-Bacon Act, contracts for services provided under the Service Contract Act, and contracts to provide certain concessions on federal lands. Covered employees must be allowed to accrue 1 hour of paid leave for every 30 hours worked, up to a maximum accrual of 56 hours per year. Alternatively, employees can be given a lump sum of 56 hours at the beginning of each year to use during the year. Unused leave will carry over to the next year, subject to the 56-hour accrual cap. Unused leave need not be paid upon termination of employment, but if the employee is rehired within 12 months the unused balance must be reinstated.

Employees may use the paid leave (1) for their own illness, injury, or medical condition; (2) to care for a child, parent, spouse, or domestic partner or any other individual related by blood or affinity whose close association with the employee is the equivalent of a family relationship who has an illness, injury, or medical condition; or (3) for treatment or legal proceedings related to domestic violence, sexual assault, or stalking. Leave must be provided in increments no greater than one hour. Employees who are absent for three or more consecutive days may be required to provide documentation of their need for leave if notified of the requirement that they do so before they return to work.

15.6 Leave as a Reasonable Accommodation

A medical leave of absence might be a reasonable accommodation under the Americans with Disabilities Act or Fair Employment and Housing Act for an employee with a disability (see Section 14.4). Such a leave might be required under the following circumstances:

- The employer is not covered by the CFRA because it has fewer than five employees;
- The employee is not eligible for FMLA/CFRA leave because they have not worked for at least 12 months for the employer, because they have not worked for at least 1,250 hours in the year before the leave; or
- The employee has exhausted their 12 weeks of FMLA/CFRA leave.

You cannot place an arbitrary limit on the duration of such leave, such as 30 days. Leave as an accommodation must be provided so long as it does not produce an undue hardship. There is no bright line regarding when a leave becomes an undue hardship for an employer, but the following guidelines might be helpful:

- A short leave of up to two weeks would almost never amount to an undue hardship if an employee could take a vacation of the same duration.
- A better argument for the leave amounting to an undue hardship can be made the more important the position to the employer's operations.
- Where the employee on leave holds a position for which there is substantial turnover, it will be very difficult to argue that it would be an undue hardship to provide the leave when you will likely be hiring for that position when the employee is ready to return to work.
- Indefinite leave, where the employee has no idea when they will be able to return to work, is not required.

Unlike under the FMLA/CFRA, you need not continue paying for health insurance coverage for employees who are on leave as a reasonable accommodation. You may issue them a COBRA notice so that they must bear the cost of the insurance.

Like under the FMLA/CFRA, you may require the employee to provide a current medical certification of their need for leave as a condition of granting or renewing a medical leave. If such a certification expires and the employee fails to return to work or submit a new certification, you may terminate the employee for unauthorized absence, but you should provide at least one written warning to the employee before doing so.

15.7 Military Leave

Both California and federal law provide for military leave, but the federal law provisions are more extensive. The federal military leave law applies to employers of as few as one employee. Employees who are called to active duty in the military services, including reservists and members of the National Guard called to federal service, are entitled to up to five years of job-protected leave. Employees may, but may not be required to, use their accrued vacation time while on military leave. Employees may not use accrued sick leave while on military leave, however. An employee's employer-provided health coverage is not affected by military leaves of 30 days or less. For absences of more than 30 days, the employee must be allowed to continue coverage for up to 24 months in a manner similar to COBRA continuation, by paying 102 percent of the premium.

An employee who completes military service is entitled to reinstatement unless separated from military service on a bad conduct discharge or on other than honorable conditions. The employee is not entitled to reinstatement, though, if you can establish that circumstances have so changed as to make re-employment impossible or unreasonable. For example, you may be excused from re-employing the employee when an intervening reduction in force would have included that employee. Yet you may not refuse to re-employ the employee because another employee was hired to fill their position during their absence, even if re-employment might require termination of the replacement employee.

Military leave is unique in that a returning employee is not entitled to be reinstated to the job they held before going on leave but rather to the job the employee would have attained if their employment had not been interrupted due to military service. This is known as the "escalator principle." The employee must be restored to the position, seniority, status, and rate of pay to which they would have likely advanced had they not taken military leave. If an opportunity for promotion that the employee missed during military service is based on a skills test or examination, then you must give the employee a reasonable amount of time to adjust following reinstatement, and then give the skills test or examination. Nonetheless, the employee must be qualified for the escalator position. You must make reasonable efforts to help the employee become qualified to perform the duties of this position but you are not required to place the employee in a higher position than the employee held when they left if the employee cannot, after your reasonable efforts, qualify for the higher position. In such a situation the employee would need to be reinstated in the position that they left. Upon reinstatement, moreover, the employee is credited with all seniority and other rights and benefits the employee would have had if they not gone on leave.

Another distinct feature of military leave is the restriction on terminating an employee following return from leave. Such an employee may not be terminated except for cause within 180 days if the leave was between 30 and 180 days, and within one year if the leave was for more than 180 days.

15.8 Military Spouse Leave

Under California law, employers of 25 or more employees must provide up to ten days of unpaid leave to an employee who is a spouse of a member of the military who is on leave from military deployment. The employee must provide notice to the employer within two business days of learning that the employee's spouse will be on leave that the employee intends to take such a leave. You may require the employee to provide written documentation of the spouse's leave status.

15.9 Jury Duty or Witness Leave

You must grant a leave of absence to employees who are called to serve on a jury or to appear in court to testify pursuant to a subpoena or court order. This requirement applies to employers of all sizes.

Exempt employees must be paid for the time they spend on jury duty unless they are absent from work and perform no work for an entire workweek. Nonexempt employees need not be paid for jury service.

15.10 Voting Leave

An employee who does not have sufficient time to vote in a statewide election outside of working hours must be permitted, without loss of pay, to take enough working time that, when added to voting time available outside of the workday, will enable the employee to vote. The maximum working time that may be taken is two hours, and it must be at the beginning or end of the employee's shift. The employee must give at least two working days' notice of their need for time off to vote.

15.11 Leave for Victims of Crimes

California law requires job-protected leave for employees who are the victims of certain crimes, or whose family members are victims of such crimes.

Victims of Violent or Serious Felony Crime or Crime of Theft or Embezzlement

Employees must be allowed time off work to attend court proceedings related to a violent or serious felony crime or a felony involving theft or embezzlement committed against the employee or the employee's spouse, registered domestic partner, child or stepchild, parent or stepparent, or sibling. You may require the employee to provide you with written documentation of the scheduled court proceeding. This leave is unpaid, but employees may use accrued paid sick leave, vacation, or PTO time.

Victims of Certain Crimes to Attend Court Proceedings Regarding Victims' Rights

Employees who are victims of certain crimes are entitled to take leave to appear in court to attend proceedings where the rights of victims of the crime are at issue. Employees may take time off if they or their spouse, parent, child, sibling, or guardian is a victim of any of the following crimes:

- Vehicular manslaughter while intoxicated;
- Felony child abuse likely to produce great bodily harm or a death;
- Assault resulting in the death of a child under eight years of age;
- Felony domestic violence;
- Felony physical abuse of an elder or dependent adult;
- Felony stalking;
- Solicitation for murder;
- A serious felony such as murder, attempted murder, rape, arson, home burglary, robbery, kidnapping, and carjacking;
- Hit-and-run causing death or injury;
- Felony driving under the influence causing injury; or
- Certain sexual assaults.

This leave is unpaid. Employees may take vacation time or PTO but not paid sick leave.

15.12 Leave and Accommodations for Victims of Qualifying Acts of Violence

California law requires that employers provide job-protected leave and reasonable accommodations, where needed, for victims of "qualifying acts of violence." Such acts include:

- Domestic violence;
- Sexual assault;
- Stalking; or
- Any act, conduct, or pattern of conduct that includes (i) bodily injury or death to another; (ii) brandishing, exhibiting, or drawing a firearm or other dangerous weapon; or (iii) a perceived or actual threat to use force against another to cause physical injury or death.

A "qualifying act of violence" exists regardless of whether anyone is arrested for, prosecuted for, or convicted of any crime.

Time Off to Obtain Restraining Order or Injunctive Relief

Employees who are victims of qualifying acts of violence may take time off work to obtain or attempt to obtain a restraining order or other injunctive relief to help ensure their own health, safety or welfare, or that of their child. This right is applicable to employees of employers of all sizes. You may require that the employee show you documentation of the court proceeding. Employees may use vacation or PTO for such leave.

Additional Leave Rights of Employees of Employers of 25 or More Employees

Employers of 25 or more employees must allow employees who are victims of qualifying acts of violence, or whose family members are victims of qualifying acts of violence to take time off work for the following additional purposes:

- To obtain or seek to obtain relief from a court, such as a restraining order or other injunctive relief;
- To seek or obtain medical attention for, or to recover from, injuries;
- To seek or obtain services from a domestic violence shelter or similar victim services organization;
- To seek or obtain psychological counseling or mental health services;
- To participate in safety planning;
- To relocate or secure a new residence or enroll children in a new school;
- To provide care to a family member who is recovering from injuries;
- To seek or obtain civil or criminal legal services;
- To prepare for or attend any civil, administrative or criminal legal proceeding; or
- To seek, obtain or provide childcare or care to a dependent adult if necessary to ensure the safety of the child or dependent adult.

A family member for purposes of this law includes a child, parent, grandparent, grandchild, sibling, spouse, domestic partner, or a "designated person" whose association with the employee is the equivalent of a family relationship.

You may require that the employee show you documentation of the reason for this leave. Employees may use vacation or PTO for such leave. The maximum amount of leave an employee may take for these purposes where the employee is the victim of a qualifying act of violence is 12 weeks in any 12-month period. Where a family member is the victim of a qualifying act of violence, you may limit the leave taken to five days for relocation and 10 days for other statutory purposes.

Leave taken for these purposes is offset by the amount of any FMLA/CFRA leave already taken in the same 12-month period. An employee does not have a right to leave under this law that exceeds the amount of leave available under FMLA/CFRA.

Reasonable Accommodation

Employees who are known victims of a qualifying act of violence are entitled to a reasonable accommodation for the employee's safety while at work. A reasonable accommodation may include the implementation of safety measures, such as a transfer, reassignment, modified schedule, changed work telephone number, changed workstation, or installation of a lock. It might also include assistance in documenting a qualifying act of violence or a referral to a victim assistance organization. You must engage in an interactive process to identify a reasonable accommodation (see Section 14.6). You are not required to provide an accommodation that would amount to an undue hardship.

15.13 School Leaves

Employees who are parents or guardians of a child suspended from school have the right to take unpaid leave to appear at the child's school for reasons related to the suspension. This right applies to employees of employers of all sizes.

Employers with 25 or more employees working at the same location must allow employees who are a parent, stepparent, grandparent, or guardian of a child of the age to attend kindergarten or grades 1 through 12, or to be placed with a licensed childcare provider, to take up to 40 hours per year of unpaid time off under certain circumstances:

- To find, enroll, or re-enroll the child in school or with a licensed childcare provider, or to participate in activities of the school or licensed childcare provider. The employee must be given reasonable notice to the employer of such absence and time off for these purposes may be limited to eight hours per month.
- To respond to a "childcare provider or school emergency," which includes a request that the child be picked up or an attendance policy that prohibits the child from attending school or a childcare provider (for example, where a child has a contagious illness); a child having behavioral or discipline problems; a school or childcare provider that closes unexpectedly; or a natural disaster such as fire, earthquake, or flood occurs.

The employee is required to use available vacation or PTO for such absences.

15.14 Volunteer Emergency Responder Leave

All employers must permit employees who are volunteer firefighters, reserve police officers, or emergency rescue personnel to take time off work to perform emergency duty in such a role.

Employers of 50 or more employees must permit employees who are volunteer firefighters, reserve police officers, or emergency rescue personnel to take leaves of absence not exceeding 14 days per year to engage in training for such roles.

15.15 Civil Air Patrol Leave

Employers of more than 15 employees must permit employees who have been employed for at least 90 days and who are members of the Civil Air Patrol to take up to 10 days per year of unpaid leave to perform Civil Air Patrol duty. You may require the employee to produce documentation verifying the employee's eligibility to take such leave. You may not require employees to use vacation, PTO, or sick leave while on Civil Air Patrol Leave.

15.16 Organ or Bone Marrow Donor Leave

Employers of 15 or more employees must provide up to 30 business days per year of paid leave for an employee who has been employed for at least 90 days to donate an organ to another person. Employees who donate bone marrow to another person must be given up to 5 days of paid leave per year. The measuring year begins on the date the employee's leave begins.

You may require an employee to use up to two weeks of earned vacation, sick leave, or PTO for organ donation and up to 5 days of earned vacation, sick leave, or PTO for bone marrow donation. Organ donors may take an additional 30 business days of unpaid leave.

15.17 Alcohol or Drug Rehabilitation Leave

Employers of 25 or more employees must reasonably accommodate an employee who wishes to voluntarily enter and participate in an alcohol or drug rehabilitation program unless an undue hardship would result for the employer. An employer in such a situation must provide unpaid leave to the employee, but the employee can use any accrued leave balance. This leave law will apply where an employee who is a current user of illegal drugs (and thus is not protected by the Americans with Disabilities Act or the California Fair Employment and Housing Act) requests a leave but is not eligible for protected leave under FMLA/CFRA.

15.18 Bereavement Leave

Employers of five or more employees must allow employees who have been employed for at least 30 days to take up to 5 days of bereavement leave for the death of a spouse, child, parent, sibling, grandparent, grandchild, domestic partner, or parent-in-law. The 5 days need not be taken consecutively, but they must be taken within three months of the date of the death of the family member. The leave need not be paid, but the employee must be allowed to use accrued vacation or sick leave while on bereavement leave. The employee may be required to produce proof of the family member's death, such as a death certificate, published obituary, or other written verification of death or memorial services from a government agency, religious institution, or funeral home.

15.19 Leave for Reproductive Loss

Private employers of five or more employees and all public sector employers must provide employees up to five days of job-protected leave for a reproductive loss event defined as a miscarriage, stillbirth, unsuccessful assisted reproduction, failed adoption, or failed surrogacy. The leave is unpaid but the employee may use vacation or paid sick leave. The leave need not be taken consecutively but it must be completed within three months of the reproductive loss event. Employees need not provide documentation of the reproductive loss event in connection with a request for such leave. The maximum allowable amount of reproductive loss leave is 20 days within a 12-month period.

CHAPTER 16

Conducting Workplace Investigations

Over the last two decades the focus of most lawsuits for harassment and discrimination has shifted. In the early days of harassment lawsuits the focus was on the acts of harassment, which were often shocking and egregious. Years of million-dollar verdicts, employers' implementation of strict policies against harassment, and training of managers and employees have eliminated much of the blatant workplace harassment that once occurred. Today, the focus in harassment and discrimination lawsuits is less on the alleged misconduct and more on what the employer did to investigate and correct the misconduct.

Every internal harassment or discrimination complaint presents an opportunity to win a lawsuit—or to avoid one altogether. Virtually every lawsuit for harassment or discrimination starts with some type of complaint, either internally or through an outside agency or attorney. Even if the complaint comes from the outside, a prompt and objective internal investigation may still be crucial to successfully defending the claim. By contrast, a poorly conceived or ineptly executed investigation can create more liability than the alleged misconduct itself.

16.1 Legal Reasons for Conducting Careful Investigations of Workplace Misconduct

There are numerous legal reasons why an employer should conduct prompt and effective investigations of workplace misconduct.

The Employer's Obligation to Take All Reasonable Steps to Prevent and/or Correct Discrimination and Harassment

California law affirmatively obligates an employer to "take all reasonable steps to prevent discrimination and harassment from occurring." This law provides a separate ground for a lawsuit against an employer besides the alleged misconduct itself when harassment or discrimination is proven and when it is additionally shown that the employer failed to take steps to prevent or properly remedy the harassment or discrimination. Conducting a prompt, objective, and comprehensive investigation in response to a complaint of harassment, therefore, will assist in establishing a defense to a "failure to prevent" claim. Comprehensive and objective investigations of harassment complaints may also aid an employer in establishing the *Faragher/Ellerth* defense to a harassment claim under federal law or the "avoidable consequences" defense under state law (see Section 13.5).

Avoidance of Punitive Damages

In California, an employer cannot be held strictly liable for punitive damages for the acts of managers who are not "officers, directors or managing agents" of the company, and a "managing agent" is a manager who is sufficiently senior in the company that they have the ability to make or change corporate policies. Most managers and supervisors at the operating level would not qualify as managing agents under this definition. An employer may be liable for punitive damages for the misconduct of a lower-level manager, however, if it ratifies the conduct of such manager. An employer's failure to conduct an adequate investigation of a complaint of harassment or discrimination, or its failure to take appropriate corrective action following an investigation, may be deemed ratification of the misconduct and may subject the company to exposure for punitive damages.

Avoidance of Claims of Negligent Retention

Even if an internal employee complaint of harassment or other misconduct does not result in a lawsuit, if the complaint is not investigated adequately and corrective action taken when warranted, and the misconduct continues, third parties (such as vendors, customers, or independent contractors) who are later victimized by such misconduct may sue for negligent retention, among other claims.

Defense Against Wrongful Termination Claims

A poorly conducted investigation that leads to termination of the accused can potentially lead to a wrongful termination lawsuit by that individual. Even if an employee is employed at will, they may still claim to have been terminated for an unlawful reason, such as race, sex, age, or national origin discrimination, or in retaliation for having complained about unlawful activities. However, a thorough and objective investigation can overcome a wrongful termination claim in many instances. In *Cotran v. Rollins Hudig Hall Int'l, Inc.* (1998), the California Supreme Court held that an employer need not prove conclusively that harassment occurred to successfully defend a wrongful termination lawsuit by the accused harasser. Rather, the court held that an employer need show only that, at the time the termination decision was made, acting in good faith and following an investigation that was appropriate under the circumstances, it had reasonable grounds for believing the harassment occurred.

16.2 Initiating the Investigation

An investigation should be initiated when evidence of employee misconduct surfaces. Oftentimes this will occur as a result of an employee complaint. Complaints can come in a number of forms and from a variety of sources, including:

- Verbal complaint by an employee to a manager;
- Verbal complaint by an employee on the employer's complaint hotline;
- Verbal complaint by an employee to HR;
- Verbal complaint by an employee during an exit interview;
- Written complaint by an employee;
- Verbal or written report by an employee that another employee is being harassed or mistreated;
- Charge of discrimination filed with the U.S. Equal Employment Opportunity Commission (EEOC) or the California Civil Rights Department (CRD);
- Letter from an attorney representing an employee or employees; and
- Lawsuit alleging harassment or other misconduct.

When such a complaint is received, it should be acted on as soon as reasonably possible. Prompt action will reinforce the notion that the employer takes such complaints seriously.

Initially, you should determine the nature of the complaint. Does it allege a violation of law, company policy, or something else? Many employers have a zero tolerance policy against harassment. This means that an act need not be unlawful to violate company policy. For example, the law requires that harassment be "severe or pervasive" to be unlawful. An employee's making a single off-color remark is probably not enough by itself to be deemed unlawful harassment by a court, but such a remark nonetheless may violate the employer's zero tolerance policy. Depending on whether the complaint arises internally, or via a communication from a lawyer or government agency, the distinction between an alleged violation of law or of company policy may be important.

Some conduct of which employees may complain internally does not amount to a violation of law or company policy but rather involves merely the exercise of proper management discretion or the maintenance of proper discipline. Examples include complaints by employees that they cannot have the shift they want or that their manager wrote them up unfairly. Although such complaints should be examined for any evidence of unlawful retaliation or discrimination based on a protected category (for example, race, sex, national origin, age, or disability), in the absence of such evidence a formal investigation need not be conducted. Rather, HR should contact the complaining employee and inform them that the conduct that is the subject of the complaint does not appear to address a possible violation of any law or company policy. The employee should be given the opportunity to provide any further information in support of the complaint. If none is provided or if it still does not appear that the complaint involves a potential violation of any law or company policy, the matter may be closed, and the employee should be so notified in writing.

If the complaining employee is no longer employed and has elected to pursue legal action, you must still conduct an investigation. Sometimes there is a concern that investigating a complaint that is the subject of pending legal action may create evidence (in the form of documentation of misconduct) that can be used against the employer. Though this may occur, the misconduct is likely to be documented anyway in the course of the investigation by the EEOC or the CRD, or in the discovery phase of a lawsuit. If a manager or other employee is guilty of the conduct charged in a lawsuit, it is far better for the employer to establish such guilt via an objective investigation and terminate the employee than to retain the employee in the hope that the misconduct will not be proven in court. In most such cases the misconduct is easily proven in court, and the employer will be portrayed as having perpetrated a cover-up that can lead to a disastrous result in court. Pursuit of a prompt and thorough objective investigation can help prevent exposure to punitive damages in a current lawsuit, as well as help prevent further lawsuits by other employees. ***If a discrimination charge or lawsuit is pending, however, guidance of legal counsel should be obtained at the outset of and during the course of the investigation.***

What About Anonymous Complaints?

Anonymous complaints should be investigated in the same manner as those with a complainant whose identity is known. The method of investigation will depend on the details provided in the anonymous complaint. If the complaint is sufficiently detailed the investigation should proceed in the same manner as any other complaint. If the complaint is only vague or general it should not be ignored. Rather, an environmental assessment should be conducted to determine if there is inappropriate conduct occurring. Such an assessment would involve interviewing the employees in the work group regarding how they interact with one another and with their supervisor, and if they have experienced or witnessed any behavior that is inappropriate or has made them uncomfortable.

16.3 Selection of the Investigator

One of the first considerations is to determine who will serve as the investigator. There is no legal requirement that an outside investigator be used. Investigations of most types of employee misconduct may be conducted internally by HR professionals, provided that the assigned investigator has sufficient training and experience in the conduct of investigations of workplace misconduct. A novice investigator should not be assigned to investigate allegations of serious misconduct. An outside investigator should be considered when:

- No sufficiently trained and experienced internal investigators are available;
- The accused is in the "chain of command" above the internal investigator who might be used (such as when the accused is the CFO or CEO, and HR reports to one of those officials); and
- The misconduct involves suspected criminal acts (such as sexual assault or embezzlement), and an investigator with law enforcement experience is preferable.

If an outside investigator is retained, California law requires that such person be either an attorney or a licensed private investigator. HR professionals may lawfully conduct internal investigations but may not be retained to conduct outside investigations. An employer should not have its regular outside employment lawyer conduct an investigation of employee misconduct if it wishes to have that lawyer serve as defense counsel in the event of a lawsuit, as a lawyer cannot effectively serve as both advocate and witness in the same case.

16.4 Placing the Accuser and/or the Accused on Paid Leave

If the accuser is still employed and is under the supervision of the accused, consider placing the accuser, the accused, or both on a paid leave of absence during the investigation. This helps (a) prevent intimidation or retaliation by the accused; (b) avoid disruption of the workplace via the accused, the accuser, or both attempting to line up witnesses or supporters on their behalf; and (c) generally reduce tension in the workplace caused by the complaint and investigation.

If the allegations against the accused are serious, ordinarily the accused should be placed on leave of absence pending the completion of the investigation regardless of whether the accuser is still employed. If the accuser is particularly upset or emotional, the accuser should be placed on leave as well. Use care, however, in placing an accuser on leave against their will, as the accuser may later claim that the leave was actually a retaliatory termination.

16.5 Preparation for the Investigation

Before the investigation commences, the investigator should take some time to examine the context in which the complaint arose. To start, the investigator should obtain and review the personnel files of the accused and the accuser. With respect to the file of the accused, the investigator should ascertain the following:

- Did the employee sign an acknowledgment of the employee handbook, the company's policy against harassment, or any other relevant policies?
- Did the employee receive supervisor training regarding harassment and discrimination if such training was required?
- Has the employee been disciplined in the past for similar types of misconduct?

With respect to the file of the accuser, the investigator should examine the following factors:

- Did the employee sign an acknowledgment of the employee handbook and the company's policy against harassment? Has the employee been disciplined recently or by the accused manager such that the complaint might have been brought for revenge or in an attempt to block termination or further discipline?
- Has the employee made prior complaints about similar types of alleged misconduct on the part of the accused or others?
- Has the employee been disciplined for conduct similar to that which is the subject of the complaint?

Other documents may also be useful, depending on the nature of the complaint. If video surveillance recordings for the period in question would be helpful, they should be obtained and reviewed. Managers' schedules and employees' time records may also be useful toward establishing who was present—or not—during the incidents alleged.

Access should be obtained to all emails on the employer's computer system between the accuser and the accused. If the complaint involves the sending of offensive emails, the accused's emails should be examined to determine whether similar emails were sent to other employees. If the accuser complains of unwanted sexual advances by the accused or an unwelcome relationship between the accuser and the accused, and the accuser has a company email account, the accuser's emails to the accused should be examined for statements made about the relationship, and to others about the accused's conduct or the nature of the relationship.

Personal emails and text messages might be requested from the accused, accuser, or both following their interviews by the investigator.

The investigator must also determine whom to interview and in what order. At the very least, the accuser and the accused must be interviewed, usually in that order. When the accuser and accused provide different accounts of the facts in question (that is, a "he said/she said" type of situation), other employee or nonemployee witnesses must also be interviewed if they are available.

When the accuser is no longer employed, an effort must still be made to interview them. Such an attempt may not be successful, particularly if the accuser has filed a lawsuit or charge of discrimination with the EEOC or the CRD, or is represented by an attorney, but the attempt must be made nonetheless. If unsuccessful, the investigator should document their attempt to interview the accuser. If the accuser refuses to be interviewed, the investigation should proceed based on the information set forth in any written complaint, charge of discrimination, lawsuit, or letter from the accuser's attorney.

Employee witnesses should ordinarily be interviewed at the location where they are employed, and they must be paid for the time spent in the interview. A place should be located in the facility where they work where confidential interviews may be conducted. If the accuser and accused are on leave, or are no longer employed, they ordinarily should be interviewed at a place other than the location where they are or were employed. If the accuser expresses reservations about the place proposed for the interview, an attempt to accommodate them by selecting an alternative location should be made.

Former employees (and nonemployee witnesses when applicable) should be contacted by phone, and the investigator should attempt to meet with them in person if possible. If the witness is not able or willing to meet the investigator in person, the investigator should conduct the interview by telephone.

If the accuser, the accused, or any witness is unable to speak and write English, and the investigator does not speak the language spoken by that individual, arrange to have an interpreter present for the interview. Employees who cannot write English should be permitted to write any written statement requested of them in their native language.

16.6 Conducting Interviews

Interviews of the accuser, the accused, and any witnesses should be conducted in a careful and deliberate manner, as described subsequently.

Opening Statement

Before commencing the interview, the investigator should inform each witness that the purpose of the interview is to thoroughly investigate a complaint of misconduct and to take appropriate corrective action, if warranted, because the employer takes complaints of misconduct seriously. In addition, witnesses should be informed of the following:

- Pursuant to the company's anti-retaliation policy, they will not be retaliated against for participating in the investigation, and they are to immediately contact the investigator or HR if they feel they are being retaliated against.
- Employees who are found to have been untruthful during the investigation are subject to discipline, up to and including termination.

- No conclusions will be reached until all facts are gathered and analyzed.
- Information provided during the investigation will be kept as confidential as possible so as to protect everyone's privacy, but the investigator should not grant the accuser's request that any or all information communicated during the interview be "kept just between us" or will remain "off the record."
- The accuser and accused should be informed that the results of the investigation will be communicated to them at the conclusion of the investigation and that appropriate action will be taken in the event violations of company policy are found to have occurred.

Interview of the Accuser

The investigation should begin with an interview of the accuser. If the accuser has already provided a written complaint, the investigator should use the interview to go over the written complaint with the accused. Then the accuser should be asked if the written complaint is complete or if there is additional information to be added. If the accuser has not already provided a detailed written complaint, the investigator should use the interview to obtain a detailed statement from the accuser.

If the accuser asks to have a friend, relative, coworker, or other representative present during the interview, the investigator should try to discourage their presence but should not absolutely refuse to allow such a person to be present so long as they sit quietly and do not disrupt the interview. An accuser who has an attorney will most likely want that attorney to be present for any interview. In such event, it may be appropriate for the employer's attorney to be present at the interview as well. Should an attorney or other representative accompany the accuser, the investigator should not engage in an argument or discussion with the representative, or allow the representative to ask questions or to interject in or interfere with the interview. Should such interference occur, the representative should be asked to remain quiet or to leave the interview. Should the representative continue to interfere, the interview should be terminated, and legal counsel should be consulted.

The following are guidelines for interviewing the accuser.

Begin with obtaining some background on the individual to help establish rapport and to establish context:

- How long have you worked at the company and in which positions?
- How well do you get along with your supervisor? Do you feel you can go to them with problems?
- Have you had any work-related problems before this incident? If so, how did you deal with them?
- Did you receive a copy of the employee handbook?
- Are you familiar with the company's policy against harassment?

Next, obtain the specifics of the accuser's complaint if they are not already set forth in detail in writing. For each incident reported, obtain the following information:

- When (date and time) did it happen?
- Where (specific location) did it happen?
- If touching is alleged, where on your body were you touched, and for how long? Did the accused say anything before, during, or after the touching?
- If improper language or advances were used, what were the exact words that were spoken?
- Were there any witnesses to the incident? Who were the witnesses, and what did they see or hear?
- Did you report this incident to anyone (including a coworker, friend, or family member)?
- Did you take any notes or make any diary entries regarding this incident?
- Did you send any emails or text messages or post any messages on social media regarding this incident?
- Did you see or hear the accused say or do anything similar to any other employee?

If the complaint involves emails, text messages, notes, or other written communications, ask the accuser the following:

- Did you keep copies of the emails, text messages, or writings? Where are they?
- Did you give or show copies to anyone?
- Did you respond to the emails, text messages, or writings? What did you say? Do you still have your responses?

If the complaint involves allegedly unwelcome sexual advances or requests for dates, ask the accuser the following:

- What exactly did the accused say?
- What did you say in response?
- Have you and the accuser ever socialized outside of work? In what respect, and how many times? Were other employees present?
- Did you ever go on a date with the accused?
- Did you ever have sexual relations with the accused? Where? How many times?
- Did the accused ever give you gifts or money?
- Did you ever borrow money or ask for money from the accused?
- Did the accused ever call you at home or on your cell phone?
- Did you ever call the accused at home or on their cell phone?

- If you and the accused had a consensual relationship, how long did it last? Whose decision was it to end the relationship, and why?
- Did the accused threaten you with any job-related retaliation after the relationship ended?
- Do you believe you have experienced any retaliation from the accused?
- Have you met outside of work with the accused since the relationship ended?

If the complaint involves alleged discriminatory treatment, ask the accuser the following:

- What specifically happened to you that you feel was discriminatory?
- What makes you think that what happened was on account of your protected status?
- What was your supervisor's explanation for what happened?
- Are you aware of other employees who were treated differently? Who were they, and what were the circumstances?
- Are you aware of other employees who were treated the same as you? Who were they, and what were the circumstances?

After the interview of the accuser is completed, they should be asked to put into writing all the factual detail of each of the incidents covered during the interview that were not already detailed in a prior written complaint. If the accuser is unable or unwilling to do so, the investigator should offer to write a statement from their own notes for the accuser to review and sign. Either way, the written statement should contain the following at the end:

- A statement that the writing contains an accurate and complete account of each and every incident of harassment or discrimination of which the accuser is complaining;
- A certification that the statement is signed under penalty of perjury: "I certify under penalty of perjury that the foregoing is true and correct;" and
- The accuser's handwritten signature and date of signature.

Interview of the Accused

The accused generally has no legal right to have a friend, relative, coworker, or other representative present during the interview, and the presence of such representatives should not be allowed. The only exception is with respect to union-represented employees, who have the right to the presence of a union representative during any interview or meeting that might lead to disciplinary action. An accused who is a current employee has no right to have an attorney present for the interview. Should the accused refuse to appear for the interview without their attorney, contact legal counsel.

The investigator's interview of the accused should begin with some background questions:

- How long have you worked at the company?
- In which positions?
- Did you receive a copy of the employee handbook?
- Have you received manager training on harassment in the workplace? How many times? When was the most recent training session?
- Has anyone ever brought a complaint against you for harassment or discrimination? How was that complaint resolved?

Next, ask some general questions about the accuser:

- How long have you worked with the accuser?
- What kind of employee is the accuser?
- Have you had to discipline the accuser for anything?
- Has the accuser been disciplined by other managers?
- Would the accuser have any reason to make up false allegations against you?
- To your knowledge, has the accuser complained of harassment in the past?

Next, address the specifics of the complaint. Start with broad, nonleading questions, and then narrow them to focus on each of the specific incidents alleged:

- On April 1st, did you work the same shift as Sam Server?
- Was there a time when you, Sam, and other employees were standing outside your office talking at the start of the shift?
- Did you touch Sam?
- Where did you touch Sam?
- Did you touch Sam's buttocks?
- Did you slap Sam's buttocks?
- Did you say to Sam: "Lookin' good!"?

If the accused admits that any of the specific incidents occurred, inquire as to the accuser's role in the incident, if any. For example:

- After you slapped Sam, did Sam say anything?
- Did Sam strike or touch you anywhere?

At the conclusion of the interview, the investigator should write a statement for the accused to sign that contains either admissions or refutations of the key allegations in the accused's complaint. The accused should sign the statement under penalty of perjury. If the accused admits during the interview to have engaged in the misconduct alleged but refuses to sign a statement, do not force the issue but proceed nonetheless to consider the appropriate disciplinary action.

If the accused denies allegations that have been confirmed by other witnesses, confront the accused with this fact, and inquire if the accused wants to remain steadfast in their denial of the allegations in light of their confirmation by other witnesses. If the accused remains steadfast, ask: "Do you know why the accuser and all these witnesses would say you said or did these things if in fact you did not?"

When the interview has concluded, tell the accused to remain on paid leave of absence until they are contacted with the results of the investigation.

Interview of Witnesses

Unless the accused admits the conduct alleged by the accuser, any witnesses whose names were provided by the accuser, or who otherwise might have observed the conduct in question, should be interviewed. Start with some background questions:

- How long have you worked at the company?
- In which positions?
- Do you enjoy your job?
- Who is your supervisor? How do you get along with them? Do you feel you can go to your supervisor with problems or complaints?
- Have you ever gone to HR with a problem or complaint?
- Do you feel that you could go to HR with a problem or complaint if you wanted to do so?

Then ask some broad questions regarding the general working environment:

- How would you describe the working environment at the company?
- Has anything happened at work that has made you feel uncomfortable?
- Have you had any problems in working with the accused?
- Has the accused ever said or done anything to you that you found offensive?
- Has any other employee or manager ever done anything to you that you found offensive?

Next, address the specifics of the accuser's complaint. Ask the witness whether they saw or heard each of the incidents described by the accuser that the witness reportedly observed. If the witness confirms the incident generally, ask the witness open-ended questions to elicit detail, such as the exact words the accused said or exactly where the accused touched the accuser. *Do not ask leading questions initially.* The truth is more likely to come out if witnesses can put their stories in their own words. For example, the wrong way to ask questions is as follows:

- On April 1st, did you observe Mike Manager slap Sam Server on the buttocks?
- When Mike slapped Sam, did you hear him say, "Lookin' good, baby!"?

The correct way, by contrast, is to ask questions that do not obviously suggest the answer, although eventually specific questions will need to be put to the witness to allow them to confirm or refute the account of the incident given by the accuser. For example:

- On April 1st, did you work the same shift as Mike Manager and Sam Server?
- Was there a time when you, Mike, Sam, and other employees were standing outside the manager's office talking at the start of the shift?
- Did you see Mike do anything to Sam that seemed improper?
- Did you see Mike touch Sam in a way that was improper?
- Did you see Mike touch Sam on the buttocks?
- Did you see Mike slap Sam on the buttocks?
- Did you hear Mike say anything to Sam that you thought was improper?
- Did you hear Mike say to Sam: "Lookin' good, baby!"?
- Did you hear Sam say anything in response?
- Have you ever seen Mike touch Sam in an inappropriate way on any other occasion?
- Have you ever seen Mike touch any other employee in an inappropriate way?
- Have you ever heard Mike say anything inappropriate to Sam on any other occasion?
- Have you ever heard Mike say anything inappropriate to any other employee?
- Has Mike ever touched you inappropriately?
- Has Mike ever said anything inappropriate to you?

At the conclusion of the interview, write a statement for the witness to sign under penalty of perjury that contains all the key facts related in the interview. Be sure that each fact the accuser claimed would be confirmed by the witness is in fact confirmed or refuted by the witness. Repeat this process for each witness interviewed.

Follow-Up Interview of Accuser

If the accused denies the allegations, and they are not corroborated by other witnesses, conduct a follow-up interview of the accuser:

- Inform the accuser that one or more of the allegations were denied by the accused and (if applicable) not corroborated by the witnesses interviewed.
- Ask the accuser if they wish to remain steadfast in the allegation and if so, whether any other witnesses or documents could help substantiate the allegation(s).

If additional witnesses are identified who were not interviewed previously, interview them as described previously.

Confidentiality of Investigations

You may require the accuser, the accused, and all witnesses interviewed to keep the content of the interviews confidential for the duration of the investigation. This can be important in preventing retaliation, tainting of potential witness testimony by the accuser or the accused, and damage to the reputation of the accused where the allegations are determined to be unfounded. Therefore, all persons interviewed should be instructed not to discuss their interview with any other employee while the investigation is ongoing. After the investigation is concluded, however, the National Labor Relations Board (NLRB) will examine any requirement of continued confidentiality in terms of whether its impact on employees' right to discuss their working conditions with one another is outweighed by legitimate business justifications. This standard, unfortunately, makes the lawfulness of confidentiality rules extending beyond the close of the investigation uncertain until the NLRB develops this area of the law more fully. In the meantime, one test that might be applied to whether confidentiality may be required after the close of the investigation is whether the investigation established that wrongdoing occurred. Where the complaint is not substantiated there would be a compelling interest in protecting the reputation of the accused by making the confidentiality rule permanent. On the other hand, where wrongdoing is established and one or more employees disciplined for it, the interests of employees to discuss the matter as an element of their working conditions would likely outweigh any interest in keeping the matter quiet indefinitely.

16.7 Resolving Credibility Issues and Reaching a Conclusion

After all interviews have been conducted and all relevant documents have been reviewed, the investigator will need to decide whether it is more likely than not that the allegations in the accuser's complaint are true. This is easy if the accused admits one or more of the allegations. It is more difficult if the accused denies the allegations and there is no corroboration by other witnesses. Nonetheless, a credibility determination must be made if at all possible. If the accused denies the allegations, consider the following:

- Was the accused credible in their denials of the allegations? For example, did the accused claim to "not recall" engaging in the alleged misconduct or deny it unequivocally? Was the accused excessively nervous or evasive during the interview? Did the accused look the investigator in the eye when answering the tough questions? Did the accused attempt to change the subject and place blame on the accuser without substantiation?
- Was the accuser observed by any witnesses to have been upset immediately following the incident? Did the accuser report the incident to someone (a coworker, a relative, or a friend) immediately after it occurred? Did the accuser complain to the company within a reasonable period, or wait many months to complain? Did the accuser remark to a coworker that they could use the incident against the accused in the future?
- Were any of the allegations corroborated by other witnesses who seemed credible? Were those witnesses completely neutral, or did they have a potential bias against the accused or have interests aligned with those of the accuser (for example, were they contemplating bringing their own complaints)?
- Does the accuser have any reason to be biased or want to seek revenge against the accused on account of, for example, recent discipline imposed or a promotion or raise request denied?
- Was the accuser's story plausible? Was it consistent and credibly told? Were there inconsistencies between the information provided by the accuser during the interview and information set forth in the accuser's initial complaint? Is the accuser's story contradicted by documents, such as time records, email, or text messages?
- Were the accused and accuser involved in a consensual but extramarital or other inappropriate relationship such that the accuser might have a reason to want to rewrite history to appease a spouse or significant other?

After weighing all of these considerations, a conclusion must be reached regarding the respective credibility of the accuser and the accused. Then, the investigator must determine whether the misconduct alleged in fact occurred. The standard is "a preponderance of the evidence" (more likely than not), *not* the "beyond a reasonable doubt" standard that applies in criminal cases. Moreover, the investigator should not conclude whether any laws were broken. Rather, the investigator should address only whether misconduct occurred in violation of company policies.

16.8 Use of Polygraph During Investigations

Sometimes during an investigation of employee misconduct the use of a polygraph examination may be suggested. While the Employee Polygraph Protection Act (EPPA) generally prohibits employers from using polygraph examinations in the employment context, there is an exception under EPPA for investigations of an employee reasonably suspected of being involved in an incident causing economic loss to the employer such as theft, embezzlement, or sabotage.

Subjecting such an employee to a polygraph test is not a good idea, however. You may not *require* a polygraph under such circumstances; you may only *request* it. Before you can request it, however, you must have reasonable suspicion that the employee was involved in the incident. You must provide to the employee a written notice describing (a) the loss being investigated, (b) the nature of the employee's access to the property taken or destroyed, and (c) your basis for suspecting the employee. Should the employee refuse to take the polygraph, or to start the test and later decide to terminate it, and you fire the employee anyway based on the evidence of misconduct you already had in order to request the polygraph, the employee will likely argue that you terminated them in retaliation for declining to take or continue the polygraph test. Use of a polygraph during an examination of employee misconduct can provide a savvy employee with a means of avoiding discipline for such misconduct or for pursuing a lawsuit based on that discipline. For this reason a polygraph examination should not be given during an investigation of misconduct even if it would be lawful.

16.9 Taking Appropriate Corrective Action

When the investigation is completed you must address the result of the investigation with the accuser and the accused.

There is no legal requirement that the accused be fired in every instance that harassment or other misconduct has been found to have occurred. Rather, you must take disciplinary action that is appropriate under the circumstances and that is effective in putting an end to the misconduct.

When the Allegations Appear to Be True

If, following the investigation, the allegations appear to be true, and one or more violations of company policy have been established, disciplinary action must be imposed against the accused. There is no legal requirement that the accused be fired in every instance that harassment or other misconduct has been found to have occurred. Rather, you must take disciplinary action that is appropriate under the circumstances and that is effective in putting an end to the misconduct. You must also take into account how others were disciplined in the past for similar types of misconduct, particularly when less serious forms of misconduct are involved. There are a number of options for disciplinary action, which include:

- *Termination.* This is appropriate for serious cases of misconduct, such as sexual assault, a non-consensual manager-subordinate sexual relationship, when repeated acts of misconduct on the part of the accused have been established, or when the accused had been warned or disciplined previously for similar types of misconduct.
- *Suspension without pay.* This is appropriate for less serious cases of misconduct, or when only one incident occurred versus a pattern or series of incidents. It should be accompanied by a final written warning.
- *Written warning.* This is appropriate when the conduct is relatively minor, such as one or a few inappropriate verbal remarks.
- *Sensitivity training.* This may be required in conjunction with a suspension or written warning, and is appropriate in situations when the accused is found to have made insensitive remarks or inquiries, or has engaged in unwelcome but nonsexual touching, invasion of personal space, or similar behavior. Such training can be provided either by a member of the HR staff or by an outside consultant.

Whatever discipline is imposed must be communicated in writing, and the employee disciplined should be asked to sign an acknowledgment of receipt of the written notice. When notifying the accused of the results of the investigation and of the discipline to be imposed, make references only to violations of company policy. Do not state that violations of the law have been found to occur. A copy of the written disciplinary notice should be retained in the employee's personnel file.

The accuser should be notified that appropriate disciplinary action has been taken against the accused. If the accused is terminated or has resigned, the accuser should be informed. If any lesser disciplinary action is imposed, the accuser should not be informed of the specific discipline that was imposed. Verbal communications should be followed up in writing.

When the Allegations Cannot Be Substantiated

When the allegations of the accuser cannot be substantiated, both the accuser and the accused should be notified in writing.

16.10 Creating and Maintaining an Investigative File

Upon the completion of the investigation, a special investigative file should be created and maintained separate from employee personnel files and should contain the following documents:

- The accuser's written complaint;
- Written statements given by witnesses;
- Written statement given by the accused, if any;
- The investigator's notes;
- Copies of all documents reviewed in the course of the investigation; and
- Copies of correspondence to the accused and accuser at the conclusion of the investigation.

The investigation file should *not* contain:

- Emails to or from, or notes relating to communications with, legal counsel;
- "To-do" lists for the investigation;
- The investigator's subjective impressions or editorial comments about any persons interviewed during the investigation; or
- Articles or materials on how to conduct an investigation.

CHAPTER 17

Avoiding Retaliation Claims

Retaliation is one of the most common claims appearing in California employment lawsuits. If an employee is terminated after taking a leave, complaining about harassment or discrimination, or alleging safety violations or pay irregularities, a retaliation lawsuit is likely to follow regardless of how well deserved the termination. This chapter will address the various types of retaliation claims that may arise and some strategies for avoiding them.

17.1 What Constitutes Retaliation

Termination of employment is the most commonly alleged form of retaliation, but adverse employment actions short of termination may also qualify. Examples include suspension, demotion, failure to hire, failure to promote, loss of pay, unjustified poor evaluations, or other actions that cause a substantial adverse change in the terms and conditions of the employee's employment. Acts that merely disappoint an employee, or that amount to petty slights or annoyances, do not qualify as retaliation, but where the line is drawn is not always clear. Any act or omission that prevents or interferes with an employee's ability to perform their job duties may constitute retaliation. An example would be a manager's refusal to communicate with a subordinate after they file a complaint of harassment.

17.2 Who Can Claim Retaliation

Terminated employees are the most common retaliation claimants but most anti-retaliation laws also cover job applicants and former employees who claim they were retaliated against post-termination. For example, you may not lawfully reject a job applicant solely because they filed a lawsuit for discrimination against a prior employer. Likewise, a former employee who alleges that their former employer "blackballed" them by preventing them from obtaining new employment after they filed a charge of discrimination may have a viable retaliation claim.

17.3 Retaliation in Violation of Laws Against Discrimination and Harassment

California's Fair Employment and Housing Act (FEHA) prohibits retaliation against any person who has "opposed" any practices forbidden under the act, or who has filed a complaint or testified or assisted in any proceeding under the act. Protected conduct does not just include filing a complaint with a government agency or testifying in such an agency's proceedings. Protected conduct includes raising internal complaints of harassment or discrimination. The conduct complained of does not actually have to violate the law so long as the employee reasonably believes that it does. For example, one off-color remark in the workplace would not likely be found to be so "severe or pervasive" as to constitute unlawful harassment (see Section 13.1). An employee who reports that remark to HR would likely be legally protected from retaliation, however.

A request for an accommodation of a disability or of religious beliefs or practices is also protected activity for purposes of a retaliation claim.

An employer may not retaliate against an employee by contacting or threatening to contact an immigration or law enforcement agency about the immigration status of an employee, former employee, applicant, or a family member of any such persons. Family members include spouses, domestic partners, parents, children, siblings, aunts and uncles, nieces and nephews, cousins, grandparents, grandchildren, great-grandparents, and great-grandchildren.

17.4 Retaliation in Violation of Leave Laws

The anti-retaliation provisions of the federal Family and Medical Leave Act (FMLA) and the California Family Rights Act (CFRA) are broadly written. They prohibit an employer from interfering with, restraining, or denying the exercise of (or the attempt to exercise) any right under the law to take family or medical leave. You, therefore, may not take adverse action against an employee for having requested or taken an FMLA or CFRA leave, and this protection against retaliation applies to intermittent leaves as well. You may not take into account an employee's or applicant's having taken a family or medical leave as a negative factor in hiring or promotion decisions. Moreover, you may not count FMLA or CFRA leave as an "occurrence" of absenteeism under an attendance policy.

The FMLA and the CFRA also contain provisions prohibiting retaliation for opposing or complaining about a violation of the leave laws, or for testifying or assisting in any enforcement proceeding.

California's pregnancy leave law prohibits retaliation against an employee for taking a pregnancy leave or for requesting a reasonable accommodation relating to pregnancy.

Employees who file workers' compensation claims or take workers' compensation leave are protected from retaliation by Section 132a of the Labor Code. This law has been interpreted as allowing an employer to replace (but not terminate) an employee on leave when required by business necessity. You should use caution in exercising this right, however, because employees on workers' compensation leave may also have leave rights under the FMLA and the CFRA or qualify as disabled and be entitled to leave as a reasonable accommodation. These laws provide broader protection to employees than does Section 132a (see Sections 14.8 and 15.1).

17.5 Retaliation in Violation of Whistleblower Laws

State and federal law provide numerous protections for employees who complain about violations of law as well as health or safety issues.

California's General Whistleblower Law

Section 1102.5 is California's most comprehensive whistleblower law. It prohibits retaliation against employees who complain internally as well as to any government agency about violations of law. Specifically, the law protects employees who report information to any of the following:

- A government or law enforcement agency.
- A person with authority over the employee (that is, a supervisor or manager).
- Another employee who has authority to investigate, discover, or correct the violation or noncompliance (typically, HR).
- A public body performing an investigation, hearing, or inquiry when the employee has reasonable cause to believe that the information discloses a violation of state or federal statute or a local, state, or federal rule or regulation. This law also prohibits retaliation against an employee whom the employer believes *may* disclose such information (that is, "Let's fire them before they report us").

This law also prohibits employers from retaliating against employees for refusing to participate in an activity that violates a state or federal statute or a local, state, or federal rule or regulation. It additionally forbids an employer from retaliating against (that is, refusing to hire) an individual who exercised their whistleblower rights under this law at a prior employer.

This law includes a burden-shifting provision in the event a lawsuit is filed. Once the plaintiff shows by a preponderance of evidence that their whistleblowing was a contributing factor in the employer's decision to terminate or take other adverse action against the employee, the burden shifts to the employer to prove, by clear and convincing evidence, that the termination or other adverse action would have occurred for legitimate, independent reasons even if the employee had not engaged in protected whistleblower activity.

Complaints About Unpaid Wages

Labor Code Section 98.6 prohibits retaliation against an employee for making a written complaint internally regarding unpaid wages, for filing a claim with the Labor Commissioner or for pursuing other legal action relating to any rights enforced by the Labor Commissioner (including the right to be paid wages on a timely basis), or for initiating a proceeding under the Private Attorneys General Act.

The federal Fair Labor Standards Act also contains a provision prohibiting retaliation against employees who file a complaint or initiate a legal proceeding alleging a violation of federal wage and hour law, such as the failure to pay the federal minimum wage or applicable overtime.

Complaints About Health or Safety Matters

Labor Code Section 6310 prohibits retaliation against an employee who complains internally to the employer, to their union, or to the Occupational Safety and Health Administration (OSHA), the California Division of Occupational Safety and Health (Cal/OSHA), or another government agency regarding an employee health or safety matter, or who has participated in an employee safety committee.

Refusing to Work During Certain Emergencies

Labor Code Section 1139 prohibits retaliation against an employee who refuses to report to work or who leaves work based on a reasonable belief that the workplace is unsafe as the result of a natural disaster or a criminal act. The employee must have a reasonable belief that there is real danger of death or serious injury should the employee remain on the premises. The statute does not apply to first responders, disaster service workers, employees of health care facilities, and certain other employees. The statute specifically does not apply during a health pandemic.

Complaints About Financial Fraud

The federal Sarbanes-Oxley Act prohibits retaliation against employees who complain internally to a supervisor or manager or externally to a federal law enforcement agency regarding:

- Mail fraud.
- Wire fraud.
- Fraud against a financial institution.
- Fraud involving trading of commodities.

- Fraud on shareholders.
- Violation of any rule or regulation of the Securities and Exchange Commission.

This law applies to publicly traded companies as well as to private companies that are contractors or subcontractors of publicly traded companies.

17.6 Wrongful Termination in Violation of Public Policy

Retaliation claims may also be brought in the form of claims for wrongful termination in violation of public policy. California courts recognize four types of such wrongful termination claims:

- When the employee was terminated for refusing to violate a law.
- When the employee was terminated for performing a legal obligation.
- When the employee was terminated for exercising a legal right or privilege.
- When the employee was terminated for reporting (internally or to a government agency) a violation of a constitutional provision, statute, or regulation.

An employer's violation of internal policies or violation of agreements with third parties will not support a claim for violation of public policy. The violation must be of some established public law, not of broad aspirational notions such as "stable employment," "fair treatment of employees," or "good customer service." Complaints about deficient product quality are protected if the employer is bound by laws or regulations governing product quality, such as in the food, drug, and aerospace industries. Complaints about unsafe working conditions, or an employee's refusal to work in conditions perceived to be unsafe or unhealthful, may also be protected given OSHA's requirement that employers provide a safe and healthful working environment.

A complaining employee need not be correct that the activity complained of violates the law so long as the employee has a reasonable and good faith belief that the activity is illegal. Likewise, an employee's refusal to carry out their employer's directive based on a mistaken belief that it violates the law will be protected if the employee's belief is reasonable and in good faith.

17.7 Avoiding Retaliation Claims

It often occurs that an employee who is about to be terminated shows up with a complaint, or goes out on leave, just as the hammer is about to fall. If you are not careful in handling the termination, a retaliation lawsuit is almost certain to follow.

When faced with whistleblowing or other protected activity by an employee about to be fired, take a hard and objective look at how well the reasons for the termination are documented. The best case is one in which the decision to terminate the employee was made and documented but not yet carried out when the employee complained or requested leave. You should always document a decision to terminate an employee at the time the decision is made, particularly when it may take a few days to implement the termination decision.

If the decision was not documented when made, review the documentation of the employee's performance deficiencies. Is nothing in the file, or was the employee on a final written warning? A final warning will not be helpful, however, if the employee has received multiple "final warnings" about their performance yet was not terminated until they engaged in protected activity.

Also consider the seriousness of the offense and the quality of your proof that the offense occurred. An employee caught stealing, coming to work on illegal drugs, or assaulting a customer or coworker will not have a credible whistleblower claim if your proof of the misconduct is irrefutable. It is also important, when terminations for rule violations are concerned, that the rule be clearly communicated in an employee handbook or other policy statement. For example, if you are going to terminate an employee for insubordination, be sure that the conduct fits within the definition of insubordination in the employee handbook or code of conduct.

Likewise, be mindful of the nature of the protected activity. A poorly performing employee who is handling a difficult pregnancy or who needs family leave to care for a seriously ill child will be a much more sympathetic plaintiff than the employee who responds to being placed on a performance improvement plan by going on "stress" leave or complaining of "harassment" by their boss in relation to the discipline imposed.

When documentation of an employee's performance problems is poor, and their need for leave or complaint of wrongdoing appears legitimate, you may have no good option other than to delay the termination until enough time has passed from the complaint or the conclusion of the leave such that the argument that the protected activity caused the termination will be less credible. That time should be used to document the employee's deficiencies and give them a fair chance to improve. However, do not attempt to create the documentation too rapidly. An employee who is placed on a performance improvement plan on their first day back from maternity leave or an employee who is written up five times in the first week after returning from a workers' compensation leave will have an even better case for retaliation when you finally terminate them.

CHAPTER 18

Rightful Terminations

Given all the wrongful termination lawsuits in California, employers are understandably leery of firing even the worst employee. They need not be, however. When a termination is properly set up in advance, the chances of avoiding a lawsuit are actually good. An up-to-date arbitration agreement (see Chapter 3) and a comprehensive employee handbook (see Chapter 4) are important to have in place if possible before you terminate an employee. This chapter will address how to set up a defensible termination as well as some of the laws that apply to terminations.

18.1 Setting Up a Defensible Termination

Be Sure There Is a Written Record of Prior Discipline

Sometimes employers are confused about the need for written documentation of misconduct or performance problems. Since an at-will employee may be terminated for any reason or no reason, why is documentation of a reason for termination necessary?

Establishing an employee's at-will status is vital because it prevents claims for breach of an implied contract to terminate only for good cause, but that is all that it does (see Chapter 2). It does not protect an employer from claims of discrimination, retaliation, or wrongful discharge in violation of public policy. In those cases an employer must articulate a lawful, nondiscriminatory, or nonretaliatory reason for termination. It is not sufficient merely to say that the employee was employed at will. Moreover, although the law books say that the plaintiff always has the burden of proof in a lawsuit, the practical reality is that most judges and juries expect the employer to prove that it had a good reason (or at least a lawful one) for terminating an employee, and in most cases that the employee received sufficient warnings before termination.

What is sufficient warning depends on the type and seriousness of the offense. Several warnings are advisable for minor infractions such as tardiness or simple work errors. No prior warnings are required for serious misconduct such as stealing, workplace violence, failing a drug test, or sexual assault. Other misconduct that falls in the middle should be documented in one or more prior warnings.

These warnings must be in writing because oral warnings can be difficult to prove in court. Every fired employee "forgets" about all the oral warnings that preceded their termination. Written documentation of an employee's misconduct or performance deficiencies can be essential toward refuting an unlawful motive for a termination.

fyi **Performance Improvement Plans: An Important Tool**

Performance Improvement Plans (PIPs) can be very effective both in managing employee performance and establishing that an employee had a fair warning of performance deficiencies before termination. PIPs must be written and managed properly in order to be effective, however. The eight elements of an effective PIP are as follows:

1. *Identify specific incidents where performance has fallen short.* General terms like "poor attendance," or "poor sales performance," or "uncooperative attitude" are not helpful. Instead, focus on specific examples:
   - "Unexcused absences on 4/11 and 5/2 and late for work without prior notice on 4/30, 5/5, 5/6 and 5/13."
   - "Failed to meet your sales targets in February, March, and April."
   - "Eight of the last ten meeting minutes you prepared contained multiple typographical errors."
2. *Provide specific instructions for how performance must improve.* These goals must be reasonable and attainable, and they must track examples of shortcomings highlighted in the PIP:
   - "No more unexcused absences."
   - "Be at work on time. If you must be late, call your supervisor before the scheduled start of your shift."
   - "Meet your monthly sales targets."
   - "Proofread your written work to eliminate typographical errors."
3. *Provide a reasonable amount of time to improve performance.* Give the employee 30 to 60 days to show improvement. Less than 30 days is not enough.
4. *Give notice of the consequences of failing to complete the PIP successfully.* Ordinarily, the consequence will be termination of employment or demotion to a lesser position. This should be stated.
5. *Reserve the right to extend the PIP period.* If the employee is showing some improvement, you might consider extending the PIP for another 30 to 60 days. If the employee takes a vacation or leave of absence during the PIP period, you should extend the PIP for the duration of the vacation or leave. If you do extend the PIP period, be clear that termination could occur before the end of the new period if performance is unsatisfactory.

6. *The employee should sign the PIP document.* It is important to get the employee's buy-in, if possible. If the employee refuses to sign the PIP, have two members of management sign it, indicating "Employee refused to sign." The PIP is no less valid if the employee refuses to sign it.
7. *Don't allow the employee to block the PIP.* If the employee attempts to avoid the PIP by filing a workers' compensation claim, going on medical leave, or complaining about labor law or safety violations, proceed with the PIP anyway. Otherwise, you will lose the ability to issue effective PIPs in the future.
8. *The employee's manager or supervisor should provide regular check-ins.* These meetings should be weekly or bi-weekly, and a written summary of each meeting should be given to the employee.

Review the Personnel File

Always review the employee's personnel file before terminating an employee, especially when a termination for poor performance is involved. Was the employee's last performance evaluation a positive one? Did the employee recently receive a raise or a commendation for good performance? The presence of these items need not get in the way of a termination that must occur, but you should be prepared to explain why circumstances have changed so drastically that termination is now warranted.

Review an employee's personnel file before terminating them. You will not want to learn for the first time when you walk a terminated employee out to their car that the employee is parked in the "Employee of the Month" space.

Document the Termination Decision When It Is Made

Sometimes it takes a while to effect a termination decision. It may take time to obtain approval of HR or higher management, or to gather all the persons who need to be present for the termination meeting. During that time facts can develop that could make the termination much more complicated. The employee could suffer a work-related injury, request a medical leave, or complain of harassment. Therefore, if you cannot carry out the termination right away, at least document the fact that you have made the termination decision. Send an email to HR or higher management notifying it that you have decided to fire the employee. If you plan to replace the person, start the process required to post the vacancy or recruit a replacement. This kind of documentation is incredibly helpful in court as it shows that you made the decision to terminate the employee *before* they filed a workers' compensation claim, requested leave, or complained about harassment, thus refuting the claim that the termination decision was made in response to those events. In many cases courts will award summary judgment for the employer when this evidence is available.

Put the Real Reason for the Termination in Writing

You should give the employee a letter or document stating the real reason for the termination. Never, ever, provide an untrue reason for a termination, even if you are trying to protect the feelings of the employee. To do so will make it easy for a plaintiff's lawyer to argue that you discriminated against the employee because California's jury instructions allow juries to find discrimination if the reason the employer gave for the termination was untrue.

Sometimes employers think they are protecting themselves by listing a vague reason for the termination such as "didn't work out" or "at-will termination," or by not putting anything in writing at all. This is a mistake. Never hide from the real reason for a termination, no matter how unpleasant it might be to confront the employee with the truth.

A good plaintiff's lawyer will pounce on your equivocation to make it appear that you had an illegal motive. Be clear about the reason for termination. Own it and be prepared to defend it.

Do Not Give Too Many Reasons for a Termination

The more reasons you list for a termination, the less credible they all become. If you are terminating an employee for failing to meet productivity standards, leave it at that. Resist the temptation to "pile on." Do not also state that the employee was tardy, submitted late expense reports, wasted time on the internet, or other reasons. For one thing, it is almost certain that other employees also engaged in such trivial misconduct yet were not fired. More importantly, adding a lot of reasons makes it appear that you lack confidence in the primary reason for the termination.

fyi ▸ What Not to Say When Terminating an Employee

Say the wrong thing during a termination meeting and you can transform a strong and defensible termination into a wrongful discharge lawsuit. Here are some examples of what you should *not* say:

1. *"We are laying you off."* A layoff is a termination due to lack of work. It should never be used to try to make a performance-based termination more comfortable. Too often employees are told they are being laid off when their employer has already started recruiting their replacement. If you lay off an employee, you cannot replace them until some time later when business improves. Moreover, a layoff of only one employee looks very suspicious.

2. *"We are exercising our employment-at-will rights."* Employment-at-will only protects against claims for breach of implied contract to terminate only for good cause, but hardly anyone sues on this ground today. Most employment lawsuits allege discrimination or retaliation, and in these cases the employer must show a legitimate, non-discriminatory reason for why the employee was terminated. You should give this reason for the termination.
3. *"You're just not a good fit."* This is not a good reason to give if the employee is in a protected classification such as race, national origin, age, sexual orientation, etc., as it suggests that the employee's protected classification is the reason they are not a good fit. It's better to say, "You are not meeting the requirements of the job."
4. *"We are terminating you for stealing."* Unless you have a confession or video evidence, you should not give a reason for a misconduct termination that you cannot prove. Instead of accusing an employee of stealing it is better to say, "money was missing from your cash drawer," or "you left the store with merchandise in your backpack."
5. *"We are terminating you for job abandonment."* If you use this reason, be sure the conduct meets the definition of job abandonment in your employee handbook. "No call, no show" might be the better description if there is such a policy in your handbook. Note that you cannot count protected paid sick days toward a finding of job abandonment, and you may not terminate an employee for job abandonment who fails to return as scheduled from FMLA/CFRA leave.
6. *"We are terminating you for cause."* If the employee is employed at will, you do not need good cause to terminate. If you say you are terminating the employee for cause, however, a court could find that employment-at-will does not apply, that a "for cause" standard applies, and that you failed to satisfy it.
7. *"We will give you a positive reference."* This statement tends to negate your good reasons for terminating the employee. You should only give neutral references (dates of employment and last position held) on former employees, anyway.

18.2 Severance Agreements

A severance agreement that includes a release of claims is a good option to consider when an employee needs to be terminated but there is little or no prior documentation of misconduct or performance problems. If the employee signs the severance agreement, the risk of a lawsuit is almost entirely eliminated. A valid release of claims must be knowing and voluntary to be enforceable. It is important, therefore, that severance agreements be written, as far as possible, in simple language that the employee can understand. A severance agreement that runs ten pages or longer and contains dense legalese is not ideal and in fact may be vulnerable to attack should a departing employee have second thoughts about having signed the agreement. Moreover, a severance agreement must meet additional requirements to be enforceable.

It Must Provide Consideration Beyond That to Which the Employee Is Entitled

For a severance agreement to be enforceable in California the employee must be given something of value over and above that to which they are already entitled to receive. If an employee is owed accrued vacation pay or a bonus, payment of those sums will not provide lawful consideration to support a release of claims. Valid consideration usually consists of severance pay (when the employee is not already entitled to severance under an employment contract, severance plan, or company policy), payment of COBRA continuation premiums for some period of time, outplacement assistance, or some combination of them.

It Should Include a Provision That All Wages Due Have Been Paid

A release of wages concededly due is not enforceable in California. A severance agreement may, however, express the agreement of the departing employee that all wages due have been paid. All severance agreements should contain such a provision, as well as an acknowledgment of the amount of accrued vacation or paid time off (PTO) due at termination, that such amount was paid, and that such payment was not conditioned on the employee signing the severance agreement.

It Must Include Section 1542 Language

Section 1542 of the California Civil Code provides that "a general release does not extend to claims which the creditor or releasing party does not know or suspect to exist in his or her favor at the time of executing the release, which if known by him or her must have materially affected their settlement with the debtor or released party."

This provision must appear verbatim in any release of claims in California, and there additionally must be language clearly stating that the employee waives this provision and intends to release all claims known or unknown at the time the severance agreement is executed.

Notification of Employee's Right to Consult an Attorney

Severance agreements must contain language notifying the employee that the employee has the right to consult an attorney regarding the agreement. You must also give the employee a reasonable time period of at least 5 business days in order to do so. Since severance agreements for persons 40 years of age or older must provide for at least a 21-day period to consider signing the agreement (see below), this 5 business day waiting period only applies to persons under the age of 40.

Special Provisions Apply to Federal Age Discrimination Waivers

The federal Older Workers Benefit Protection Act (OWBPA) imposes special requirements on waivers of federal age discrimination claims. Severance agreements for departing employees who are 40 years of age or older must therefore contain a recitation that the employee:

- Is waiving, among other claims, any and all potential claims for age discrimination under the federal Age Discrimination in Employment Act.
- Is receiving consideration in exchange for their waiver and release of claims over and above that to which they are already entitled.
- Is advised of their right to obtain the advice of legal counsel of their choosing before executing the severance agreement.
- Is not releasing any claims that may arise after the execution of the severance agreement.
- Will have up to 21 days to consider the severance agreement before executing it.
- May revoke the severance agreement at any time within seven days from the date they execute it.

Further language must be provided advising the employee how to revoke the severance agreement should they wish to do so. On account of this right to revoke the release within seven days of signing it, severance pay should not be due under the agreement until the eighth day after the departing employee's execution of the agreement, or on the next business day if the eighth day falls on a weekend or holiday.

When two or more employees are terminated on the same day or within a short period of time for the same reason (a reduction in force, for example), if at least one of them is age 40 or older the following additional language must be included in the severance agreement:

- A provision stating that the employee has up to 45 days to consider the severance agreement before executing it (as opposed to the 21-day period that applies to single-employee terminations).
- A provision stating that the employee has up to 45 days to consider the eligibility information presented along with the severance agreement.
- Typically as an Exhibit A to the severance agreement, a three-column chart containing, in the first column, a list of all the positions in the "decisional

> unit" of the organization affected by the terminations; in the second column, the ages of all employees in that position who are eligible for severance (because they are being terminated); and in the third column, the ages of all employees in that position who are not eligible for severance (because they are not being terminated).

The purpose of this list is to disclose information from which the employees contemplating signing the severance agreement can determine whether they might have a valid claim of age discrimination based on the ages of those employees who were terminated versus the ages of those who were not. The *decisional unit* for the purposes of this list is the department, location, or identifiable group of employees in which the terminations occurred. Examples might be the "engineering department," the "San Diego office," or "salaried managers at the Stockton manufacturing plant."

Confidentiality Provisions

The National Labor Relations Board (NLRB) has taken the position that severance agreements that prohibit the employee from disclosing the terms of the agreement or other terms and conditions of employment violate Section 7 of the National Labor Relations Act (NLRA), which protects employees' right to engage in concerted activity for their mutual aid and protection. The only exception, according to the NLRB, is that confidentiality may be required as to the amount of severance compensation provided. Severance agreements for executives and managers, who are not covered by Section 7, would also be exempt from the NLRB's restriction on confidentiality. Severance agreements for other employees should require confidentiality only as to the amount of severance, and they should additionally include this disclaimer:

> Nothing in this Agreement prevents or restricts Employee from enforcing their Section 7 rights under the National Labor Relations Act, participating in Section 7 activity (including the right to communicate with former coworkers and/or third parties about terms and conditions of employment or labor disputes, unrelated to the amount of the Severance Pay under this Agreement) or other otherwise cooperating with the National Labor Relations Board's investigative process through investigation, testimony, or otherwise with an administrative agency or court.

Nondisparagement Provisions

If a severance agreement includes a nondisparagement provision, such a provision must not prohibit the disclosure of information about unlawful acts in the workplace.

In fact, nondisparagement provisions must contain the following statement: "Nothing in this agreement prevents you from discussing or disclosing information about unlawful acts in the workplace, such as harassment or discrimination or any other conduct that you have reason to believe is unlawful."

Other Limitations on Severance Agreements

Although the release of claims provision in a severance agreement may contain a covenant not to sue, it may not prohibit the employee from filing a charge of discrimination with the U.S. Equal Employment Opportunity Commission or the California Civil Rights Department. Likewise, the Securities and Exchange Commission takes issue with provisions prohibiting employees from reporting securities law violations to that agency. Therefore, to avoid an attack by one of these agencies on a severance agreement, a provision should contain language stating that the agreement does not prohibit the employee from filing charges with or reporting violations of law to any law enforcement agency, but that the employee waives any monetary recovery from the employer as the result of any such charge or complaint.

In addition, in California, releases of workers' compensation claims are not valid unless signed by a workers' compensation judge. A general release of claims, therefore, will not bar an employee from filing a workers' compensation claim, and a release of workers' compensation claims in a severance agreement will be invalid without a workers' compensation judge's approval.

18.3 Reductions in Force

Before implementing a reduction in force (RIF), you should create a matrix containing all employees in each of the departments, locations, or other working units to be affected by the RIF along with their demographic data: race/ethnicity, sex, age, length of service, and any additional information that might increase the risk of terminating a particular employee such as a disability, a pending workers' compensation claim, or a recent return from medical leave. You should then examine the matrix to ensure that the terminations are not adversely affecting older employees or a particular sex, race, or ethnicity. For each employee in a protected classification you should be prepared to defend why that person was chosen for termination versus other employees in the same working unit who are not in a protected classification. If the defense is weak, you should consider reordering the RIF or offering severance to those employees in exchange for a release of claims.

In reality, almost every RIF will affect employees in one or more protected classifications. This is not a reason to cancel a reduction that is warranted for business reasons, but identifying potential exposure and addressing it beforehand can prevent lawsuits later.

18.4 WARN Acts

The federal and California Worker Adjustment and Retraining Notification (WARN) Acts must be considered whenever a large number of employees are terminated in a RIF or plant closing. These two laws differ in some significant respects.

Federal WARN Act

The federal WARN Act applies to employers of 100 or more full-time employees (or 100 or more full-time or part-time employees who together work at least 4,000 hours per week exclusive of overtime). It applies to the following situations:

- Plant closings involving 50 or more full-time employees who suffer an *employment loss* at a single site of employment in a 30-day period; and
- Mass layoffs involving more than 500 full-time employees, or between 50 and 499 full-time employees and at least 33 percent of the workforce, who suffer an *employment loss* at a single site of employment in a 30-day period.

"Employment loss" is defined as (a) termination other than for cause, resignation, or retirement; (b) a layoff exceeding 6 months; or (c) reduction in hours of more than 50 percent in each month of any six-month period. "Full-time" means employees who are employed for an average of 20 or more hours per week and for more than 6 of the 12 months preceding the date when notice is required. This definition is significant because employees who have worked for fewer than 6 months as of the date notice is required need not be counted in determining whether the thresholds for the notice requirement are met.

The federal WARN Act also has a "90-day rule," which provides that employment losses for two or more groups of employees at a single site of employment occurring within a 90-day period that individually do not meet the threshold for required notice, but would meet the threshold if combined, will require WARN notice unless the employer can prove that the employment losses are the result of separate and distinct actions or causes.

The federal law requires that at least 60 days' notice (or pay in lieu of notice) be given before any covered plant closing or mass layoff. Notice must be given to affected employees individually or to their union if they are represented by a union, to the Workforce Services Division of the California Employment Development Department (EDD), and to the chief elected official of the local jurisdiction in which the plant closing or mass layoff occurred.

Notice need not be provided to employees who are offered a transfer to another worksite within a reasonable commuting distance, or when a transfer is offered regardless of distance and the employee accepts the transfer. Notice is also not needed when the plant closing or layoff is the result of the completion of a project or undertaking, and the affected employees were hired with the understanding that their employment would be limited to the duration of the project or undertaking. Nor is notice required in the event of a strike or lockout in a labor dispute. Notice is also not required in a merger or acquisition when the employees of the seller are hired by the buyer on the effective date of the merger or acquisition.

A reduced amount of notice may be given if the employer is actively seeking new business or capital that, if obtained, would have enabled the employer to avoid or postpone the shutdown and the employer reasonably and in good faith believed that providing timely notice would have prevented it from obtaining the new business or capital. The full 60 days of notice is also not required when the plant closing or layoff is the result of unforeseen business circumstances or a natural disaster. As much notice as possible must still be given in these situations, however.

California WARN Act

California's WARN Act applies to "covered establishments," which are industrial or commercial facilities in which 75 or more "persons" have been employed during the year before the date upon which notice is required. Both full-time and part-time employees should be counted to determine whether this threshold has been met, and all employees who have worked at the facility during the preceding year should be counted, as opposed to counting only the number of employees employed on the date notice is required. All employers that own or operate at least one "covered establishment" are covered by the statute.

At least 60 days' notice is required in the event of a mass layoff, relocation, or termination at a covered establishment. "Mass layoff" means a layoff during any 30-day period of 50 or more employees at a covered establishment, regardless of the percentage of the workforce affected. As under the federal WARN Act, employees who have worked for fewer than six months as of the date notice is required need not be counted in determining whether the threshold for a "mass layoff" has occurred. "Relocation" is defined as a move to another location more than 100 miles away. "Termination" is defined as "the cessation or substantial cessation" of industrial or commercial operations at a covered establishment. There is no minimum employee threshold for relocations and terminations under California law.

Temporary holiday or seasonal shutdowns require 60 days of notice under California's WARN Act if 50 or more employees are affected, even if the shutdown lasts only a few days or weeks.

Unlike the federal WARN Act (which applies only to layoffs exceeding 6 months in duration), California's WARN Act applies to layoffs and furloughs of any duration that involve 50 or more employees in a 30-day period. Even temporary layoffs of short duration due to a downturn in workflow therefore require 60 days' advance notice if 50 or more employees are affected. Likewise, where seasonal shutdowns occur, such as closing between Christmas and New Year's, or during the summer months, at least 60 days' advance notice of such shutdowns must be given.

WARN notice is not required when the plant closing or mass layoff is the result of a completion of a particular project in the construction, drilling, mining, logging, or motion picture industries, and employees were hired with the understanding that their employment would be limited to the duration of the project. Likewise, WARN notice is not required for seasonal employees who were hired with the understanding that their employment would be seasonal or temporary.

Notice is not required under California law when the buyer of assets hires enough of the seller's employees such that 50 or more employees do not lose their jobs as a result of the transaction. The employees hired by the buyer must remain in the same positions they had with the seller, and at the same rate of pay and seniority (if applicable) and with the same benefits.

Notice is not required in the event of a physical calamity or act of war. Nor is notice of a plant closing or relocation required when, under certain conditions, the employer was actively seeking capital or business and a WARN notice would have precluded the employer from obtaining the business or capital. California's WARN Act does not have an unforeseen business circumstances exception.

Consequences of Failing to Provide WARN Notice

Failure to provide WARN notice when it is required can create substantial financial exposure for an employer. Employees who were entitled to notice but did not receive it may generally recover pay and benefits for the period during which notice was not given, to a maximum of 60 days. Employers that do not provide required notice may also be liable for fines and penalties under both federal and state law, plus attorneys' fees for the employees who sue to collect wages, benefits, and penalties. As these suits may easily qualify as class actions, they are often filed when WARN notice is required but not provided.

18.5 Employee Resignations

An employee who resigns need not be permitted to rescind the resignation later. The same result applies even if the employee claims not to have been in their "right mind" when resigning, and even if the employee in fact was suffering from a mental disorder at the time of resignation. An employer need not accommodate such an employee by rescinding the resignation.

May an employee who gives two weeks (or some other amount) of notice be terminated immediately? That depends on whether you have a policy in your employee handbook or otherwise requiring two weeks' notice of termination, or whether the employee has a contract requiring that a specific amount of notice be given. If so, you may terminate the employee immediately, but if you do not pay the employee for the notice period the employee would likely have a valid claim for breach of contract.

If there is no policy or contract requiring prior notice of resignation (as would be the case with at-will employees), an employee who gives notice of resignation need not be paid for the notice period. Note, however, that in such a circumstance the EDD is likely to find that the employee was terminated and determine that the employee is eligible for unemployment insurance benefits. Such a result may generally be avoided by paying the employee for the notice period unless the employee can show "good cause" for resigning (see Section 18.7).

18.6 Documents to Provide to Terminating Employees

In addition to their final paycheck (see Section 7.27), federal and state law requires that terminating employees be given the following documents:

- COBRA notice. Employers of 20 or more full-time equivalent employees must provide the federal COBRA notice, which may be accessed at https://www.dol.gov/agencies/ebsa/laws-and-regulations/laws/cobra. This notice should be mailed to the employee's home and addressed to the employee and employee's spouse, or to the employee "and Family" if the spouse or family are covered by the plan. Employers of 19 or fewer employees that provide health coverage through an insurance company must provide notice to the insurer, which will then issue a notice to the employee under Cal-COBRA. Self-insured employers of fewer than 20 employees are not covered by Cal-COBRA.
- California EDD unemployment benefits pamphlet DE 2320, which may be accessed at https://www.edd.ca.gov/pdf_pub_ctr/de2320.pdf.
- Written notice to employees who are terminated or laid off as to their change in employment status. No specific form of notice is required but a sample notice may be accessed at https://edd.ca.gov/en/Payroll_Taxes/Required_Notices_and_Pamphlets.
- Employers of 20 or more employees must provide the Department of Health Care Services Health Insurance Premium Payment (HIPP) notice, DHCS 9061, which may be accessed at https://www.dhcs.ca.gov/services/Documents/DHCS-9061.pdf.

18.7 Unemployment Insurance

Employees in California who lose their jobs through no fault of their own are generally eligible for unemployment insurance benefits. These benefits, which may range from $40 to $450 per week depending on earnings during a 12-month "base period," are administered by the EDD and are funded by employer taxes. A person will not be eligible for unemployment benefits if they meet any of the following criteria:

- They were an independent contractor and not an employee;
- They are not able to work (for example, are on disability);
- They are not available to work (are on a vacation out of state, for example);
- They resigned without good cause;
- They were terminated for misconduct related to work; or
- They are not actively looking for work each week for which benefits are claimed.

Good cause for resigning may exist if:

- The employer moves the place of employment beyond a reasonable commuting distance;
- The employee moves to accompany their spouse or domestic partner who moves to a place from which it is impractical to commute;
- There are safety or harassment issues in the workplace that the employee has unsuccessfully attempted to correct;
- The employee must leave the workplace to protect themself or their family from domestic violence; or
- The employee must care for a seriously ill family member who is unable to care for themself.

Inherent in the notion of "good cause" is that the reason for leaving work must be compelling. Good cause, therefore, typically will not be found to exist when the employee resigns to look for a better job, to return to school, because of the inconvenience of a normal commute, or as the result of a general dissatisfaction with pay, working conditions, or management.

An employee terminated for misconduct related to work will not be eligible for unemployment benefits, but active and serious misconduct is required for this exclusion to apply. Poor work performance, errors, or mistakes will not qualify. Not all violations of company policy will qualify as misconduct, moreover. Occasional tardiness or absenteeism will likely not qualify, especially if the employee complied with prior notice requirements. When relatively minor offenses are involved, one factor the EDD will consider is whether the employee received prior documented warnings.

If a former employee files a claim for unemployment benefits, you will receive a Notice of Claim Filed. You must respond to this notice, indicating the reason for the employee's departure, within ten days of the mail date of the notice. This does not provide much time for you to complete the response. The EDD may call you and conduct a follow-up interview by phone if it needs more information. Then the EDD will make its determination of whether the employee is or is not eligible for benefits, and the agency will mail you a Notice of Determination. It is not up to the employer in California whether a departed employee will be able to collect unemployment benefits. The EDD will reach its own determination regardless of whether you oppose the unemployment claim.

Should the EDD award unemployment, you have 20 days from the mail date of the Notice of Determination to file an appeal with the California Unemployment Insurance Appeals Board (CUIAB), which will hold a hearing before an administrative law judge. You may attend such hearing in person or by telephone, but the hearing will be recorded, and you will be required to testify under oath and provide copies of relevant documents to the judge. If future litigation with the former employee appears likely, you should consider whether pursuing an appeal of a grant of unemployment benefits is a good idea because:

- The standard for determining eligibility for benefits is favorable to the ex-employee;
- Failure to appeal will result in charges to your employer account but will have no impact on any future litigation; the results of an EDD determination or a CUIAB appeal are not admissible in a lawsuit in court;
- If the ex-employee is able to collect unemployment, they may be less inclined to sue;
- If you appear at the hearing and testify under oath without thorough preparation, you may say something that could be used against you in a later lawsuit. Although the result of the CUIAB appeal is not admissible in court, your recorded testimony under oath at the CUIAB hearing may be used to impeach your testimony in a later court case; and
- If the ex-employee wins the appeal, they may think "the judge thought I had a great case" and decide to sue in the hope of a repeat victory in court.

CHAPTER 19

Unions and Labor Relations

The law regarding private-sector labor relations in most industries is federal; the statute that is the basis for most federal labor relations law is the National Labor Relations Act (NLRA). Federal law preempts state law in most instances, but California does have a few important laws governing strikes and picketing.

19.1 Coverage of the NLRA

The NLRA governs most private-sector employers. The exceptions are:

- Airlines and railroads (they are covered by the Railway Labor Act);
- Agricultural employers (these are covered by the California Agricultural Labor Relations Act);
- Government agencies; and
- Very small businesses (jurisdictional standards vary by type of business).

A common misconception is that the NLRA governs only those employers that have union-represented employees. In fact, however, the NLRA governs virtually all private-sector employers, including nonprofits such as hospitals and universities, with only those exceptions noted above. In recent years, the National Labor Relations Board (NLRB), the federal agency that enforces the NLRA, has targeted non-union employers for having policies that could potentially interfere with employees' right *to form or join unions or engage in concerted activity for their mutual aid and protection*. These rights, among those set forth in Section 7 of the NLRA, are at the core of the NLRA and are the primary basis for the NLRB's scrutiny of nonunion employers.

19.2 Employees' Rights under the NLRA

Section 7 of the NLRA provides employees with four basic rights:

- To engage in concerted activity for mutual aid and protection;
- To form, join, or assist unions;

- To bargain collectively over wages, hours, and working conditions; and
- To refrain from any of the foregoing.

One example of concerted activity is a strike in which employees together refuse to work in a dispute over wages, benefits, job security, safety, or other workplace issues. Most often strikes are called by unions during negotiations over a collective bargaining agreement, but a union is not required for a protected strike to occur. For example, if acting in a concerted manner to protest wages or working conditions, nonunion employees may walk off the job or refuse to accept voluntary overtime.

In recent years, the NLRB has expanded the scope of protected concerted activity "for mutual aid and protection" among nonunion employees. Nonunion employees may organize informally to protest some issue related to their wages or working conditions. Concerted activity can occur as simply as when one employee speaks to management as representative of a group of employees about a workplace issue, or when two or more employees communicate with each other about their pay or a work issue such as sexual harassment or an attendance policy. An employee does not need to have the consent or participation of coworkers to act in a concerted manner. Instead, the NLRB will find purely individual conduct to be concerted if the employee seeks to incite other employees to group action, or if the employee's individual conduct relates to a matter of group concern, as opposed to merely a personal complaint.

The NLRB has recognized that concerted activity is manifest differently in today's technological workplace than in the industrial workplace of 1935 when the NLRA was enacted. Accordingly, the NLRB has applied Section 7 in recent years to social media, email communications, and confidentiality policies.

19.3 Unfair Labor Practices Under the NLRA

Section 8 of the NLRA sets forth a list of unlawful conduct called unfair labor practices. Section 8(a) addresses employer unfair labor practices:

- Section 8(a)(1): Interference with employees' Section 7 rights;
- Section 8(a)(2): Domination or interference with a union (for example, maintaining a "company union");
- Section 8(a)(3): Discrimination against employees to encourage or discourage membership in a union;
- Section 8(a)(4): Retaliation for filing charges with or giving testimony before the NLRB; and
- Section 8(a)(5): Refusal to bargain collectively with a union in good faith.

Section 8(b) addresses union unfair labor practices:

- Section 8(b)(1): Restraint or coercion of employees in their exercise of their Section 7 rights or of an employer in its selection of representatives for collective bargaining;
- Section 8(b)(2): Causing an employer to discriminate against an employee in violation of Section 8(a)(3);
- Section 8(b)(3): Refusal to bargain collectively with an employer in good faith;
- Section 8(b)(4): Engaging in illegal secondary boycott activity;
- Section 8(b)(5): Requiring excessive membership fees;
- Section 8(b)(6): Causing an employer to pay for services not performed; and
- Section 8(b)(7): Illegal recognitional picketing by uncertified unions.

An unfair labor practice case commences when an employee, employer, or union files an unfair labor practice charge with a regional office of the NLRB. The regional office investigates the charge, and if it finds the charge to have merit, issues an unfair labor practice complaint against the employer or union. A hearing is then held before an administrative law judge in which an attorney from the office of the NLRB's General Counsel prosecutes the case. After the hearing the judge issues a decision. If the judge upholds the complaint, they may order a wrongfully terminated employee reinstated with lost wages to be paid by the employer, or order that the employer or union cease and desist from further unlawful activity. Typically the judge orders that the employer or union post a notice of the finding of a violation as well. The judge does not have the power to award compensatory damages (such as for emotional distress), punitive damages, or attorneys' fees.

The judge's decision may be appealed to the entire NLRB. In most cases, three of the NLRB's five members review a judge's decision and either affirm or reverse it. The NLRB's decision can then be reviewed by a U.S. Circuit Court of Appeals.

19.4 The Process by Which Employees Select a Union as Their Bargaining Representative

Section 9 of the NLRA sets forth the process by which employees may select a union as their bargaining representative. Employers should understand not only the formal process by which a union can become certified as a bargaining representative of a group of employees but also what motivates employees as they consider whether to vote for a union.

How Does Union Organizing Get Started?

Union activity usually starts with employee dissatisfaction over pay, benefits, job security, safety, or relations with management. When union organizers arrive at the scene, they attempt to convince the unhappy employees that a union will solve their problems. Employers can therefore take some meaningful steps toward preventing a union from gaining a foothold. These include the following actions:

- *Maintain competitive pay and benefits.* Whereas employees are unlikely to seek union representation over a small pay difference, they will be more motivated to do so when they are substantially underpaid compared to competing businesses (especially those whose employees are represented by a union), or when their health plan or other benefits are considered inferior in the industry.
- *Ensure that supervisors are effective managers and communicate well with the employees they supervise.* They must be good listeners as well as good communicators, and if the employees they supervise do not communicate well in English, they should be able to speak their subordinates' native language. Rank-and-file employees regard their direct supervisor as "the company" in many respects, and if they view their supervisor as ineffective, insensitive, or aloof they may soon become alienated. Supervisors who do not relate well to their subordinates should be retrained or replaced.
- *Maintain a genuine "open door" policy so that employees feel welcome to bring issues and concerns to HR and senior management.* Do not have such a policy just on paper; show employees that you mean it. Senior managers and HR staff should be visible to employees, and when presented with a problem or concern, they must address it promptly. Unions often try to convince employees that they need a "voice" (that is, the union). Employees should feel that their own voices are heard.
- *Without endangering your status as an at-will employer, maintain an atmosphere in which employees feel that they need not fear for their job security, that they are fairly treated, and that the most qualified candidates are promoted.* Managers' decisions to terminate employees should be reviewed by HR to ensure consistency across the company. If reductions in force are necessary, be forthright and candid with employees about the reasons for the layoffs, and use objective criteria (such as length of employment, prior experience, or numerical performance data) to select employees for layoff, not supervisors' subjective evaluation of employees.
- *Consider implementing a seniority system.* If seniority is commonly used in your industry you should consider adopting such a system so that employees will not feel that they must elect a union to gain seniority protection.
- *Move disgruntled employees out of the organization.* These employees usually spread negativity to others, often causing them to mistrust management and view the future pessimistically.

The NLRB's Process for Conducting Union Elections

Under current NLRB law, there are two ways in which a union may become the bargaining representative for a unit of employees.

The Traditional Method

Under the traditional method, the union starts the process by filing a Petition for an Election with the NLRB's regional office that has jurisdiction over the employees involved and serving a copy of the petition on the employer. This petition may be filed electronically. Along with its petition, the union must submit a showing of interest from at least 30 percent of the employees it seeks to represent. Usually this showing is in the form of authorization cards signed by employees and stating that the employee wishes for the union to represent them. In practice, unions often try to obtain a showing of interest of more than 50 percent before filing a petition for an election so as not to waste their time with a group of employees among whom they have the support of less than a majority. In its petition the union must disclose its position on the appropriate bargaining unit, voter eligibility, and other issues regarding the election.

Upon receiving the petition, the NLRB will notify the employer of the petition and send the employer a Notice of Hearing. It will also send the employer a Notice of Petition for Election, which the employer must post within two business days and also distribute electronically if it customarily communicates with employees electronically. The NLRB will determine if the employer and union can agree on the bargaining unit, ballot language, date, time, and place for the election. If no agreement is reached, the NLRB will hold a hearing eight calendar days from the date the petition is filed. The employer must file its Statement of Position by noon the day before the hearing; that statement must contain the employer's position on whether the proposed bargaining unit is appropriate and on details of the election such as date, time, and place. The employer's Statement of Position must also include an electronic alphabetized list of all employees in the proposed unit with their full names, work locations, shifts, and job classifications. If the employer contends that other employees must be included in the unit, or employees proposed by the union to be in the unit should not be included, respective similar lists of those employees must also be provided.

At the hearing an agent of the NLRB will accept testimony from the union's and employer's witnesses to determine the scope of the bargaining unit in which the union election will be conducted. The NLRB will consider whether employees in a proposed bargaining unit share a "community of interest." If so, the NLRB will likely determine that the bargaining unit is appropriate. Such a unit may encompass a single department, a single employee craft, an entire plant, or multiple facilities. Factors the NLRB considers in determining whether a unit is appropriate include:

- Common supervision;
- Similar wages, benefits, and working conditions;
- Interchange between employees in the unit and outside the unit;
- Similarity of skills; and
- Integration of operations.

At this hearing the NLRB agent will also determine who will be eligible to vote in the election. Managers and supervisors are never eligible to vote. Absent agreement by the parties, guards and office clerical employees will not be included in a plant-wide unit but may be union-represented in separate units. Temporary employees are not eligible to vote, but employees on leaves of absence may vote if they have a reasonable expectation of returning to work. However, litigation over whether individual employees are eligible to vote in the election will be deferred until after the election is conducted. The parties may submit closing oral arguments at the hearing but are not allowed to submit post-hearing briefs without permission from the NLRB's Regional Director.

Following the hearing, the NLRB's Regional Director will issue a Decision and Direction of Election that defines the bargaining unit in which the election will occur and sets a date for the election. The election will be set on the earliest date practicable (there is no longer a 20 business day waiting period). Within 2 days of the issuance of the Decision and Direction of Election, the employer must transmit to the NLRB and the union an electronic alphabetized list of all employees eligible to vote, along with their full names, work locations, shifts, job classifications, and their home addresses, plus their home and cell phone numbers and their personal e-mail addresses if the employer has such information.

During the period preceding the election, the employer has the free speech right to communicate with its employees and urge them to vote against the union. Supervisors may speak individually with employees, or group meetings may be held, although the NLRB requires that such meetings be only voluntary and not mandatory. You should notify employees that meetings with management to discuss the merits of union representation are voluntary and that there will not be any negative consequences for employees who choose not to attend.

During these discussions with employees you may highlight the negative aspects of union representation such as mandatory union dues and fees, the high salaries often paid to union officials, corruption on the part of union leadership, the possibility of strikes or lockouts, and union fines. You may discuss negative consequences that occurred at other businesses where employees chose union representation, and you may state your firm opposition to unions. You may inform employees that if they choose a union, there is no guarantee that they will earn more money or have better benefits. You may not, however:

- Threaten employees that if they elect the union they will lose their jobs, or that you will shut down the operation, refuse to negotiate with the union, or refuse to agree to a union contract;
- Interrogate employees about their union activities or their views on unions;
- Promise employees a benefit, such as a pay raise or a new health plan, if they vote to reject a union; or
- Spy on union organizers or on closed union meetings.

You also must not solicit grievances from employees with the express or implied promise to fix them, as the NLRB interprets such conduct as undermining the union.

You are prohibited from terminating employees for union activity. The proponents of unions are not always model employees, and there may be a temptation to terminate them. If you terminate them during a union campaign they will almost certainly file unfair labor practice charges with the NLRB. In response you will have to show that they were terminated for legitimate reasons not connected with their union activities, or the NLRB will order their reinstatement with back pay.

The representation election is by secret ballot and is supervised by an NLRB agent. Alternatively, a mail ballot may be used if in-person balloting is not practical. To win, the union must obtain a majority of all valid votes cast. The losing party may file objections to the election based on the other party's misconduct, and if the NLRB finds merit to the objections, it may hold a hearing. Otherwise, the NLRB will certify the results of the election if the union lost or certify the union as the collective bargaining representative if the union won.

A New Alternative Method

In 2023, the NLRB announced a new method by which a union can become the bargaining representative of a unit of employees. In lieu of filing a Petition for an Election with the NLRB, a union instead may present to the employer authorization cards signed by a majority of employees in a proposed bargaining unit and demand recognition as the representative of those employees. Previously, an employer faced with such a demand could simply decline to recognize the union and the union would need to file its petition with the NLRB. Now, if the employer does not wish to recognize the union as bargaining representative based on the authorization cards, it must file an RM petition with the NLRB within two weeks for a secret ballot vote to resolve the union's claim of majority status. A secret ballot election will then be held, following the same procedure as is outlined above. During that period, if the employer is found to have committed one or more unfair labor practices that would have justified setting aside an election, the NLRB will not order a new election but instead will order the employer to bargain with the union. Both the traditional method for a union to become the bargaining representative of a unit of employees as well as the new alternative method make it more difficult to defeat a union organizing effort once it has begun. This makes it all the more important that an employer take proactive steps in advance, as outlined in the beginning of this section, to prevent a union from getting traction among its employees.

19.5 Collective Bargaining

Once a union is certified as the bargaining representative of a group of employees, negotiations over a labor agreement begin. The union and employer must bargain in good faith over wages, hours, and working conditions. These negotiations, especially regarding an initial labor agreement, may take several months to complete. Neither side is legally required to agree to any specific proposal, but there must be genuine give-and-take as the parties attempt to reach agreement. Either party's refusal to bargain in good faith is an unfair labor practice. The employer must respond to union requests for information regarding subjects for bargaining. Such information may include financial information and information on benefit plans.

One common topic of negotiations is a ***union security clause***. The employer and union may not agree to require that all employees in the bargaining unit must become members of the union. Employees represented by a union may be required to pay the costs of the union representing them, called an ***agency fee***, except in "right-to-work" states where such provisions are prohibited. California is not a "right-to-work" state.

Most collective bargaining agreements contain an arbitration provision under which the union and the employer agree to arbitrate all disputes arising under the agreement. Most such agreements also include a provision that employees may not be terminated except for just cause. This requires that employee terminations in a union environment meet a higher standard than when employees are employed at will. Except in instances of the most egregious misconduct, the union will file a grievance over most employee terminations, and if the union and employer cannot agree on the resolution, the matter will be decided by a neutral arbitrator.

19.6 Obtaining Relief from California Wage and Hour Requirements Through Provisions in a Collective Bargaining Agreement

Unionized employers may obtain some relief from California wage and hour law requirements by including specific language in a collective bargaining agreement (CBA).

Overtime

As noted in Chapter 8, under California law overtime must be paid at time-and-a-half for (1) all hours over 8 in a workday, (2) all hours over 40 in a workweek, and (3) for the first 8 hours on the seventh day of work in a workweek. Double time must be paid for (1) more than 12 hours per day in a workday and (2) more than 8 hours on the seventh day of work in a workweek.

These requirements do not apply to an employee covered by a valid CBA if the agreement expressly provides for the wages, hours of work, and working conditions of the employees, and if the agreement provides premium wage rates for all overtime hours worked and a regular hourly rate of pay for those employees of not less than 30 percent more than the state minimum wage. A CBA therefore may provide for overtime pay that is less generous than is required by California law. For example, it need not provide for daily overtime or double time. Rather, the CBA need only provide for payment of overtime as specified in the CBA itself. A CBA cannot, however, waive the overtime provisions of the Fair Labor Standards Act.

A CBA also may provide for an alternative workweek of four ten-hour days or a "9/80" arrangement without the need for a secret ballot among affected employees and the other required procedures (see Section 8.9).

The expiration of a collective bargaining agreement generally will not result in covered employees becoming subject to California's overtime provisions if a new agreement is negotiated in due course and the parties agree to maintain the prior contract terms during negotiations. Only if the employer were unilaterally to impose new terms and conditions of employment upon expiration of an agreement would the employees come under the protection of California's overtime laws.

Meal Periods

California's meal period requirements (see Section 9.1) do not apply to an employee covered by a valid collective bargaining agreement that expressly provides for the wages, hours of work, and working conditions of employees, and expressly provides for (1) meal periods for those employees, (2) final and binding arbitration of disputes concerning application of its meal period provisions, (3) premium wage rates for all overtime hours worked, and (4) a regular hourly rate of pay of not less than 30 percent more than the state minimum wage.

What is not clear at this point in the development of the law is whether the conditions placed by state law on meal periods are overridden by the required language in a CBA. These state law requirements are that the meal period be at least 30 minutes in duration, that it be completely duty-free, that it begin before the end of the fifth hour of work, that a second meal break be provided for employees who work more than 10 hours, and that an hour of pay must be provided to employees who do not receive a compliant meal break. A union may waive, on behalf of the employees it represents, meal periods before the end of the fifth hour of work if an employee works no more than 6 hours.

Vacation Pay

California law requires that accrued vacation pay and PTO be paid out upon termination of employment (see Section 7.21) *unless otherwise provided by a CBA*. Thus, a CBA may include a "use it or lose it" provision requiring employees to use their vacation by a specific deadline or else have it expire.

Construction, Drilling, Logging and Mining Industries

There are further exemptions from California wage and hour laws available under Wage Order 16 covering employers in the construction, drilling, logging, and mining industries. These include exemptions from the rest break requirements (so long as rest breaks are provided under the CBA), transit time between where employees enter the secured perimeter of the worksite and when they arrive at their place of work (which must be paid unless a CBA provides otherwise), and claims under the Private Attorneys General Act (PAGA) (provided specific language is included in the CBA).

19.7 Strikes and Lockouts

Both the union and the employer must bargain in good faith until they reach agreement on a contract, or until they reach an impasse where no further bargaining is likely to be fruitful. A union may go on strike anytime, without prior notice, unless it is subject to a contractual "no strike" clause. However, unions in the health care sector must give ten days' notice before a strike. Certain strikes are not protected, including intermittent strikes, partial strikes, and sit-down strikes.

Once a valid impasse is reached, the employer may unilaterally implement its "last, best, and final" offer. In addition, upon reaching a valid impasse, the employer may lock out the employees to pressure them to accept the employer's contractual offer. In a strike or lockout over economic issues, the employer may permanently replace strikers and not reinstate them at the conclusion of the strike unless there is evidence of the employer's intent to punish or retaliate against the strikers for striking. You therefore should develop a business justification for replacing strikers and avoid making statements suggesting animus against the strikers.

If the union strikes over an unfair labor practice on the part of the employer, the strikers must be reinstated at the conclusion of the strike, which limits the employer's leverage during the strike. It is important, therefore, for the employer to try to avoid committing any unfair labor practices before or during a strike.

Federal Restrictions on Strikes and Picketing

The NLRA prohibits secondary boycott picketing, which is picketing designed to induce a neutral employer to cease doing business with an employer the union is striking. A typical secondary boycott situation occurs when a union pickets employees of a supplier or subcontractor of the struck employer, inducing them not to cross the picket line and go to work. For this reason many employers experiencing a strike will establish a "reserved gate," which is an entrance to be used exclusively by employees of suppliers and subcontractors. Should the union picket the reserved gate, it would be subject to an unfair labor practice charge for a secondary boycott. Employers may also sue unions under federal law for monetary damages caused by secondary picketing.

Secondary boycott picketing is distinguished from handbilling and other publicity. Unions are permitted to notify members of the public, including customers of a business, that they have a labor dispute with an employer that produces goods sold by the neutral business. Such publicity is lawful so long as it does not have the effect of preventing employees of the neutral employer from going to work. For example, a union on strike against a producer of a certain brand of beer could lawfully distribute flyers to customers of a supermarket urging them not to purchase that brand of beer. The union, however, could not lawfully picket the supermarket to induce the supermarket's employees to engage in a work stoppage as such would amount to a secondary boycott.

California Laws Affecting Strikes and Picketing

California law imposes restrictions on employers that replace strikers. Any advertisement, solicitation, or other communication used to hire striker replacements must clearly state that a strike or lockout is in progress. California law also prohibits employers from hiring "professional strikebreakers," defined as persons who worked for two or more employers in the past five years where there was a strike or lockout in progress. This law may be preempted by federal labor law, however, which clearly recognizes the employer's right to replace strikers. An employee employed by a temporary services agency and supplied to an employer with a strike or lockout underway must be paid their wages on a daily basis under California law.

California also imposes restrictions on courts' ability to enjoin picketing. Employers may obtain injunctive relief against violence on the picket line, threats of violence, and mass picketing in such numbers as to block the ingress and egress of traffic to the employer's property. Courts, though, are not permitted to enjoin peaceful picketing, and unions are specifically permitted to picket or distribute flyers on any public street "or any place where any person or persons may lawfully be." This law has been interpreted to allow picketing and handbilling on private property outside retail stores and other businesses. A court in California, therefore, does not have jurisdiction to enjoin picketing or handbilling as trespassing on exterior private property. The picketing or handbilling must be peaceful, and picketers and handbillers are not permitted to enter stores or other private buildings.

California law also imposes limits on when and how courts may enjoin even violent or other unlawful picketing. Before issuing an injunction the court must hear live testimony in open court, and the court must expressly find that:

- Unlawful acts have occurred or been threatened and are likely to occur or continue unless an injunction is issued;
- A union against which the injunction is sought must have authorized the unlawful conduct that is sought to be enjoined;
- Substantial and irreparable injury to the employer's property will occur if the injunction is denied;
- Greater injury will occur to the employer if the injunction is denied than will occur to the union if the injunction is granted;
- The employer has no adequate remedy at law;
- Law enforcement agencies with jurisdiction over the picketing are unable or unwilling to provide adequate protection; and
- The employer has not failed to comply with any obligation imposed by law, and has not failed to make every reasonable effort to settle the labor dispute by negotiation or by mediation or voluntary arbitration.

19.8 Decertification and Withdrawal of Recognition

Just as a union may gain rights to represent a unit of employees, it may lose those rights as well. Bargaining unit employees or the employer may petition the NLRB to conduct an election to determine whether the union commands the support of a majority of the employees. For an employer to file such a petition, it must have a good faith belief, based on objective evidence, that a majority of employees no longer favor union representation. Alternatively, an employer that can make such a showing may simply withdraw recognition from the union.

There are limits to when such activities may occur. They may not take place during one year following certification of the union as the bargaining representative, nor may they occur during the first three years of the pendency of a union contract.

For the NLRB to conduct a decertification election, a nonsupervisory employee must file a petition with the NLRB accompanied by a showing of interest indicating that at least 30 percent of the employees no longer want to be represented by the union. The NLRB will proceed to set an election, and if a majority of eligible voters rejects the union, it will be decertified as the employees' representative.

CHAPTER 20

Workplace Safety and Health

At the federal level, workplace safety and health are regulated by the Occupational Safety and Health Administration (OSHA) which is part of the U.S. Department of Labor. Federal law allows OSHA to approve state plans under which state governments may manage workplace safety and health law compliance in their state. California is one such state that has its own plan, and in California workplace safety and health are regulated by the Division of Occupational Safety and Health, known informally as Cal/OSHA. Cal/OSHA regulations, called Safety Orders, provide various standards and requirements that employers in the state must meet. Cal/OSHA enforces these standards and requirements via workplace inspections and a process of citations and penalties against employers for violations. Cal/OSHA regulations cover virtually all employers and employees in the state, including state and local government employees.

Some of Cal/OSHA's Safety Orders, such as the one requiring that an employer maintain an Injury and Illness Prevention Plan (IIPP), apply to all employers. Other standards are more specific and apply only to certain industries or work functions, or to specific situations. Unlike under federal law, there is no Cal/OSHA catch-all "general duty standard" that requires employers generally to maintain a safe and healthful workplace. However, Cal/OSHA administrators often cite employers for "failing to maintain an effective IIPP" when they determine an unsafe condition is present in a California workplace. Moreover, Cal/OSHA requirements exceed those of federal OSHA in several instances. A comparison of Cal/OSHA and federal OSHA requirements is beyond the scope of this chapter, but what is important to know is that in California, the Cal/OSHA requirements apply.

20.1 Injury and Illness Prevention Plan

Every employer in California must develop and implement a written IIPP. The IIPP is not merely a document to be written and filed away. It is the foundation for each employer's approach to providing a safe and healthy workplace for its employees. The IIPP must be tailored to a specific workplace but each IIPP must include the following elements:

- Responsibility;
- Compliance;
- Communication;
- Hazard assessment;
- Accident/exposure investigation;
- Hazard correction;
- Training and instruction; and
- Recordkeeping.

A sample basic template for an IIPP document may be found at https://www.dir.ca.gov/dosh/dosh_publications/iipp.pdf. To be effective, however, an IIPP must be more than just a template document. It must address the unique challenges, processes, and procedures that exist at a particular company or plant.

Responsibility

The responsibility section of the IIPP must list the name, title, and contact information of the person(s) in the company with overall responsibility for ensuring that the company maintains an effective IIPP.

Compliance

The compliance section should include the company's established safety policy or a commitment to providing a safe and healthy workplace. It should also indicate what steps the company will take to enforce the safety policy, such as disciplining employees who engage in unsafe work practices, retraining employees where necessary, recognizing and rewarding employees with excellent safety records, or keeping a posted record of days worked without injury.

Communications

The communications section should describe the schedule under which safety meetings are held, as well as describe other means used to communicate with employees about safety such as periodic topical email communications. If the company elects to have a labor/management safety committee to help communicate safety issues to employees, the committee should be referenced in the communications section. This section should also include instructions for supervisors and employees to report hazards and provide employees with the option of reporting hazards anonymously with assurances of no reprisals.

Hazard Assessment

The hazard assessment section should identify the person(s) in the company who will conduct periodic inspections to identify and evaluate workplace hazards. It should also include the schedule for making those internal inspections. A schedule for periodic inspections of all operations should be provided, as well as for the conduct of inspections following the introduction of new substances, processes, procedures, or equipment that might represent a new safety or health hazard, or upon management's discovery of a new safety or health hazard.

Accident/Exposure Investigation

This section should identify the person(s) in the company who will conduct investigations of workplace injuries, illnesses and accidents, hazardous substance spills or exposures, and other safety incidents. Such responsibility can be placed on a single person, such as a director of safety, upon each department head, or upon all managers and supervisors when an accident occurs in the area they supervise. This section should explain that accident investigation is a systematic method for collecting factual information that makes it possible to accurately reconstruct the accident and determine the underlying reasons for the cause of the accident so that preventive measures may be implemented in the future. It should emphasize that the investigation is a *fact-finding, not a fault-finding* exercise. This section should require prompt investigation of accidents and submission of an accident investigation report as soon as possible following an accident.

Hazard Correction

This section should include a statement that all unsafe or unhealthy working conditions or practices will be evaluated and corrected in a timely fashion and that the corrective action taken will be documented. It should state that any identified unsafe work practices will be immediately corrected by providing the employee(s) involved with retraining.

Training and Instruction

The training and instruction section should include a list of all of the types of safety training that are provided to employees and when the training is provided. It should state that training will be provided, at a minimum:

- To all new employees;
- To employees given new job assignments who have not previously been trained;
- Whenever new substances, processes, procedures, or equipment are introduced that amount to a new potential hazard;
- Whenever the company is made aware of a new or previously unrecognized hazard; and
- To familiarize supervisors with hazards to which employees under their immediate direction and control may be exposed.

The IIPP for a construction industry employer should specifically state that supervisory employees shall conduct toolbox or tailgate safety meetings with their crews at least every ten working days.

Generally, employee training should cover:

- Safe work practices in the particular workplace;
- Employees' role and responsibility in maintaining a safe workplace;
- How and to whom to report health or safety hazards;
- When personal protective equipment (PPE) is required and how to use it; and
- What to do in case of an accident or other emergency.

A list of specific training requirements for particular jobs and industries may be found at http://www.dir.ca.gov/dosh/dosh_publications/TrainingReq.htm.

The training and instruction section should include a template of an employee training record for employees to sign every time they receive a training session.

Recordkeeping

The recordkeeping section should describe which records will be made and maintained and for how long. Employers of ten or more employees must keep records of all scheduled and periodic safety inspections, including documentation of any unsafe practices or unhealthy conditions identified and how they were corrected, for at least one year. Employers of fewer than ten employees may elect to state that they will keep inspection records only until the hazard has been corrected.

Likewise, this section should state the company's policy for keeping documentation of safety and health training provided to employees. Employers of ten or more employees must keep these records, including title of training program, name of trainer, and date of training, for at least one year. Employers of fewer than ten employees may state that they will maintain documentation only of training provided to employees with respect to hazards they may encounter at work upon hire or when assigned new duties.

Reduced Documentation Required of Small Employers

Employers with fewer than 20 employees that (1) are not in an industry on the Department of Industrial Relations (DIR) "high hazard" industries list and that have a workers' compensation experience modification rate of 1.1 percent or less, or (2) are in an industry on the DIR's "low hazard" industries list may limit their written documentation of their IIPP to the following:

- The identity of the person(s) with authority and responsibility for implementing the IIPP;

- The scheduled periodic inspections to identify unsafe conditions and work practices; and
- The training and instruction provided to employees.

Cal/OSHA's "high hazard" industries list may be found at http://www.dir.ca.gov/dosh/documents/hhu-list-2025-2026.pdf. Its "low hazard" industries list may be found at http://www.dir.ca.gov/doshpol/low-hazard-industries.pdf.

20.2 Emergency Action Plan

Employers in California with ten or more employees must maintain a written Emergency Action Plan which covers at least the following topics:

- Procedures for emergency evacuation, including type of evacuation and exit route assignments;
- Procedures to be followed by employees who remain to operate critical plant operations before they evacuate;
- Procedures to account for all employees after emergency evacuation has been completed;
- Procedures to be followed by employees performing rescue or medical duties;
- The preferred means of reporting fires and other emergencies; and
- Names and job titles of persons or departments who can be contacted for further information or explanation of duties under the plan.

In addition, employers must establish an alarm system to notify employees of fires or other emergencies, and they must designate and train a sufficient number of employees to assist in the evacuation of other employees. All employees must be provided training on the Emergency Action Plan:

- Upon its implementation;
- Whenever an employee's responsibilities under the plan change; and
- Whenever the plan is changed.

The written Emergency Action Plan must be reviewed with each new employee and must be kept in the workplace where it may be reviewed by employees.

20.3 Fire Prevention Plan

California employers with ten or more employees must maintain a written Fire Prevention Plan that includes the following items:

- Potential fire hazards, and their proper handling and storage procedures;
- Potential ignition sources (such as welding, smoking, and others) and their control procedures;
- The types of fire protection systems or equipment in place to control any fires that might occur;
- Names and job titles of those persons responsible for maintenance of fire protection systems and equipment; and
- Names and job titles of those persons responsible for control of accumulated flammable or combustible waste materials, if any.

The plan also should describe how the employer will control the accumulation of flammable and combustible waste materials so that they do not contribute to a fire emergency. Employees must receive training regarding the fire hazards inherent in the materials and processes to which they are exposed, and new employees must receive orientation to those parts of the plan the employee must know to protect themself in the event of an emergency. The Fire Prevention Plan must be kept in the workplace where it may be reviewed by employees.

20.4 Hazard Communication Program

All employers in California must have a written Hazard Communications Program. This program should include:

- A list of the hazardous chemicals known to be present in the workplace, including the product identifier for each;
- The methods the employer will use to inform employees of the hazards of nonroutine tasks (for example, cleaning reactor vessels), and the hazards associated with chemicals contained in unlabeled pipes in their work areas;
- A description of how Cal/OSHA's requirements for labels and other forms of warnings will appear on containers of hazardous chemicals in the workplace;
- A description of how and when safety data sheets (previously known as "material safety data sheets") will be obtained from the manufacturer or importer of each hazardous chemical used in the workplace; and
- A description of the training that will be provided to employees with respect to hazardous chemicals in the workplace.

In multiemployer workplaces, the Hazard Communication Program must include the methods employers will use to inform employers sharing the same work area of the hazardous chemicals present and suggestions for appropriate protective measures, including the following:

- How the employer will provide access to safety data sheets to other employers or make them available in the workplace;
- How the employer will inform the other employers of any precautionary measures that must be taken to protect employees during normal operations in the workplace and in foreseeable emergencies; and
- How the employer will inform the other employers of the labeling system used in the workplace.

Required Employee Training

Employers must provide training on hazardous chemicals in the workplace to existing employees, to new employees, and whenever a new chemical hazard is introduced into the work area. Such training must include:

- Informing employees that training on hazardous chemicals in the workplace is required by law;
- Informing employees of any operations in their work area where hazardous chemicals are present;
- Informing employees of the location of the Hazard Communication Program and safety data sheets for all hazardous chemicals in the workplace;
- Training on how to detect the presence or release of a hazardous chemical in the work area (such as by operation of monitoring devices or visual appearance or odor of hazardous chemicals when released);
- Training on the physical, health, simple asphyxiation, combustible dust, pyrophoric gas hazards, and other hazards of the chemicals in the work area, measures they can take to protect themselves from these hazards, emergency procedures, and use of personal protective equipment (PPE) where appropriate;
- An explanation of how to read safety data sheets and the labels received on shipped containers of hazardous chemicals as well as the labeling system used in the workplace for hazardous containers; and
- Informing employees of their right (1) to personally receive information on hazardous chemicals to which they may be exposed, (2) to have their physician or collective bargaining agent receive information regarding such hazardous chemicals, and not to be discharged or discriminated against on account of their exercise of their rights with respect to hazardous substances in the workplace.

If an employer receives a new or revised safety data sheet indicating significantly increased risks to, or measures necessary to protect, employee health compared to the information on the prior safety data sheet, the new safety data sheet must be provided to affected employees within 30 days.

Proposition 65

California nongovernmental employers of ten or more employees are subject to Proposition 65, the Safe Drinking Water and Toxic Enforcement Act. Every year, California publishes a list of chemicals known to cause cancer or reproductive toxicity (this list may be found at https://oehha.ca.gov/proposition-65/proposition-65-list).

Compliance with the requirements of the Cal/OSHA Hazard Communication Standard is considered to be compliance with Proposition 65. If chemicals on the Proposition 65 list are covered under the employer's Hazard Communication Program, no further compliance is required. If chemicals on the Proposition 65 list are not addressed in the Hazard Communication Program (for example, where safety data forms are not available), then a clear and reasonable warning must be provided to employees via signage or labeling stating that they may be exposed to chemicals that are known to cause cancer or reproductive harm.

20.5 Heat Illness Prevention Plan

All California employers with employees working outdoors must have a Heat Illness Prevention Plan, either as a separate document or as a component of its IIPP. The plan must be written in English and in the language understood by a majority of the employees affected, and it must be made available to employees at the worksite. It must, at a minimum, include explanations for how the following requirements will be met:

- Procedures for the provision of water and access to shade;
- High heat procedures for when temperatures exceed 95 degrees Fahrenheit;
- Emergency response procedures; and
- Heat acclimatization procedures for employees.

Employers should note that Cal/OSHA enforcement staff give priority attention to employer compliance with Heat Illness Prevention Plan requirements.

Requirements to Provide Drinking Water and Shade

Employees working outdoors must have access to potable drinking water that is fresh, pure, suitably cool, and provided free of charge. Where drinking water is not plumbed, enough water must be transported to the worksite to provide at least one quart of water per employee per hour. Employees must be encouraged to drink water frequently; employees must not be limited to drinking water only during their paid rest breaks (see Section 9.2).

When the temperature exceeds 80 degrees Fahrenheit the employer must provide one or more areas of shade which must be open air or that is ventilated or cooled.

A shaded area can be natural or artificial. There must be a large enough shade area to accommodate the total number of employees on a meal or rest break at any given time (see Section 9.4), such that they are able to sit normally without coming into contact with one another. Where temperatures do not exceed 80 degrees Fahrenheit, you must provide shade as described above or provide "timely access" to shade at an employee's request.

Employees must be allowed to take a cool-down break in the shade when they feel the need to do so to protect themselves from overheating (see Section 9.4). An employee taking such a cool-down break (1) must be monitored and asked if they are experiencing symptoms of heat illness, (2) must be encouraged to remain in the shade, and (3) must not be returned to work until the signs and symptoms of heat illness have abated, with a minimum of five minutes spent in the shade. Employees whose symptoms do not subside quickly must be given first aid or access to emergency medical services.

"High Heat Procedures"

When the temperature exceeds 95 degrees Fahrenheit, employers in the following industries must implement "high heat procedures":

- Agriculture;
- Construction;
- Landscaping;
- Oil and gas extraction; and
- Transportation or delivery of agricultural products, construction materials, or other heavy materials such as furniture, lumber, freight, cabinets, or industrial or commercial materials, except for operation of an air conditioned vehicle where the employee is not responsible for loading or unloading the vehicle.

"High heat procedures" include:

- Ensuring that effective communication by voice, observation, or electronic means is maintained so that employees can contact a supervisor when necessary;
- Observing employees for alertness and signs of heat illness by, for example, having a supervisor monitor no more than 20 employees, establishing a "buddy system" among employees, or regularly communicating with employees by radio or cell phone;
- Designating at least 1 employee at a worksite as authorized to call for emergency medical services, but allowing all employees to call for such services if the designated employee is unavailable;
- Reminding employees throughout the shift to drink plenty of water; and

- Holding a pre-shift meeting to review the high heat procedures, to encourage employees to drink plenty of water, and to remind employees of their right to take a cool-down break when necessary.

Acclimatization Requirements

Cal/OSHA regulations require that all employees working outdoors be closely observed by a supervisor or designee during a "heat wave," which is defined as any day when the predicted high temperature will be at least 80 degrees Fahrenheit and at least 10 degrees Fahrenheit higher than the average high daily temperature in the preceding 5 days. Also, an employee who has been newly assigned to a "high heat" area must be closely observed by a supervisor or designee for the employee's first 14 days on the job.

Required Employee Training

Training on the following topics must be provided to employees (including supervisors) before they begin work that might expose them to the risk of heat illness:

- Environmental and personal risk factors for heat illness, and the added heat load on the body caused by exertion, clothing, and PPE;
- The employer's procedures for providing water, shade, cool-down breaks, and access to first aid, as well as employees' ability to exercise their rights to these protections without retaliation;
- The importance of frequent consumption of small amounts of water (four cups per hour) when the work environment is hot and employees are sweating;
- The concept, importance, and methods of heat acclimatization;
- The different types of heat illness, their common signs and symptoms, and appropriate first aid and/or emergency medical response;
- The importance of employees reporting immediately any signs or symptoms of heat illness in themselves or in coworkers;
- The employer's procedures for responding to signs or symptoms of heat illness, including how emergency medical services will be provided if necessary;
- The employer's procedures for contacting emergency medical services and, if necessary, for transporting employees to a point where they can be reached by an emergency medical services provider; and
- The employer's procedures for ensuring that, in the event of an emergency, clear and precise directions to the worksite can and will be provided to emergency responders, and for designation of a person to summon emergency medical services when required.

Supervisors must additionally be given training on the following:

- Procedures the supervisor must follow to implement the various requirements for preventing and responding to heat illness;
- Procedures the supervisor must follow when an employee exhibits signs or reports symptoms of possible heat illness, including emergency response procedures; and
- How to monitor weather reports and to respond to hot weather advisories.

20.6 Repetitive Motion Injuries (Ergonomics)

Employers do not need to have a specific ergonomics program unless all of the following occur:

- Two or more repetitive motion injuries (RMIs) were reported to the employer in the last 12 months;
- The RMIs were musculoskeletal injuries that a licensed physician objectively identified and diagnosed;
- The RMIs were predominantly caused (i.e., 50 percent or more) by a repetitive job, process, or operation; and
- The employees incurring the RMIs were performing the same repetitive motion task, such as word processing, assembly, or loading.

Should an employer meet this test it must implement an ergonomics program that consists of the following:

- **Worksite evaluation:** Each job, process, or operation must be evaluated for exposures that have caused RMIs.
- **Control of exposures:** Any exposures that have caused RMIs must be corrected in a timely manner or, if not capable of being corrected, be minimized to the extent feasible by, for example, work station redesign, adjustable fixtures or tool redesign, or administrative controls such as job rotation, work pacing, or work breaks.
- **Training:** Employees must be provided training that includes an explanation of (1) the employer's program, (2) the exposures which have been associated with RMIs, (3) the symptoms and consequences of injuries caused by repetitive motion, the importance of reporting symptoms and injuries to the employer, and methods used by the employer to minimize RMIs.

20.7 Bloodborne Pathogens

Employers having employees who are subject to occupational exposure to bloodborne pathogens are required to implement a written Exposure Control Plan. Bloodborne pathogens are microorganisms present in human blood that can cause disease in humans. They include hepatitis B virus (HBV), hepatitis C virus (HCV), and human immunodeficiency virus (HIV). Employers subject to this requirement include hospitals and clinics, medical and dental practices, and ambulance companies and emergency medical services agencies.

Exposure Control Plan

The first step in creating an Exposure Control Plan is to prepare an exposure determination, which contains the following:

- A list of job classifications in which *all* employees have occupational exposure; and
- A list of job classifications in which *some* employees have occupational exposure, along with a list of all tasks and procedures or groups of closely related tasks and procedures that are performed by employees who have occupational exposure.

This exposure determination must be made without regard to the use of personal protective equipment.

The Exposure Control Plan must additionally contain:

- The schedule and method of implementation for each of the applicable elements of the Cal/OHSA bloodborne pathogens standards, which may be found at https://www.dir.ca.gov/title8/5193.html;
- The procedure for the evaluation of circumstances surrounding exposure incidents;
- An effective procedure for gathering the information required by the Sharps Injury Log;
- An effective procedure for periodic determination of the frequency of use of the types and brands of sharps involved in the exposure incidents documented on the Sharps Injury Log;
- An effective procedure for identifying currently available engineering controls and selecting such controls, where appropriate, for the procedures performed by employees in their respective work areas or departments;
- An effective procedure for documenting patient safety determinations made where a licensed healthcare professional directly involved in the patient's care determines, in the reasonable exercise of clinical judgment, that use of engineering controls will jeopardize the patient's safety or the success of the medical, dental, or nursing procedure involving the patient; and

- An effective procedure for obtaining the active involvement of employees in reviewing and updating the exposure control plan with respect to the procedures performed by employees in their respective work areas or departments.

Sharps Injury Log

A Sharps Injury Log must be maintained that records each exposure incident involving a sharp, including the following information if available:

- Date and time of the exposure incident;
- Type and brand of the sharp involved in the exposure incident;
- A description of the exposure incident that includes the job classification of the employee, the department or work area where the exposure incident occurred, the procedure the employee was performing at the time of the incident, how the incident occurred, and the body part involved in the exposure incident;
- Whether the sharp had a protective mechanism and whether it was activated at the time of the injury;
- If the sharp had no engineered injury protection, the injured employee's opinion as to whether and how such a mechanism could have prevented the injury; and
- The injured employee's opinion about whether any engineered, administrative, or work practice controls could have prevented the injury.

Each exposure incident must be recorded on the Sharps Injury Log within 14 working days of the date the incident is reported to the employer, and the information in the Sharps Injury Log must be recorded and maintained in such a manner as to protect the confidentiality of the injured employee.

Personal Protective Equipment

Where occupational exposure to bloodborne pathogens remains after implementation of engineering and work practice controls, the employer must provide, at no cost to the employee, appropriate PPE such as gloves, gowns, laboratory coats, face shields or masks, eye protection, mouthpieces, resuscitation bags, pocket masks, or other ventilation devices. PPE must not permit blood or other potentially infectious materials to pass through to or reach the employee's work clothes, street clothes, undergarments, skin, eyes, mouth, or other mucous membranes under normal conditions of use and for the duration of time which the protective equipment will be used.

Required Training

Employers must provide all employees with occupational exposure training during working hours at the time of the initial assignment of the employee to work where occupational exposure may occur, and at least annually thereafter. The training must include:

- An accessible copy of the Cal/OSHA standard on bloodborne pathogens and an explanation of its contents;
- A general explanation of the epidemiology and symptoms of bloodborne diseases;
- An explanation of the modes of transmission of bloodborne pathogens;
- An explanation of the employer's Exposure Control Plan and the means by which the employee can obtain a copy of the written plan;
- An explanation of the appropriate methods for recognizing tasks and other activities that may involve exposure to blood and other potentially infectious materials;
- An explanation of the use and limitations of methods that will prevent or reduce exposure including appropriate engineering controls, administrative or work practice controls, and personal protective equipment;
- Information on the types, proper use, location, removal, handling, decontamination, and disposal of personal protective equipment;
- An explanation of the basis for selection of PPE;
- Information on the hepatitis B vaccine, including information on its efficacy, safety, method of administration, the benefits of being vaccinated, and that the vaccine and vaccination will be offered free of charge;
- Information on the appropriate actions to take and persons to contact in an emergency involving blood or other potential infectious materials;
- An explanation of the procedure to follow if an exposure incident occurs, including the method of reporting the incident, the medical follow-up that will be made available, and the procedure for recording the incident on the Sharps Injury Log;
- Information on the post-exposure evaluation and follow-up that the employer is required to provide for the employee following an exposure incident;
- An explanation of the signs and labels and/or color coding required for biohazardous waste and sharps waste; and
- An opportunity for interactive questions and answers with the person conducting the training session.

Employers must provide additional training when changes, such as introduction of new engineering, administrative or work practice controls, modification of tasks or procedures, or institution of new tasks or procedures affect employees' occupational exposure. The additional training may be limited to addressing the new exposures created.

20.8 Workplace Violence Prevention Plan

California employers must have a Workplace Violence Prevention Plan in effect. The plan must be in writing and be easily accessible to employees. It may be incorporated into the employer's IIPP or be a separate stand-alone document. It must include all of the following:

- Names or job titles of the persons responsible for implementing the plan. If there are multiple persons responsible for the plan, their roles must be clearly described.
- Effective procedures to obtain the active involvement of employees and authorized employee representatives in developing and implementing the plan, including, but not limited to, through their participation in identifying, evaluating, and correcting workplace violence hazards; in designing and implementing training; and in reporting and investigating workplace violence incidents.
- Methods the employer will use to coordinate implementation of the plan with other employers, when applicable, to ensure that those employers and employees understand their respective roles, as provided in the plan. These methods shall ensure that all employees are provided the required training and that workplace violence incidents involving any employee are reported, investigated, and recorded.
- Effective procedures for the employer to accept and respond to reports of workplace violence, and to prohibit retaliation against an employee who makes such a report.
- Effective procedures to ensure that supervisory and nonsupervisory employees comply with the plan.
- Effective procedures to communicate with employees regarding workplace violence matters, including (1) how an employee can report a violent incident, threat, or other workplace violence concern to the employer or law enforcement without fear of reprisal, and (2) how employee-reported incidents and concerns will be investigated and how employees will be informed of the results of the investigation and any corrective actions taken.
- Effective procedures to respond to actual or potential workplace violence emergencies, including (1) effective means to alert employees of the presence, location, and nature of workplace violence emergencies, (2) evacuation or sheltering plans that are appropriate and feasible for the worksite, and (3) how to

obtain help from staff assigned to respond to workplace violence emergencies, security personnel, and law enforcement.

- Procedures to develop and provide the required training.
- Procedures to identify and evaluate workplace violence hazards, including scheduled periodic inspections to identify unsafe conditions and work practices. Inspections must be conducted when the plan is first established, after each workplace violence incident, and whenever the employer is made aware of a new or previously unrecognized hazard.
- Procedures to workplace violence hazards that are identified.
- Procedures for post-incident response and investigation.
- Procedures to review the effectiveness of the plan and revise the plan as needed, including procedures to obtain the active involvement of employees and authorized employee representatives in reviewing the plan. The plan must be reviewed at least annually, when a deficiency is observed or becomes apparent, and after a workplace violence incident.

The employer must establish and maintain a violent incident log, and record for each incident of workplace violence:

- The date, time, and location of the incident;
- The workplace violence type or types involved in the incident;
- A detailed description of the incident;
- A classification of who committed the violence, including whether the perpetrator was a client or customer, family or friend of a client or customer, stranger with criminal intent, coworker, supervisor or manager, partner or spouse, parent or relative, or other perpetrator;
- The circumstances at the time of the incident, including whether the employee was completing usual job duties, working in poorly lit areas, rushed, working during a low staffing level, isolated or alone, unable to get help or assistance, working in a community setting, or working in an unfamiliar or new location;
- A description of where the incident occurred, such as in the workplace, parking lot, or other area outside the workplace, or other area;
- The type of incident, including whether it involved (1) an attack with a weapon, (2) a physical attack without a weapon (such as biting, choking, grabbing, hair pulling, kicking, punching, slapping, pushing, pulling, scratching, or spitting), (3) a threat of physical force or threat of the use of a weapon or other object, (4) sexual assault or threat, including rape, attempted rape, physical display, or unwanted verbal or physical sexual contact, (5) an animal attack, or (6) some other incident;

- The consequences of the incident, including whether security or law enforcement was contacted and their response, and actions taken to protect employees from a continuing threat or from any other hazards identified as a result of the incident; and
- Name and job title of the person completing the report and the date the report was completed.

The employer additionally must provide training to all employees when the plan is established and annually thereafter. The training must cover:

- The employer's plan, how to obtain a copy of the employer's plan at no cost, and how to participate in development and implementation of the employer's plan;
- The requirements of the law regarding workplace violence prevention;
- How to report workplace violence incidents or concerns to the employer or law enforcement without fear of reprisal;
- Workplace violence hazards specific to the employees' jobs, the corrective measures the employer has implemented, how to seek assistance to prevent or respond to violence, and strategies to avoid physical harm;
- The violent incident log maintained by the employer; and
- An opportunity for interactive questions and answers with a person knowledgeable about the employer's plan.

Employers must maintain records covering workplace violence incidents and investigations, training, hazard identification and correction, and related matters for at least 5 years, and copies of such records must be produced to employees and their representatives for examination and copying within 15 days of request.

20.9 Injury and Accident Reporting Requirements

Employers must report immediately by telephone or email to the nearest District Office of the Division of Occupational Safety and Health any death or serious injury or illness of an employee occurring in a place of employment or in connection with any employment. The nearest District Office may be found at https://www.dir.ca.gov/DOSH/DistrictOffices.htm. "Immediately" means as soon as practically possible but not longer than 8 hours after the employer knows or with diligent inquiry would have known of the death or serious injury or illness. A "serious injury or illness" is one which requires inpatient hospitalization for more than 24 hours for reasons other than medical observation, or in which the employee loses a limb or suffers any serious degree of permanent disfigurement. Whenever a state, county, or local fire or police agency is called to an accident involving an employee's death or serious injury or illness, the agency must notify the nearest office of the Division of Occupational Safety and Health by telephone immediately. The actions of first responders do not relieve the employer of its obligation to contact the Cal/OSHA office, however.

A report of a workplace fatality, serious injury, or illness must contain the following information if available:

- Time and date of the accident;
- The employer's name, address, and telephone number;
- The name and job title, or badge number of the person reporting the accident;
- The address of the site of the accident;
- The name of person to contact at site of the accident;
- The name and address of the injured employee(s);
- The nature of the injury;
- The location where the injured employee(s) was (were) moved to;
- The identity of law enforcement agencies present at the site of accident; and
- A brief description of the incident and whether the accident scene or instrumentality has been altered.

Employers should refrain from presenting hastily assembled reports regarding the causes of injuries and accidents. The employer may choose to inform Cal/OSHA enforcement officers that an incident is still under investigation and that no preliminary report is available.

Employers also must complete an "Injury and Illness Incident Report" (Cal/OSHA Form 301) for all work-related injuries and illnesses that require medical treatment beyond first aid, or that result in missed days of work or work restrictions, loss of consciousness, diagnosis of a significant injury or illness, or death (regardless of length of time between the injury and death). The report must describe the accident and the injuries suffered. It is not submitted to Cal/OSHA but it must be retained for at least five years and produced upon request during any Cal/OSHA investigation or upon the request of any employee, former employee, or their union.

Employers, except employers of 10 or fewer employees or employers in specific low hazard industries listed in Appendix A to Section 14300.2 of the Cal/OSHA reporting regulations, additionally must keep a log of work-related injuries and illnesses on a document called a Form 300. The injuries and illnesses should be logged as they occur, and a separate log must be maintained for each of the employer's locations. The Form 300 must be made available to employees, former employees, and their union upon request.

If you are required to keep a Form 300 log of injuries and illnesses, at the end of each year you must complete a summary of all injuries and illnesses on a different document, Form 300A, and post the document where it can be viewed by employees between February 1 and April 30 of the following year. Data on injury and illness types, days of work missed, and the like are aggregated on the Form 300A. Employers of 250 or more employees must electronically report the information on Form 300A to Cal/OSHA on an annual basis. Employers of between 20 and 250 employees must electronically report the information on Form 300A to Cal/OSHA if they are in an industry listed in Appendix H to the Cal/OSHA reporting regulations. Other employers do not have to electronically report the information on their Form 300 to Cal/OSHA unless notified by Cal/OSHA to do so.

20.10 Responding to a Cal/OSHA Investigation

Cal/OSHA will conduct an investigation in response to:

- Complaints of workplace hazards filed by employees, employee representatives, or others;
- Reports of serious violations received from law enforcement; and
- Reports of accidents resulting in serious injury or illness or death.

Cal/OSHA also conducts targeted inspections of employers in "high hazard industries" with high rates of preventable injuries and illnesses and workers' compensation losses (see Section 20.1). Finally, Cal/OSHA conducts programmed inspections in mining and tunneling, petroleum refining, and the underground economy.

Employees may file a workplace safety complaint by calling or emailing the nearest Cal/OSHA District Office. The identity of the complaining employee will not be revealed unless the employee otherwise requests. If the identity of the complaining employee is nonetheless determined, note that California law prohibits retaliation against an employee, or a family member of an employee, who reports a workplace safety violation to a government agency or their employer or union.

When an OSHA Investigator Visits

Most Cal/OSHA inspections occur without prior warning. The investigator will simply show up, show their credentials, and request the employer's consent to the inspection. You may refuse to consent to an inspection which has not been authorized by a search warrant except for places open to the general public. Cal/OSHA can usually obtain a search warrant in a short period of time, so insistence upon a warrant is not always the best strategy. The advantages of allowing warrantless entry include having more control over the inspection. The investigator must ask your permission to see various areas of a facility during a warrantless inspection. Consenting to a warrantless inspection may demonstrate good faith and helps to prevent an adversarial interaction. However, supervisors and managers should not agree to participate in tape-recorded interviews and should refrain from signing declarations or witness statements prepared by a Cal/OSHA investigator.

It is possible to request a short postponement of the inspection to enable the appropriate representatives of the employer (HR or safety manager, for example) to be present. It is not wise to allow an inspection to proceed without a management representative present who is familiar with workplace safety issues.

The Opening Conference

An opening conference allows the Cal/OSHA investigator to explain the purpose of the inspection. The investigator will usually indicate whether the inspection was prompted by a complaint, an accident, or is a general programmed inspection. The compliance officer will also disclose the specific areas to be inspected, whether samples or photographs will be taken, whether employees will be interviewed, and which documents will be reviewed. The investigator also may request that an employee representative (or union representative if the company is unionized) be present. The investigator will also ask for the identity of any contractors or subcontractors working at the facility.

Document Inspection

The investigator will ask to see your IIPP, your Form 300 logs (if you are required to maintain them) for five years, and any other documents your organization is required by Cal/OSHA standards to maintain. You should request a reasonable amount of time (at least five working days) to provide the requested documents. Note that Cal/OSHA has authority to issue a subpoena for documents not produced within a reasonable amount of time.

Walk-Around

The investigator will want to conduct a physical inspection of the location. You have the right to accompany the investigator during this tour and you should do so. The employee representative also has the right to accompany the investigator on this tour. The investigator may take photographs and samples. If this occurs you should ask for duplicates or take similar photographs and samples.

During the walk-around, the compliance officer will look to ensure that the mandatory Cal/OSHA poster describing the rights and responsibilities of employers and employees is on display.

Employee Interviews

The investigator will likely want to interview some employees. A representative of the employer should be present during interviews of any supervisory or management employee. If any written statement is given, the employee giving the statement should request a copy of the signed statement. Representatives of the employer are generally not permitted to be present during interviews of nonmanagement employees, although on certain occasions employees may request that their supervisor stays with them while they are being interviewed.

You may wish to give employees copies of their health and safety training records, to refresh their recollections before being interviewed. In any event, any employees interviewed have the right to receive a copy of their statement, and this right should be explained to the employees.

The Closing Conference

At the end of the investigation the investigator will hold a closing conference with the employer's representative. At this time the investigator will address any safety violations the investigation has identified. The investigator also may discuss potential penalties, correction of violations, and the law against retaliation against any employees who might have complained about safety violations.

If the investigator finds conditions that could violate Cal/OSHA Safety Orders you might receive a citation. The citation will describe the alleged violation, list the relevant Safety Orders, and affix civil monetary penalties. The penalties will be based on the seriousness of the alleged violations. The citation must be issued within 6 months of the date Cal/OSHA opened its investigation. You may appeal the citation to the Occupational Health and Safety Appeals Board within 15 business days of receiving the citation.

20.11 Expanded Cal/OSHA Penalties

Cal/OSHA is authorized to issue two types of expanded penalties against employers.

Enterprise-Wide Violations

A presumption will arise that an employer has committed an "enterprise-wide" violation, or a violation at multiple worksites, if Cal/OSHA finds that either:

- The employer has a written policy or procedure that violates any Cal/OSHA standard, rule, order, or regulation; or
- Cal/OSHA has evidence of a pattern or practice of the same violation or multiple violations committed by that employer involving more than one of the employer's worksites.

There is no requirement that Cal/OSHA investigate other worksites or observe other violations in order to issue a citation for an enterprise-wide violation. This means that employers can be cited for worksites that have not been inspected, based entirely on a written policy in effect at only one of the employer's worksites.

Employers should review their policies and procedures so as to ensure that none of them violates any Cal/OSHA standard, rule, order, or regulation.

Egregious Violations

Cal/OSHA also may issue penalties for "egregious violations." Such a penalty may be issued for each employee who is exposed to the violation. Cal/OSHA may find that an employer has committed an "egregious violation" in any of the following situations:

- The employer, intentionally, through conscious, voluntary action or inaction, made no reasonable effort to eliminate a known violation;
- Violations resulted in worker fatalities, a worksite catastrophe, or a large number of injuries or illnesses;
- Violations resulted in persistently high rates of worker injuries or illnesses;
- The employer has an extensive history of prior violations;
- The employer has intentionally disregarded its health and safety responsibilities;
- The employer's conduct, taken as a whole, amounts to clear bad faith in the performance of its duty to provide a safe work environment; or
- The employer has committed a large number of violations so as to undermine significantly the effectiveness of any safety and health program that might be in place.

Appendix of Cited Cases

AMN Healthcare, Inc. v. AYA Healthcare Services, Inc., 28 Cal.App.5th 923 (2018).

Armendariz v. Foundation Health Psychcare Services, Inc., 24 Cal.4th 83 (2000).

AT&T Mobility LLC v. Concepcion, 563 U.S. 333 (2011).

Castro-Ramirez v. Dependable Highway Express, Inc., 246 Cal.App.4th 180 (2016).

Cotran v. Rollins Hudig Hall Int'l, Inc., 17 Cal.4th 93 (1998).

Doe v. Department of Corrections, 43 Cal.App.5th 721 (2019).

Dynamex Operations West, Inc. v. Superior Court, 4 Cal.5th 903 (2018).

Iskanian v. CLS Transportation, 59 Cal.4th 348 (2014).

Meritor Savings Bank v. Vinson, 477 U.S. 57 (1986).

S.G. Borello & Sons, Inc. v. Dept. of Industrial Relations, 46 Cal.3d 341 (1989).

Index

E

X

Y

Z

Printed and bound by CPI Group (UK) Ltd, Croydon, CR0 4YY

Printed and bound by CPI Group (UK) Ltd, Croydon, CR0 4YY

17/09/2026

14964328-0001